SURVIVING FAMILY LIFE

Also by Josleen Wilson

Live Longer—Control Your Blood Pressure
(with Dr. Max Feinman)

The Passionate Amateur's Guide
to Archaeology in the United States

SURVIVING FAMILY LIFE

BY SONYA RHODES, D.S.W.
WITH JOSLEEN WILSON

G. P. Putnam's Sons
New York

The authors gratefully acknowledge permission to quote from the following
sources:
E. P. Dutton & Co., Inc., for *When We Were Very Young* by A. A. Milne. Copyright
© 1924 by E. P. Dutton & Co., Inc. Renewed 1952 by A. A. Milne.
The Family Service Association of America for "Some Dynamics of the Middle
and Later Years" by S. Cath, from *Crisis Intervention: Selected Readings,* ed. H. J.
Parad, 1965, pp. 182–183. And for "The Place of In-Laws in Marital Relationships,"
from *Social Casework,* October 1975, p. 486.
Marriage and Divorce Today for *Marriage and Divorce Today Newsletter,* July 14,
1980, p. 3. Copyright © 1980 by Marriage and Divorce Today, an Atcom Publication,
2315 Broadway, NY, NY 10024.
The New York Times Company for "Family Myths" by Beth Hess, from *The New
York Times,* January 9, 1979. Copyright © 1979 by The New York Times Company.
And for "Shift in Family Structure Said to Affect Child Care," by Robin Herman,
The New York Times, May 2, 1980. Copyright © 1980 by The New York Times
Company.
News Group Publications, Inc., for "When Was the Last Time You Called Your
Mother?" by L. Wolfe, *New York* Magazine, May 7, 1979. Copyright © 1979 by News
Group Publications, Inc.
W. W. Norton & Co., Inc., for *Uncommon Therapy: The Psychiatric Techniques of
Milton H. Erickson, M.D.,* p. 64., by Jay Haley. Copyright © 1973 by Jay Haley.

Library of Congress Cataloging in Publication Data

Rhodes, Sonya.
  Surviving family life.

  Bibliography: p.
  1. Family—United States. 2. Life cycle, Human.
3. Family therapy. I. Wilson, Josleen, joint author.
II. Title.
HQ536.R46   306.8   80-24240
ISBN 0-399-12507-8

ACKNOWLEDGMENTS

I am indebted to my colleagues, friends, patients, and family for their contributions to this book. Some knowingly lent their enthusiasm, criticism, and support. Others unknowingly provided background, inspiration, and emotional intensity, which enriched my understanding of family life.

My first professional work at the Jewish Family Service of New York City gave me the rare opportunity to study family therapy with some of the best-known family therapists of the day. I observed firsthand the therapeutic approaches of Nat Ackerman, Shep Sherman, Frances Beatman, Arthur Leader, Celia Mitchell, Dick Auerswald, and Ross Speck.

Two women at JFS made an immeasurable impact on my life, shaping my personal growth as well as my professional development. Jeanne Katz, my casework supervisor for four years, patiently and lovingly taught me the basic theory and technique of family therapy. Elsa Leichter's magnetic personality infused her teaching style. Under her tutorship, I discovered the power of the group process and the hypnotic effects of countertransference. As role models and mother figures, Jeanne and Elsa helped me discover my strengths and know my limitations.

In my next professional job I took a giant step toward professional autonomy. I thank Gloria Warshaw for her vote of confidence and encouragement, and her unique leadership as director of the Family Counseling Service, Inc., in Hackensack, New Jersey.

Among my closest friends are colleagues who offer the unbeatable combination of intellectual stimulation and comradeship. Ellie Amel and Judy Lang had the wisdom and love, sense of humor and perspective that helped me as I struggled with concepts for this book.

My friends Emily Chou and Michael Abramson inspired this project by proving that it wasn't an impossible dream to write and publish a book. And Jean Marzollo's experience as a writer and her common sense and optimism gave me invaluable support throughout. I am especially grateful to Gail Koff, June and Harold Wise, Patricia Holzman, Suzanne Moore Pyle, Susan

Strang, and Anita Jacobson for sharing their insights about family life. Elise Robinson, who has been an unofficial member of our family for over eight years, gave generously of her time and love throughout this project.

My co-author, Josleen Wilson, and I especially want to thank Neil Felshman for his professional review and criticism of the final manuscript.

At the core of this book are the people in the families I've worked with. Their dreams, longings, and fears mirror everyone's life-long quest for intimacy. This book is a testimony to their courage to be known and to care about each other.

I especially thank my mother, whose trust and confidence has been a sustaining force, and my sisters, who showed me the power of families, thereby making a very special contribution to this work.

Last, I thank my family—Bob, Justin, and Jennifer. They know what this book is about.

—Sonya Rhodes

In memory of my father
—SR

CONTENTS

SURVIVING FAMILY LIFE

INTRODUCTION

More than a year after my father died I realized that we were still hiding the truth about the way it happened. At a family reunion my mother and sisters and I, my aunts, uncles, and cousins moved dreamlike through the charade of a happy gathering. We spoke fondly of my father, and we smiled and talked and laughed. But tension flickered around the room like electricity through a frayed wire as we all danced away from the truth.

I knew that all families had secret pacts loyally kept and forever binding. It is part of my job as a family therapist to help troubled families bring their fears into the open and discover the secrets and myths that so often bring pain and disruption. But I had never before faced the secrets in my own life. It would eventually bring me much closer to my own family, and to those families I worked with.

From the day we're born until the day we die, families are powerful influences, whether we call once a week, get together for dinner on weekends, see each other only at weddings and funerals, or remain completely aloof. Single, married, or divorced, family ties are our most intense personal attachments.

This is true even though the family is no longer a structured social unit with rigidly defined roles. Today it may be communal, unmarried, single-parented, or extended. It's an adaptable organism, with a constant purpose: to nurture and protect, to encourage and support growth, to show love. But other emotions go with the territory.

Mothers and fathers, sisters, brothers, husbands, wives, and children are experts at arousing passion, longing, pain, and even fear. Our families force us to show the most primitive emotions and display the most childish behavior. Against them we wage our fiercest battles for independence.

Some surrender to family pressure and allow families to swallow them up. Others try to protect themselves from the voraciousness of family relationships by almost total detachment. Membership exacts too big a price, we say, so to hell with it. Some of us swing back and forth between the two extremes of overcloseness and complete detachment without striking a balance. We kid ourselves that we've got it all together but our confidence evaporates with the distant tremor of the next family gathering.

Family struggles center around the conflict between individual rights and the needs of the family. Is it possible to be free and yet close to the people we love? Parent and child, we are tossed back and forth on a sea of conflicting desire.

To have fulfilling, intimate relationships without losing a sense of self, we need to understand how families work and how the past influences present and future relationships. For everything we know about loving we learned in our original families.

For many of us, family life is a battleground from which we flee in defeat. In a frantic search for freedom, we look inward. We try to become more assertive and independent, to discover what we want for ourselves, and how to be relieved of the guilt we carry as part of our baggage when we leave our families.

But to complete the journey of discovery we need to transcend self-absorption. None of us exists alone in the world. When we learn to survive in our own families, we find a way to meet others' needs and retain our own integrity.

SEVEN STAGES OF FAMILY LIFE

Whether it is a commune in California or a remarried household in New York, every family can anticipate a similar series of stages that evolve as a cycle: a man and woman make a commitment to each other, children are born and grow up, responsibilities increase and are taken away, marriage often cools, careers develop and subside, ties are broken and reshaped, loved ones grow old and die.

All families move through a cycle of stages, and each stage has built in, predictable crises.[1] In the many families I have worked with over the years, certain crises were clearly and repeatedly revealed in their history.

There are seven specific stages in the life cycle of every family, and in each stage a "normal" crisis will occur that requires change from everyone in the family.[2]

Stage 1   Early Marriage
Stage 2   Coping with Parenthood
Stage 3   When Children Go to School
Stage 4   Families with Adolescents
Stage 5   The Shrinking Family
Stage 6   The Empty Nest
Stage 7   Three Generations Together

Every stage of family life has special problems and themes, and in each stage the family faces a major turning point.

What Is Crisis?

A normal crisis is a turning point or transition in the ebb and flow of family life. It may have varied moods and extremes, depending on the family's basic pattern. Some families smoothly make the transition from one stage to the next with only a slight rumbling to show that new patterns have evolved. Others shift in fits and starts. And some get bogged down in one stage and cannot move at all. Getting stuck can mean trouble. (A child may reflect the family's strain by developing problems in school or showing some other serious symptom. A mother may become depressed, a father starts to drink heavily. It can be much worse.)

At best, these turning points are sensitive times for all families. At worst, family members suffer psychiatric problems.

Every family has weak spots or problems that aggravate the turning point. Usually these problems are invisibly recorded in the past and passed along from generation to generation. In this sense, every newly married couple can be either burdened or enlightened by "inherited" family patterns.

Unpredictable events at the vulnerable turning points may further complicate the process. An unexpected stress event (death of a loved one, illness, job or financial loss) that occurs on the cusp of a turning point can create a severe crisis for even the healthiest family.

Once children are born, the family may find itself straddling more than one stage at a time. Stages often overlap as children help the family enter passages of profound change and move through its life cycle.

In the life cycle of the family, change is natural, though often wrenching. Change upsets the family's rhythm and generates emotional intensity for everyone, but how well the family copes with change determines whether it will move forward or become self destructive. Couples who effectively handle the turning point of one stage, automatically find it easier to face the next crisis.

Surviving family life depends on a willingness to work through the predictable crises of family life with the people we love. It requires humor and resilience and a desire to create solutions that work for all family members.

In my own life I know the struggles and conflicts that are an inevitable part of family life. I am not a detached observer. Some stories told in this book find their sources in my own family life. Others are based on experiences of families I have worked with as a staff clinician, community consultant, and family therapist in private practice. However, in each "case history," names, occupations, locations, and family composition and backgrounds have all been changed, and experiences blended to create a single story. Thus, no one "case" relates to any one real famiy, each being a composite distilled from my personal and professional experiences, which often as not is more "true to life" than any single story could be.

The characters are mainly second- and third-generation Americans of Irish, Italian, Eastern European, and Anglo-Saxon ancestry, reflecting the population of this country in its more urban areas. Some families are poor, others economically privileged; most are middle-class. In the main, they are two-parent families, as are 84 percent of families in the American population.[3] But some are two-paycheck families, some traditional nuclear families, some blended families.

In family therapy, things often happen quickly. There is an immediacy that does not occur in standard individual therapy, and difficulties are sometimes resolved on the spot. But family therapy is a new and complex discipline. Most families still struggle for survival on their own. Families that actually enter therapy are no different from others. Their problems are very much the same, and any family—in or out of therapy—can go completely out of control. With an understanding of the basic family cycle I think families often can work through typical crises by themselves. Just knowing that these problems are not unique but are similar to those faced by other families and, in fact, can be expected, and resolved, gives families the courage to work together.

The existence of a recognizable pattern—of these distinct stages in the life of the family—is a comforting reality. I believe it's possible to have families where all members are fulfilled and no one is sacrificed for the sake of another or for the sake of the family as a whole.

In a society where things are disposable and people dispensable, men and women and children seek a place that is secure and dependable, a place to retreat from the world, where emotional needs are met and batteries recharged. This is what I believe most of us want and look for in family life. We long for emotional contact, for affection we don't compete for, and closeness we needn't earn.

Stage 1
EARLY MARRIAGE: INTIMACY OR GAMES?

Turning Point: To fight for love or give it up

Chapter 1

ROMANCE—DISILLUSIONMENT—INTIMACY

Taking the Plunge

Margo Richman awoke one Saturday morning just after Christmas and couldn't remember where she was. She gazed at the gray satin comforter that slipped across the bed when she stretched her legs and looked at the view through the french windows that opened out to a pale morning sky and silver mountains beyond. Early skiers, specks of bright color on the barely trampled snow, glided slowly down the mountainside.

The sound of the shower in the adjacent bathroom jogged her memory. Her companion for a long weekend in the Italian Alps was a wealthy stockbroker she had seen a few times over the last several months, a middle-aged married man whose money allowed him to turn an otherwise ordinary affair into the grand tour. Margo knew she was a *divertissement*. She did not blame him for this, and in fact she felt no strong emotional connection at all. When she began to cry, tears slipping almost accidentally down her cheeks, she couldn't imagine what was wrong with her. This was not her first affair.

When she had been in her twenties Margo had had a succession of lovers, but relationships had not deepened. She had wanted more, and finally walked out on a man she lived with for two years when he said he wasn't ready for marriage. Six months later, he married the girl across the hall. On her thirtieth birthday Margo hardened herself against love.

"I had spent too much time worrying about this guy or that one, trying to figure out what he was thinking or what I was feeling. I thought it was time to get on with my life."

Margo had a reputation as a journalist with style but not much ambition. Over the next few years she devoted herself to work and succeeded in moving a previously sluggish career. She made it to the staff of a national newsmagazine and could soon pick her own assignments. Her love life,

21

which she had ignored for several years, was revived. She had several more lovers.

"I began to understand the masculine view of sex," she observed. "It has more to do with power than masculinity, and men are usually the ones with the power. Anyway, for the first time in my life, I used sex in purely physical terms, rather than as the usual tangle of emotions that had always confused me." Margo fulfilled her sexual desires with the most attractive partner she could find, whether it was for a week or a night. She was convinced that at last she was immune to love and its aftermath. So the stockbroker, presently soaking in the shower, meant neither more nor less than any of the others.

But Margo couldn't stop crying. She cried off and on for the next two days until, tears held tremulously in check, she packed her bags and caught a plane back to New York.

At home, she felt better. But she was changing in some way that was unfamiliar.

Margo met Greg Cresson in the reception room of her office building. "I was going out for lunch and I saw him standing there, talking to a friend of mine. I took one look at him and knew I had to meet him. The sensation was so strong it was like a bell going off. I veered off course and walked directly toward him. My friend introduced us. If she hadn't, I would have introduced myself and spirited him away. As it was, we all went to lunch together and from that moment on, Greg and I were inseparable."

The attraction was mutual, though from the beginning they seemed to have nothing in common except their oppositeness. Greg appeared detached and coolly intelligent. Margo was open and down to earth. She was vibrant, he was cynical. She adored him, and he couldn't stay away from her.

Greg was no stranger to love affairs. Women were a big part of his life, and his elegant room in a New York hotel was a magnet for female visitors. He clearly liked it that way. Women came and went in his life with the regularity of commuter trains: there had been a few layovers, but by and large they arrived and departed according to his schedule.

"He was so exciting to be around," Margo said. "He didn't live by the ordinary rules that most people follow. He was building this new resort on a deserted island—how many people do you meet who own their own island?"

At the time, Greg was involved in a multimillion-dollar real-estate deal in the Caribbean. He traveled back and forth between an office on St. John, which had the nearest access to his new resort, and New York, where his financial backers were located. Once the deal was settled, he planned a decade of building and profit making.

"But this was really the most exciting time for him," Margo continued. "All he talked about was plans, surveys, contacts, and financial wheels within wheels. He was so fired up and enthusiastic."

The love affair between Margo and Greg bloomed within the excitement of his dream. When he was out of town, the telephone wires burned with midnight conversations. In New York, there were little dinners at the best restaurants, followed by nights of sexual fantasy in his hotel room. Some weekends, high on Acapulco Gold, they flew to San Juan, others they spent lying in the sun on the terrace of Margo's apartment.

"Some of my friends thought Greg was a show-off and a big talker. But I loved his swagger and bravado. I was touched by his almost child-like boasting because I knew that underneath he was a vulnerable, sensitive man. That was our secret. He and I both knew it, but no one else did."

Margo was something of a show-off herself. She thrived on being unconventional, and Greg was amused when one day he walked into her office unannounced and found her puffing a huge Havana cigar while three or four other reporters lounged around her desk loudly arguing about thoroughbred bloodlines.

Margo was happier than she had ever been. Greg never gushed or fawned over her, he never mentioned love, yet she knew he felt the same excitement she did. Margo went on shopping sprees, buying quarts of French perfume and expensive lingerie. For the first time in her life, she lingered happily in the men's department at Saks and purchased quantities of cashmere socks, grotesque ties, and silk shirts.

A long time afterward Greg would remember that he was tiring of the fast pace. But he hesitated to say so. Margo loved action and novelty, and he was afraid to disappoint her.

But Margo, too, wanted a change. The wide edge of glamour was fun, but she couldn't seem to get close enough to Greg. As they lay next to each other on a secluded beach in Tortola, Margo, her eyes barely open against the sun, tested the emotional water. "Why don't we stay home for our next junket and play house? I think I need a rest." Greg, a little roughly, started to make love to her.

After that Greg began to spend more time in New York. His trips to the island dwindled, and finally, without saying why, he decided to make his base in New York. He gave up his hotel room and moved into Margo's apartment. Margo thought she was extremely pleased.

Almost immediately, everything started to go sour. To a certain extent Margo recognized what was happening. "I knew it was one thing to be in love with someone who wasn't around much, but I wasn't sure how to be in love in an everyday way. I wanted to try, but it wasn't as much fun anymore." If Greg noticed anything, he didn't mention it.

Everyone reaches a turning point in romance when the relationship either dies out or it moves toward greater intimacy. In this instance the turning point coincided with, or perhaps was brought on by, Greg's move into Margo's apartment, which radically increased the amount of time they spent together. But if Greg hadn't made the move, the turning point would have occurred in some other way or the affair might have eventually fizzled out.

Suddenly they were living together. No romantic arrivals and departures in the middle of the night. No expensive hotels with room service, no need for telegrams and long-distance calls. They were together, and now they were straining to be polite when they felt tired and wanted to be alone.

Greg began to brood. He withdrew into silence and seemed to be waiting for something. Margo also waited. She thought he was unhappy with her, but was too proud to ask him what she had done wrong. "If he didn't like me anymore," she said later, "I didn't want to know about it. I thought if I could be brighter or more fun he would love me again."

Occasionally they spent an evening out, but there was a false gaiety in the air. Now Margo, tired of trying to look cheerful, also began to retreat. They became completely isolated from one another and each felt disappointed.

The accusations began. "You don't talk to me," Margo told him. This was her gambit. As long as she blamed Greg, he would never suspect that, like him, she was afraid to talk openly about risky issues. With every new accusation Greg became more withdrawn, rigid, and unyielding.

We think that when we are in love, the other person should magically know what we feel. This is only true in a general sense. But much cannot be guessed at or superficially transmitted like signals along a telegraph wire. Thoughts must be fully spoken with the heart, mind, and voice. If Margo and Greg could not put into words what they felt and wanted from each other, they would never survive the turning point.

One thing they never discussed was money. Margo hadn't questioned that when they used to dine out, Greg put all the tabs on his credit card. Occasionally he had borrowed twenty or sometimes fifty dollars from her for incidentals because he was out of cash. These loans were never repaid, but she didn't query him because she thought it only fair to pay part of their entertainment expenses. It had crossed her mind that she would rather pay her share than "lend" him a few dollars, but she didn't mention it.

The second month after he moved in, Greg didn't contribute to the rent, and he seldom bought groceries. Once in a while, when he went out to a meeting, he would say casually, "I need cab fare . . . can you let me have a ten?" Margo would give him whatever cash she had. She couldn't bring herself to ask him why he didn't have any money.

After several weeks Margo found the courage to confront Greg. One Monday morning, after a grim weekend, she brought it up just before she left for work. "Greg, is something wrong?"

"No."

"Are you sure? You seem very low."

"I don't know why you say that."

"For one thing, you don't say much . . . I can't tell what's going on with you."

"It's nothing."

"What about the resort—you haven't mentioned it in weeks."

"Let's talk about it tonight."

Margo left for work. But, having finally and unsuccessfully tried to talk to Greg, she felt even more frustrated than before. She couldn't concentrate on her work, and at noon she called him on the telephone and said she was coming home for lunch.

Over sandwiches they didn't eat, Greg told Margo that the money from his backers hadn't materialized and he had lost his real-estate options along with his own investment. The fantasy island was gone.

"Why didn't you tell me?"

"It doesn't help to talk about it."

"What are you going to do now?"

"I don't know—I'll get something going."

Their talk ended there, with the vague promise that they should discuss things more, although in the following weeks they never spoke of it again. But something had changed between them. Although Margo was no longer certain about her feelings for Greg, she was relieved to know that his problems were unrelated to her.

At this time of her life, Margo was established as an independent person. She was ready for an important relationship. The question was, was Greg the right one?

Even after admitting his business failure, Greg tried to keep up a good front. He continued to boast, but now Margo knew there was little behind the bravado. Unhappy with the present, he spoke of past triumphs. He began talking about other women. As he described sexual affairs of the past, Margo felt humiliated. His obvious relish in describing some former conquest didn't make her feel any better about his sexual withdrawal from her. It had been weeks since they slept together, and they had never discussed it.

Margo was certain that Greg didn't love her. She had lost some of her confidence and felt unfeminine. But she was afraid to say so. She didn't want Greg to know that she was so insecure.

The truth was that Greg had lost his dream and his business, he was running out of money, and Margo was all he had left. He was terrified she would leave him. He was so ashamed that he needed her that he pretended he didn't.

At this point it was just a matter of time before they split up. "I was just waiting until he got on his feet,' Margo said. "I couldn't stand being with him anymore."

Communication between them was now cross-wired on every level. But they couldn't quite give it up. "It had been so fabulous at first," she continued. "I couldn't believe everything turned out so awful. The worst was that it had all happened to me before. I had seen dozens of my affairs suddenly go bad. I was sick of it. I think that's why I wanted to try again.

"But I knew I had to do something different. I wasn't certain what to do. But at the times I hated him most, I gritted my teeth and tried to move closer to him."

Margo looked for ways to show Greg that she cared for him. She made a fabulous breakfast on Sunday morning. Greg devoured the meal and left the table without helping her clean up. She was crushed. She had sent him a strong message, and she expected a loving response.

However, while she was sensitive to these slights, she didn't pick up the important signals Greg sent when he held her hand crossing the street or waited up for her at night if she had to work late. Most of all, he began to share his dreams and spoke of his past failure.

In a few months Greg started to get on his feet again, developed another project, and shook himself out of his depression. The desperation was gone from the relationship; but so was the romance. What was left?

One day, sitting in the back of a taxi, Margo said, "Greg, why don't we call it a day. I think that's what you really want."

Greg didn't answer. The traffic clogged and clanked around them. Margo pressed. "Well, what do you think?"

"Let's discuss it some other time."

The cab was trapped in an intersection. Margo jumped out, and Greg quickly lost sight of her on the crowded sidewalk. She spent that afternoon and evening at a friend's house and didn't return home until after midnight. Greg was in bed, asleep. She turned on every light in the apartment and roused him.

"Damnit, Greg, I asked you something. Don't just put me off."

"I told you we'd talk about it some other time."

"I need to know now."

"Don't you understand?"

"Understand what?"

"Let's leave it alone."

"It? What it?"

"Us. Let's stay together."

"Well, Jesus Christ, why didn't you say so?"

"I did."

"You didn't—you said . . ."

"What do you think I meant?"

* * *

"I don't know how we had lasted that long," Margo said, "but finally it all started to fall into place. We just weren't tuned in. I was thinking about myself and trying to measure my reactions, and making up what he was thinking. He was doing the same thing. We each knew what we felt and thought, but didn't have the slightest idea what was going on in the other's head."

Two more years passed before Greg and Margo fell in love again. "I remember it very clearly," Margo said. "One morning I was standing in front of the bathroom mirror looking for wrinkles under my eyes, when Greg came in behind me. He put his arms around me and rested his head against my shoulder, and I felt the oddest sensation. In that split second we fell in love."

The Nature of Intimacy

Falling in love creates a state of harmony which makes being together perfect. You dissolve into one another's souls. "He will see me for what I really am." "She senses my innermost feelings." "She can read my mind."

Falling in love is blissful. It is also misleading. The state of perfect unity, fused spirits, and blurred bodies cannot (and should not) last forever.

The odd thing about falling in love is that it is both profound and superficial—profound because the connection is primitive and powerful and occurs without conscious effort; superficial because it's not sophisticated enough to sustain the many subtle aspects of separate personalities. When you fall in love, you recognize only one side of a person. When you fall *out of love*, you begin to discover someone's full personality. That is why disillusionment is the road to real love.

Although disillusionment ends some relationships, it's a necessary step toward intimacy. Disenchantment forces us to come to terms with who our partners are; not who we think they are or who we would like them to be, but who they *really* are. Then we can achieve a greater understanding and acceptance of ourselves and our partners.

This is what commitment is about. The word *commitment* is often used loosely, usually in the shallow sense of making a decision or promise. "I want him to make a commitment." ("Marry me.")

Only when two people make an effort to understand each other are they truly committed. *Commitment* means "I care enough about you to try to understand you and consider you." But it's a risky business, because we might be misunderstood or dumped if we reveal ourselves. But it's the only way. Commitment is a prerequisite to intimacy.

Greg and Margo were used to taking private professional risks, but not to laying themselves on the line with other people. They had to learn to take personal risks.

Chapter 2

WHAT ARE RELATIONSHIPS MADE OF?

THE NEUROTIC/EROTIC CLICK: COMPLEMENTARITY

Marriages are not made in heaven. And love does not conquer all. Love and marriage are based on unresolved conflict, vulnerability, neurosis, and illusion.

Family therapists have a lot of ideas about what makes "it" happen between two people. "Out of the millions of people in the world, how did you two get together?" Dr. Don D. Jackson, a pioneer in family therapy, used to ask couples in an attempt to understand the complex needs that bring two people together.[1]

Instant attraction between two people is based on superficial qualities that we consciously admire, but also on something else—a mysterious quality that two people pick up with a personal radar, a vulnerability that we sense in one another.[2] This hidden quality is so powerful that someone can walk through a room crowded with people and gravitate toward the one person with whom he or she shares an attraction: the fatal enchantment. This powerful force produces the emotional click we call chemistry.

This natural attraction functions surprisingly well. When the chemistry works, each person picks up on the positive aspects of the partner's behavior and learns from him or her, acquiring something of the other's style and approach to living. The slob learns to be a *bit* neater, while the fiend for cleanliness becomes less compulsive; the spender makes purchases more prudently, and the worrier panics less as the bills pile up; the angry one grows less volatile as the restrained one becomes more assertive; the workhorse relaxes and has more fun at the same time that the carefree partner becomes more organized.

This positive exchange takes place when partners allow each other room to change, to expand, and to take on some of their own coloration and manners.

First impressions are the primary clues to the mysterious mix that determines our choice of partners. They are also clues to our secret hopes and dreams. "He looked so sure of himself." "She was such a live wire." These first impressions reveal the foundation of the ensuing relationship.

From this first moment we are subliminally aware of the traits we love (and hate) in our new romantic partners. That doesn't mean that every attraction turns into a deep relationship. But flirtations that endure arise out of the magnetic emotional field between partners. This magnetism is a charge both positive and negative—a bond that links and may also bind.

Family therapists believe that couples share the same basic insecurities. But the strategies each adopts over the years to handle his or her conflict are different and usually opposite. Couples sense their similarity, and their opposite manner of coping attracts them to each other. They "fit" together because although their basic vulnerabilities are the same, their styles of coping with life are different. This dovetailing is called complementarity,[3] on which all relationships are based.

On the surface complementarity seems simple: opposites attract. His bossiness is balanced by her submissiveness. Her liveliness counters his shyness. His impulsiveness is tempered by her cautiousness. But no matter how different a couple appears to outsiders, at heart they are the same people.

Complementarity is more profound than the balancing of outward characteristics, though. Genuine complementarity is shaped around deeper human conflicts: independence and dependence, sensuality and sexual inhibition, aggressiveness and passivity, self-confidence and self-doubt. These elements are at the heart of complementarity. Even when the superficial aspects of complementarity are absent, these deeper attractions still exist.[4]

Positive Complementarity

Complementarity works extremely well when each person has a good sense of individual identity and is open to learn from her or his partner. Each begins to become more of a whole person.

The cool, detached man is attracted to the warmer, more outgoing woman. He remains at a slight distance from people, almost never talking about his deeper feelings. He lives largely in his mind. She appears open and down to earth. Yet she too is afraid that she will be engulfed by people she loves or who love her. She is in continual conflict, leaping out and withdrawing. When she gets too close, she recoils.

Their relationship over a period of time works for them. She warms him up, keeps him in the center of reality, and adds depth to his life. While loving her, he gives her freedom and doesn't overwhelm her with demands for constant intimacy. She learns to relax more, to take relationships in her stride, and not run away from conflict. He has become more like her, and she has grown to be something like him.

People fall in love with people with the same kinds and levels of problems.[5] When partners recognize this similarity, they can help each other. When they don't, they can torture each other, each trying to make the other solve the problem that both have.

By taking on something of the other's style, partners can grow and change together. They benefit from having the same problem because they can understand each other when nobody else understands either one of them.

This last is the beauty of complementarity and the key to making it work in a positive manner. Partners in conflict need to learn from each other without swallowing each other up. We can learn by trying to understand our partners. And to know them is to know ourselves.[6]

Negative Complementarity

In a less positive way the sexually exuberant male marries the sexually timid female. On a deeper level they share a fundamental fear of being possessed (being passionate, being out of control) and express it in two different ways. He flaunts his sexuality, boasts of his exploits, and goes from one woman to another in a frenzy of passionless relationships. She retreats. She's a cold fish, he says. She says he's oversexed. It's a perfect no-win situation because each can point a finger at the other. The relationship can't be satisfying unless they each face the fact that they're afraid of closeness.

In the same way the person who freely spends money shares a core conflict with his partner who is miserly and watches every dollar, paying each bill the day before it's due. They may take opposite sides, but both are deeply concerned about whether they are deserving. One is self-denying and the other self-indulgent. If they continue to stay on extreme opposite sides, their relationship is doomed.

Relationships cemented in opposite styles are negative in complementarity. Partners hide behind each other.[7] Rather than helping each other change, each emphasizes the other's imperfections. "I'm okay. You're not." These couples find fault with and blame each other for their problems. Instead of changing themselves, they try to make each other over.[8]

The wife of a successful businessman was often depressed and despairing; sometimes she couldn't get out of bed in the morning. She was shocked to hear her husband speak of his own fears and doubts, because she never knew he had any. In this relationship each partner did double duty: she carried all his insecurities, he carried all her competence.[9] This is complementarity at its worst.

In other relationships one partner may be phobic and the other daring. The fearful partner has undisclosed strengths; the daring partner hides secret fears. It always works this way. There are no exceptions.

We choose people because we believe they're different from us, and we like the difference. We want to be more like them.

A retiring, shy woman chose someone who seemed more daring. After a while something happened. She got upset when he jumped from one business to another, when he failed to meet his financial responsibilities, when he could not adhere to the simplest rules of personal obligation—in short, when he could not be more like her. Why, she asked, was he out cooking up another get-rich-quick scheme when he should get a steady job and pay the rent? She had forgotten how much she loved his sense of fun and rebelliousness. She now wanted him to be like her. After all, she had put aside frivolity in favor of responsibility.

Her solution was to put him aside in the same way that she had put aside that disowned part of herself. She knew him so well because she had the same problem taking risks, but erred on the side of caution instead of recklessness.

This is always the dilemma. We choose someone because we want to be more like them; then we're upset when they aren't more like us. And like every other aspect of complementarity, there is always an opposite condition. Sometimes we get upset *because* our partners are the same as we. We try to get them to do the things we can't do for ourselves, and hate them when they can't. One wife found that she became most irritated with her husband when she tried to get him to do something she didn't want to do herself. "I would nag him to pay the bills until I was in a rage and completely frustrated. It was years before I realized that I was nagging him because I didn't want the responsibility of handling the money. We finally realized that we both had the same problem meeting financial obligations."

Going to Extremes

Extreme complementarity almost never works because neither partner, like a child on one end of a seesaw, can balance himself or herself alone. He is always a half-person, a fragmented personality looking for someone else to make him or her whole and provide balance. Each is desperately attracted to people who seem, at least on the surface, to fill in the missing part.[10]

There are usually elements of both positive and negative complementarity in any relationship. The more grown-up and emotionally mature partners are when they meet, the more positive their "fit." When people have some idea of who they are, they are less likely to be pushed into false role-playing in order to give themselves definition.[11]

Tony Mosca was an emotional live wire who was immediately attracted to his wife the first time he saw her. She was a tall, slender blonde dressed in a pale blue silk dress that made her look both elegant and reserved. He was friendly and energetic. Linda cooled him off, and he warmed her up. Alone, she tended to get too reserved, too aloof. He tended to get crazy.

Tony was always close to emotional overload and wished he could put a lid on his outbursts. Linda's social, Philadelphia-based family had trained her to squelch passion by means of reason. She avoided being "overemotional," but worried that she was lifeless. She longed to be spontaneous and passionate.

Together Tony and Linda achieved a balanced position between aloofness and hysteria. But this positive complementarity could reverse and push them to extremes.

"Sometimes when he gets violently upset," Linda said, "it scares me. I turn all cold inside."

"When she gets like that," Tony countered, "it makes me even more angry because she doesn't feel anything. I go out of control."

In times of stress Linda's coolness infuriated Tony and pushed him too far. The more rational and detached she became, the more he raved.

Neither Tony nor Linda could express anger directly and realistically. Tony's tantrums excluded real communication as effectively as Linda's silence and withdrawal. When he got out of control, he proved to both of them that emotions were dangerous.

Tony and Linda were good for each other when they helped each other become more whole. They were bad for each other when they pushed one another to extremes and created rigid, polarized shadows of people. Then he dubbed her "ice maiden," and she coolly responded that he was neurotic.

It is this darker side of complementarity that turns romantic visions into marriages that drive people crazy.[12] People get locked into their roles and are not permitted, or do not permit themselves, to change.

Positive complementarity helps partners become more whole, helps each person to grow. Negative complementarity keeps two people one-dimensional and forces each to stay the same; relationships based on negative complementarity are fertile grounds for fault finding and trying to change the other person.[13]

MARRIAGE CONTRACTS

It has become fashionable to put the rules and regulations of marriage in writing. As a result, many couples are writing marriage contracts, specifying the mutual obligations in the relationship: money, life-style, child rearing, housekeeping, leisure time. These contracts attempt to equalize sex roles, anticipate and resolve potential conflicts, and impose a quasi-legal structure on an institution that needs bolstering.

Such contracts add weight to the relationship and help partners express their expectations of one another as well as their fears (one new husband wrote into his contract that his wife must tell him if she had an extramarital affair). Often in the process of writing a marital contract, important differences are revealed and partners begin to see each other more clearly.

Marriage contracts are attempts to deal rationally with conflicts, bring issues out into the open, and give couples a way to discuss emotional issues in a cool, fairly detached manner. What's more interesting than which partner does the dishes is *how* they arrive at the decision. The decision-making process is more important than the decision itself.

For example, do they draw straws, negotiate and compromise, or debate endlessly until one is worn out and the other wins by default? Does one partner overpower the other? Do they listen and respect each other's position or belittle and diminish each other's arguments? Are they committed to arriving at a solution that feels satisfactory to both?

The way couples influence each other, the subtle ways in which they exploit or respect each other's weaknesses, and the ways they avoid some problems and recognize others are the guts of the marriage contract that never appear on paper.

Clear recognition of problems is the benefit of written contracts. The danger is that rigidity or sterility will creep into the relationship and take the spontaneity and discovery out of marriage. Marriages need to be more, not less, dynamic. Written contracts can get bogged down in trivia such as who cleans the bathroom rather than the real issues around which marriages are built: independence, anger, power, loyalty, and trust. Some couples are so busy working out their dishwashing schedules that they don't attempt to explore deeper issues.

One bride and groom in their mid-thirties worried constantly about losing their identity in marriage: everything, they agreed, had to be fifty–fifty. Each paid exactly half the rent with his or her own check. Each declared ownership of his or her own household property; there were to be no transgressions. "If we ever split up," the bride used to say, "we know exactly who owns what." She blushed furiously if anyone made a social gaffe and referred to her as Mrs.————. She was even annoyed if someone referred to her husband as "your husband" (as in, "How's your husband?"). If they needed anything, financially or otherwise, they didn't turn to each other; they turned instead to friends or parents.

Both were so busy defining the boundaries of their individual lives that they never merged into a couple. And after a year and a half they were no longer married. The only argument was about how to divide the wedding presents.

Written and sometimes spoken contracts are of value when they make each partner aware of their expectations of each other, including their needs and fears. And the clue to making contracts work is to keep them flexible. Some couples build in an option so that they automatically review their contract every year. However, the probable rigidity and superficial quality of most written marital contracts outweigh their potential value, and for most people they have only a modest benefit.

These written agreements are not what family therapists refer to when they speak of marriage contracts. All couples have contracts. These agreements on the nature of their relationship are seldom even verbalized, let alone written down. Yet they are even more binding because they bind the mind and soul.

SECRET CONTRACTS

Every couple "writes" a contract from the very beginning of the relationship. Ask any couple ten years after they met what their first meeting was like—everyone remembers it clearly—and you'll find that all the elements of the relationship were laid out in that first encounter.

I was very young when I met my husband, and we have lived several lifetimes together since, yet I can remember and see as clearly as yesterday that all the elements in our first meeting are present in our marriage today. It was a noisy early morning at the breakfast table of a ski house in Vermont. We looked each other over, but didn't exchange a word. We rode in the same car all the way to the ski slopes, still not speaking.

In the ticket line I struggled to fasten my ticket to my jacket. He offered to help and tightly fastened the bright bit of pasteboard onto my zipper.

For the rest of the day, I shadowed him all over the mountain. He went up, I tagged along a few skiers behind in the lift line. He went down, I tracked him several turns behind. We didn't really speak until that evening over dinner. We were married a year and a half later.

The seemingly insignificant events of our meeting shaped the rest of our lives. Only years later did I understand that we were signaling more than we were aware of. That he rescued me from my own helplessness with the ski ticket had a secret meaning for me. I read his response to mean that I could count on him to anticipate my needs. My helplessness would be our secret, and he would take care of me. By tracking him all over the face of the mountain, I displayed my more competent and aggressive side. His continued interest showed that he wasn't put off by either of these extremes. He let me know he cared and also showed me that he liked being pursued. Unknowingly, and without a word, we had stylized all the routines of our relationship.

All the struggles of the years to come were written on this scene. Our extreme tendencies to reach out and retreat, to be helpless and competent, became visible in decidedly less attractive ways in the years that followed. But it was all there at the very first moment.

From the first encounter we signal our innermost longings and fears, even though most of us are on our best behavior. In a moment the basic rules of the relationship are present.

What are these rules about? Loving and hating, getting close and being separate, expressing tenderness, and handling conflict. Because we are making the rules we will live by, the first few years of every relationship is a period of extensive upheaval and conflict.

Dr. Clifford Sager distinguishes between a person's individual marriage contract and the couple's common contract. The first deals with what you want and what you're willing to give in marriage. The second is the set of maneuvers that we develop with our partners.[14]

Marital contracts are dynamic and should change throughout the marriage. The unspoken agreement between spouses will be partially renegotiated at each new stage of family life, sometimes in major ways. Needs change through the life of the family: between courtship and marriage, at the end of the first year of marriage, after the birth of children. Each time a change takes place, couples should explore the limits and range of their relationship.

It's not enough for one person to want change. Like written contracts, changes can be made only with the consent of all concerned parties. Partners instinctively know this but often perceive any change in the contract as a threat. Instead of talking together, one person exerts pressure; the other feels controlled. Changes must be negotiated between partners.

Marriage contracts get "rewritten" in subtle shifts and balances of power. One of the things that makes relationships interesting is the struggle for power. Power means getting what you want, and what you want today will probably not be what you want tomorrow.

Each time any family member wants a change, it shakes up the other people in his or her life. Hence the struggle for power between partners is a natural part of rewriting the contract.

Power struggles are futile when one person wants to make another person change. They are productive when you want change for yourself and will fight for it.

In the throes of her first love affair, Janice Colton found herself pregnant. A college girl from a puritanical, hard-working family, she felt God was punishing her for having sexual desires, an opinion that was confirmed a few weeks later when her boyfriend deserted her. An abortion solved the immediate problem for Janice but also added to the mountain of guilt she already carried.

Janice was a shy, studious girl who was very lonely on her own. She soon fell in love again, but in contrast to her first affair, this new love was reasonable and didn't tempt her sexually. Her new boyfriend was outgoing and confident, the oldest child in a big family and accustomed to his role as family ruler. Janice admired Larry Trull and looked up to him as a protector. Larry was attracted to her intelligence and felt he could mold her quiet brilliance into achievement.

They got married following graduation. Larry joined a big-business conglomerate and Janice perpetuated her student life, taking a part-time job and going to graduate school. Eventually she earned a master's degree and got her first professional job as a city planner.

After they had been married several years, Janice began to complain that Larry was overly protective and condescending. "I felt controlled and manipulated by him, as if my whole life was dictated by his opinions and desires. I tried to stand up for myself, but he verbally beat me down. He would outargue and outtalk me until I started to cry. Why do I always cry when things get tough?"

In retaliation Janice closed herself off sexually. Sex was an ordeal for her anyway, another obligation at the end of a long day. The lesson of adolescence had been that lust was not to be trusted, and that sexual excitement only led to trouble.

"Sometimes I think I got married to get away from sex, if that makes any sense. When Larry and I met, the sexual revolution was in full swing. Everyone had sex with everyone else. It was very confusing. Getting married took us out of all that. I didn't have to think about sex anymore." But that same security had now turned into a kind of straitjacket.

For Janice, their unspoken contract was "restrain my passion, stabilize my emotions, help me achieve my potential." For Larry, it was "lean on me and I'll protect you." And their common agreement: "We'll take care of each other so we won't have to face the world alone."

For eight years they had lived up to the marital contract. But marriage contracts are subject to change as people change. In young marriages especially the early contract is based on illusion and partial pictures of ourselves and our partners. Janice outgrew the contract. As she gained status in her profession, she no longer felt the need for Larry's protection and guidance. She wanted his respect. Larry wanted the relationship to remain the same.

It isn't unusual for one partner to choose growth while the other clings to the status quo. These opposing forces sometimes have advantages for marriage. If one partner is forced to take risks, the other can hold the line and provide stability. But wholesale change or boring stability destroys marriages. Marriage is a series of pushes and pulls.

After eight years of stability it was time for a change. But Larry couldn't handle it. He had been Janice's mentor rather than her husband. And mentors traditionally are put aside when their protegés move past them. For all his apparent self-confidence, Larry needed Janice to depend on him.

They tried to form a new relationship that would leave room for change. For a while they wavered, then suddenly switched positions. Now Janice demanded, Larry placated. Janice shouted; Larry cried.

"Now he seems so vulnerable," Janice said. "I need to protect him."

"Now she seems so confident," Larry said. "I can't live without her."

These flip versions are common in relationships based on extremes of complementarity. Instead of encouraging growth, each person was polarized by her or his role. All they could do was flip back and forth between extremes. Unfortunately there wasn't enough flexibility in their marital contract to accommodate change.

Janice ended the stalemate when she packed her bags and left. She never went back. She has learned to live alone. Larry got involved in another mentor-student affair similar to his relationship with Janice. So Janice got her change, and Larry retained his status quo, but they couldn't do it together.

ME, YOU, US

Family therapists speak of closeness and distance in relationships. They talk about *enmeshed* relationships,[15] in which there is too much togetherness. Couples fuse into a faceless lump of togetherness. Security, loyalty, and devotion are the passwords. Romance may fade, but they cling to each other out of habit.

One young couple met in high school and have been together ever since. They were apart for one "miserable" year while they attended different colleges in the same city, and they cherished their weekends together. They vowed never to be apart again. They moved in together and made their own "little nest." She thinks they're the perfect couple and talks about marriage. He's beginning to feel claustrophobic. Marriage frightens him. But being alone scares him, too. Enmeshed relationships trap, restrain, and imprison people.

At the other extreme are *disengaged* relationships,[16] in which two people maintain their distance. Personal space and privacy are jealously guarded. One newly married man and wife were so busy leading their own lives that they hadn't spent an evening together in months. It was probably just as well; the last time they were alone together at the beach, they fought the entire weekend. Excessive personal freedom brings narcissism and loneliness.

At either extreme end of the continuum—too close or too distant—there are only half-people. In the enmeshed relationship, couples fail to grow as individuals. In the disengaged relationship, they fail to grow together.

The healthiest relationships fall in between these two extremes. Each person is independent and capable of surviving with or without the relationship. You don't *need* each other to survive, but you choose to be together and have learned to depend on one another.

Extending personal freedom while staying within the rules and obligations of marriage is for many couples the ideal mixture. For others the emphasis is on unity. There is room for both styles, but extremes in either will wreck marriages. In Stage 1, couples struggle to find their unique blend of individual autonomy and mutual obligations. They are challenged to create relationships that balance commitment with freedom.

Chapter 3

HAZARDOUS RELATIONSHIP STYLES

"Marriage is," Jane Austen said in *Mansfield Park*, "of all transactions, the one in which people expect most from others, and are least honest themselves."[17]

For most of us falling in love is a passionate affair. Romance happens when two people connect to each other strongly but keep their attraction superficial. Romance may last a week or a year; six months is probably average. Then the relationship reaches a turning point. You begin to wonder if you've made a mistake. The idyllic partner is full of flaws you never saw before. You question whether you can work things out.

Sometimes fading romance is signaled by an escalating series of arguments that never seem to get resolved. At other times you may begin to notice things you don't like about your partner, irreversible flaws that you can't stand. Response to a loved one's eating habits is a common signal. One man remembered watching the woman he had lived with for six months eat yogurt from a container as the relationship was ending. "It was the most revolting thing I've ever seen," he said. "I remembered it particularly because a couple of years later I wanted to break off a relationship with another woman but was worried because I thought she loved me so much. We were eating dinner and she said, 'Do you have to hit your teeth with the fork?' Then I knew I didn't have to worry. It was our last dinner together."

Whatever it is that is going on, you find that you can't talk about it; the words stick in your throat. This is the time that many relationships go down the drain.

Sometimes the turning point occurs before marriage, but it often happens after. That's why there are so many different readings on what people think about early marriage. ("The first year is the hardest" might not be true for

38

couples who have already gone through the transition from romantic love to genuine intimacy.)

What makes some relationships fizzle out or blow up at the turning point, and others continue? It depends largely on what we bring to the affair.

First-bloom love needs to be accompanied by openness and honesty between people. Too often at the beginning of love affairs, we keep parts of ourselves hidden until "he gets to know me better." We show only what we consider our good selves. This perpetuates the illusion our lover already has going, and also puts a strain on us. It's hard to be perfect all the time. Much later, if we spring the more unworthy aspects of our characters on our new loves, we risk rejection.

The more fully people express different facets of their personalities—good and bad—from the beginning of the relationship, the less shocking the turning point will be. This doesn't mean that you can reveal yourself fully the first time you meet someone. We come to each other in pieces, and it takes time to know someone fully. But the more honest the pieces, the easier it is to achieve intimacy. Putting your best self forward all the time is not only a strain; it also keeps the relationship from growing.

Once you reach the turning point, both people must express themselves more fully, revealing hidden feelings, weaknesses, vulnerabilities, and fears. If you avoid this process, you mislead your partner and are forced to play an uneasy role that is only part true. By failing to reveal yourself as a whole person, you make a contract as an imposter. Taking the risk is tough for some people. We fear that we won't be loved if we are really known. But we aren't really loved unless we are known fully.

This is the time to find out how much you care about each other, to clarify expectations, to settle misunderstandings. It's easier at this point to talk about the things that are wrong than that are right. But if you're blaming each other, you can be sure that you're not revealing yourselves.

The turning point of Stage 1 offers an opportunity to deepen and improve the romantic affair, take it out of the realm of fantasy, and place it firmly in the real world. Instead of reaching this happy result, however, many couples set upon a disastrous course. They may vacillate between romance and disillusionment, with knock-down fights followed by passionate lovemaking. You break up, suffer for a week, and get together again in a wild romantic moment. Then it happens all over again. Sooner or later one blowup will be too much, and the relationship ends forever. Long afterward you look back on the affair as a wonderful romance that somehow didn't work out.

Others, disappointed and confused at the turning point, withdraw before the action starts, which is the one sure way to protect the fantasy that somewhere in the world the perfect mate exists (but not here). The affair may erode slowly or end abruptly in tears and accusations.

PSEUDOINTIMACY

Usually people who end relationships at the first sign of trouble are afraid
to get close. Veronica and Theo were a classic example of two people who
avoided intimacy. Neither one rocked the boat. It took a wave to swamp
it.

Veronica Lyle and Theo Muir had been dating for almost a year. She had
her own apartment but lived at his place, although it was still very much *his*
place. She had a small portion of the closet and dresser, but all the furniture
was his, and the house was run according to his wishes. Veronica never
knew exactly where she belonged. Although her personal possessions were at
her own apartment, her place had that look of neglect that comes when no
one lives in it. She went home twice a week to water her plants, do her
laundry, and pick up mail and clothes. She always felt unsettled.

In other respects Veronica and Theo shared their lives, friends, and
holidays and seemed to have a stable relationship. Veronica sensed, however,
that it was time for a change, to draw closer together and add more
definition to their affair.

She wasn't sure how to do this. Talk about feelings, desires, or troubles
was a foreign language to them. Sometimes they spoke in code.

Veronica loaded her own words, spoke between the lines, and in an effort
to detect vital signs in their relationship, mulled over every nuance in Theo's
small talk. She imbued meaningless comments with import, as if each might
be a secret proclamation of his devotion. Veronica was afraid to ask Theo
directly how he felt about her.

They had never had a fight. Several weeks ago Veronica said Theo was in
a foul mood. He withdrew, ignored her, and was self-absorbed. Veronica kept
up her charming good manners but was annoyed with his dour disposi-
tion.

Finally, she "initiated a discussion" and spoke obliquely about coping
with problems you can't do anything about, such as work. "After this
discussion," she said, "he improved." I asked what she would have done if
they were married. "I'd probably speak up, but I'm not ready to chance it
now."

Veronica didn't like living with a man without the security and trappings
of marriage, but she had never mentioned this to Theo. She planned to bring
up the subject of marriage after the New Year.

Theo had been married and divorced twice. Veronica knew he was reluctant to marry again, but she was banking on the fact that he cared enough
about her to overcome his reluctance. The main rule of their relationship
was to avoid unpleasant confrontations.[18] Veronica believed she could
change the rule after they got married.[19]

On the first Monday night in January, as they were riding up to Theo's
apartment in the elevator after an evening out, Veronica, with a slight

tremor in her voice, casually told Theo that she wanted to get married. Of the possible responses she had reviewed in her mind, she hadn't imagined the one she received. Theo said he had no intention of marrying again and had never indicated that he had, and refused to discuss it further.

The conversation was over by the time they got to the front door. They went to bed; Theo slept through the night, while Veronica sat in the dark, smoking and watching.

The next morning Veronica packed her belongings and left. She kicked herself all the way home. How could she have lived with a man for a year and completely misread him? Theo also was shocked, for he had believed that Veronica wanted things just as he did.

"WE NEVER FIGHT"

A similar but even more dangerous pattern is mutual retreat—more dangerous because as a style, it can go on indefinitely. To keep the romance going partners agree to withdraw from problems and live together in false harmony. At least one of the partners hides some major dissatisfaction, feels angry, and wants more but is afraid to say so. He or she is afraid to raise objections, because to open the door may cause the other partner to pour out all his or her grievances as well. You swallow your feelings and your complaints. How long you keep it up depends on your capacity for self-denial. To continue in the relationship means denying your own personality.

Delia Warren and Gunther Krause had been seeing each other for more than a year. They spent every other weekend together and occasionally one night during the week. Although the relationship was dependable, it didn't seem to be going anywhere.

They spent their time together at Gunther's house, watched television, and ate German-style dinners that Gunther cooked. They never went out or saw other people.

As the months passed, Delia wanted to expand their relationship. She modestly suggested a few things she'd like to do. She timidly asked if he'd like to go to a movie, and he vetoed the idea. She suggested a German restaurant, but he decided against it. She turned the radio to opera; he switched it back to popular music. In the face of Gunther's blatant indifference, all Delia's feeble negotiations collapsed.

Delia desperately wanted this relationship to work. She was lonely and had never had a lasting relationship with a man. Delia had totally given herself over to Gunther. With Gunther, she had at least found someone to be with, even if it meant hiding her feelings and her desires. She forfeited her rights in the relationship for a guarantee of companionship.

A relationship, by definition, is two people negotiating their rights with one another. What Delia had with Gunther can only be called a pseudo-relationship. Her lack of self-esteem was so profound that she was willing to settle for a false sense of companionship. She would be satisfied, she said, if only Gunther would say he cared for her. A hint would be good enough.

She grew more depressed. Underneath the depression she was angry that she was getting so little. To her the smallest act of assertion now was like revolution. But she felt that if she showed her anger, she would blow the relationship. She didn't realize that there was no relationship to blow.

How do people find themselves in this kind of predicament, willing to settle for so little? Why are we afraid of the people we love, so unsure that we will go to any lengths to obscure our real feelings, the people we really are?

Mutual retreat as a style of living together never works.[20] It causes serious problems if the couple marries and later has children. They use children to express unhappiness that cannot be openly expressed to each other. The pattern becomes entrenched, and the result is tragic. Couples who deny their disappointments in each other retreat from the battle before the skirmish even begins. These relationships sometimes look peaceful, but underneath they are fragile affairs that cannot withstand the rigors of family life.

People in love are not always at cross-purposes. Sometimes the signals are clear, and both people want the same thing. But not often. When it's time for a change, women most often seem to be the initiators, perhaps because they are more comfortable expressing emotion. Yet the initiators of change are always in a weaker position, because they ask for something. It is up to the other person to grant the change or refuse to cooperate. If the other partner doesn't cooperate, the initiator is forced into a grandstand power play, which invariably fails. To initiate change is to take a risk. However, when a relationship has something going for it and one person wants to change and states his or her wishes, negotiations usually open up the situation. People who care for each other look for ways to be happy together.

"WE ALWAYS FIGHT"

The reverse of "we never fight" is "we always fight." But the dynamic is the same: it covers up the need for intimacy and affection.

"We always fight" is based on pseudohostility,[21] which protects couples from genuine closeness. These couples find a million things to argue about: whether to have pizza or Chinese food; go biking or lie on the beach; buy shag or flat carpeting. Everything is a power struggle. Compromise means surrender and loss of self-esteem. Stubbornness prevails. Winning—or better yet, not letting the other person win—is crucial. No one's going to push me around, is the unspoken message.

For some couples who have trouble being close, arguing is an excuse for making up. After a vicious go-round, they end up making love. The fight is a prelude to passion. It heats up their relationship. Fighting keeps them from drifting apart.

Karen and Stu Sandler had been married for three years. When they came for counseling, they couldn't decide if they wanted help to stay together (marital counseling) or help in splitting up (divorce counseling). They hadn't been able to live together peacefully, but they couldn't separate, either. It was a stalemate.

As if a gong had gone off for the first round, Karen and Stu were off. They attacked, criticized, and argued from the minute they arrived until the minute they left. Their patterns were so reliable that they could depend on each other to be nasty, insensitive, withholding, unyielding, and mean.

It was impossible to get them together on anything except their disagreeing. In fact, they were exuberant when they fought and lifeless otherwise. Their power to hurt each other was awesome; few couples are as free to hate each other as these two.

The power to hurt is the darker side of the power to love.[22] Afraid to love in any other way, some couples respond to coaching on better ways to communicate. They become aware of the ways their insecurities translate into skirmishes.

But Karen and Stu had logged years of distrust. Retaliation was a sport; they were opponents in a deadly match. I didn't relish being the referee.

After several months of therapy I agreed with their assessment that their relationship was not improving. Karen was on the verge of moving out, and divorce was becoming the probable outcome.

But when Karen began to look for an apartment to sublet, Stu became conciliatory. When her search abated because she half-expected an improvement between them, he became obsessed with something she had done to him two years before. If Stu threatened to walk out, Karen suddenly held her tongue and made an effort not to call him a pig for watching football on television. But she couldn't resist sneering at his "low life" taste in restaurants.

They could vacillate about separation indefinitely without either one getting any closer to giving up on the other. There are many couples who spend their whole lives together making each other miserable.

In the midst of one heavy series of accusations and counteraccusations, I wondered who was going to get custody of their poodle, Cuddles. To my amazement, they took the question seriously and on the spot worked out a joint-custody agreement that would impress a lawyer.

At this point they really shifted gears, perhaps because they felt I was "recommending" divorce. For the next six weeks we worked on a divorce settlement, dividing property and assets in a fair and equitable negotiation.

Their divorce was the most amicable accomplishment of their entire relationship. Because they were unable to reflect on their problem, there was no way of knowing whether Karen and Stu would repeat pseudohostility in new relationships.

Chapter 4

MY FAMILY, MYSELF, AND MY SPOUSE

Imagine making love to your spouse with your parents standing over you, observing, evaluating, and criticizing your performance. This actually happens to all of us. Without even realizing it, we bring our parents into the bedroom.

To a great extent success in marriage depends on how separated we are from our parents.[23] Both lay and professional experts warn that we choose mates who have personalities similar to our parents. Beware: is your husband-to-be like your father? Does your wife act like your mother?

It's actually more complicated than that. It's not that we choose spouses amazingly like our parents, but we tend to re-create relationship patterns that are strikingly similar to our original families.[24] Current family problems are reconstructions of patterns that existed in our original families. In any marital crisis the family therapist considers what part separation from parents plays.

Separation is a psychological process, not a literal one.[25] Separating from your parents is not leaving home in a trail of dust, but separating childhood from adulthood so that you become your parents' peer; the relationship is no longer based on your being a child.

Separation means feeling whole without your parents; it means financial, emotional, and social independence; and knowing your parents as people, not as tyrants or idols. When separation is achieved, we maintain our relationship with our parents out of a mixture of feelings of continuity, obligation, and affection. Family reunions and occasions are rewarding and fun, now more adult and mutually replenishing.

Separation is the task of adolescence and young adulthood.[26] People who fail to achieve separation before they marry carry all the emotional baggage they haven't worked out with their parents into their marriage and transfer it onto their spouses.

When you are too attached to your parents, it's impossible to make a commitment to anyone else. Young couples become enmeshed in their original families and surrender their identity as a couple, often playing out unfinished family dramas from the past.

Many people who are still attached to their families see marriage as a way to separate. They want to make a break but feel so guilty about it that they look for a way out without hurting anyone. Marriage, to most mothers and fathers, is an acceptable reason for adult children to leave home. So young people—usually too young—get married, leave their original families, and carry all their problems with them.

Separating includes developing friendships with other adults outside the family. Friends should replace family as support systems. When young adults fail to develop strong friendships with their peers, they are often swamped by loneliness and a feeling of being unconnected. The apparent solution: marriage.

Separation also means that young adults have their own work patterns and personal interests. To be self-supporting is to have a sense of identity in the working world. Until recently women have missed out on this important task, seeking marriage as a way of being taken care of, and avoiding the marketplace. Society expected it, and it was an easy out.

Getting away from family, absorbing loneliness, or being taken care of are not strong enough motives to sustain a marriage.

"I MARRIED YOU, NOT YOUR FAMILY"

The most common problem young couples have is pushing their parents out of the marriage bed. Parents can intrude on the new marriage in a variety of ways. Making your spouse the most important person in your life means settling things between you and your parents, separating from them in a profound manner.

Most people who marry in their early twenties haven't finished "pulling up roots."[27] They are struggling to create a unique identity, a sense of who they are and what they believe. Marriage at this young age may inhibit personal growth, because people tend to transfer their situation with their families into their marriages.

Couples still connected to their original families fail to deal with each other and hammer out their marital contract. The major task for newly married couples is to establish the rules they will live by. This involves shifting loyalty from your family (and/or your friends) to your partner as the most important person in your life.[28]

People who have moved away from family ties often replace family with friends who are at least as close. These friendships that mimic family ties also have to be switched over. Best friends, along with parents, have to be placed outside the marriage.

To declare yourself a twosome, you need to put psychological distance between you and your parents and close friends. This is easiest when each partner is a one-some to begin with.

Couples can stop themselves from forming the exclusive relationship essential to marriage. One bride, for example, hooks her girl friends into her marriage by talking to them about her husband. Spouses should practice *not* talking about their mates with family and friends. Although, of the two, it's better to talk to your friends than your parents or in-laws.

Another wife said: "I used to tell my girl friend everything about my husband, kind of a hangover from when we were teenagers, I think—you know how girls talk endlessly about boys. Somehow I sensed that this complaining to her about my husband was interfering with our marriage. Instead of telling him my troubles, I'd tell her, and he'd never know. Now if I'm having a problem I might talk to her about it, but it's not to complain about him."

When my husband and I married, we were both still embedded in our original families. Our relationship was complicated by the work we still had before us of extricating ourselves from our families. To form a strong emotional bond, we first had to unravel the threads of old loyalties that had been reserved for our parents.[29]

We were masters at avoiding these problems. It seemed so natural, so convenient, to go to my mother-in-law's apartment for dinner several times a week. It seemed so easy for her to scout the stores for our furniture, to call the supermarket for our groceries, to hire the seamstress for our drapes. I was busy in school, and as a bride and a newcomer to New York, I wasn't familiar with the stores and shops. I had never bought a piece of furniture or cooked a meal in my life. Bob's mother became my confidante, my friend. She was, I thought, a better mother than my own, more understanding and giving. Bob seemed relieved that our marriage wasn't going to displace his family.

This rosy picture abruptly faded on the day I found myself talking to "our" gynecologist about birth control while my mother-in-law waited for me only half an earshot away. I realized that now I was inviting her to share my bed. When I went home that day, I cried for my own mother and my sisters, who were several hundred miles away, and for my father who had died the summer before.

Playing "the children" to my husband's parents meant we couldn't be adults. We had sacrificed our privacy and self-respect for free meals and convenience shopping.

It's a small miracle that Bob and I survived our early marriage. All the odds were against us. In every respect we were unprepared. Like many couples, we married too early, too rashly, naive in the blush of romance, still attached to our original families, each of us more child than adult.

Being distinct from our original families but still connected to them is not easy. Our relationship as a couple was stymied by our lack of separation from our parents.

I cried for the first two years of my marriage. Tears rolled down my face and ruined two Thanksgiving dinners. Tears soaked the sofa in the den and made blotches in my notebooks at school. At first people noticed my tears, but after the first year everyone took it for granted that I was just a crier.

My husband and I were both miserable, stunned by the discrepancy between romantic courtship and married life. Life became harder. We blamed each other and tried to make each other over. This failed completely, because we were both stubborn and equally matched in our power to hurt. One night I made a grandstand play, threw a handful of clothes into a suitcase, hurled malicious accusations, and slammed the door behind me. I sat in our car, the keys in the ignition, the motor running, ready to accelerate myself to independence. I cried some more when I realized there was no place to go.

Bob watched me from the rooftop of our building, only guessing at my dilemma. Hours later I sheepishly returned home. I have never before or since felt so alone.

Slowly it dawned on us that our marriage was in trouble because we as individuals were in trouble. We could split up or stay married. It really didn't matter much. What we had to do was grow up. We liked each other, and we were scared. We thought we might help each other become more independent and still be close the way we were when our love affair was filled with Cape Cod holidays and Vermont skiing.

Since then we have been pathetic and sometimes ugly in each other's presence. We have tempted each other with the truth and waited to see if we could bear it. Humor at the right time has saved us from feeling hopeless.

Alone, we found ourselves as separate people. Together, we discovered each other and made a family. Today, sixteen years later, I am strong enough to walk out the door, but I can't imagine doing so.

It's easier if you are a one-some before you become a twosome. Actually, in the long run, growing up together strengthened our relationship, but I believe luck was on our side.

Now we can see his family and my family regularly and enjoy being part of large, noisy extended families.

Finding a place for yourself in your partner's original family is important.[30] Some family therapists think of marriage as an integration of two families of origin.[31] When a young marriage is in trouble, therapists sometimes hold family reunions with all living members—the new couple and both extended families of origin.[32] It's quite a gathering.

One family therapist emphasizes that "the varieties of meaning that the in-laws have for the spouses sometimes include, surprisingly, a value that transcends the importance of the marital relationship itself. In fact, some spouses go through one or more marriages looking for but never able to find the 'proper' in-laws. In a sense, for them the marriage serves as a bridge that attempts, unsuccessfully, to span the unresolved gulf between themselves and their own family."[33] Some unhappy marriages go on for years because the wife or husband has such a deep attachment to in-laws.

Problems with in-laws are displaced separation problems that we have not resolved with our own families of origin.[34] If you find yourself losing sleep over your mother-in-law or sister-in-law, your relationship with your own mother or sister needs work.

RE-CREATING FAMILY DRAMAS

Lucy and Mike Lazar fought constantly, sometimes, as they said, over nothing. After only a few months of marriage, they had a particularly vicious fight; it quickly got out of hand and Mike slapped Lucy. The physical violence frightened them both, and they called that same day for a consultation.

Both came from families where warfare was a way of life, although their families had different fighting styles. Lucy's mother was the warlord in her family. "It was a daily ritual for Mother to criticize and belittle Daddy. And he depended on me for support. I was the peacemaker."

Lucy calmed her mother down and soothed her father's ego. She often diverted the battle by becoming the target of her mother's tirades. "I learned to deliberately provoke my mother so she would attack me instead of Daddy," Lucy said. In this manner the deep hostility between parents was kept manageable.

The hostility was even more circuitous in Mike's family. "When my parents divorced," Mike said, "I was about seven. It was all very vague, but Mother was very bitter and angry afterwards. They never spoke to each other again. Mother made me her ambassador. I had to ask my father for everything for my mother, especially money."

Mike also had to do all the negotiation for visiting rights, camp fees, and dentist bills. From an early age he was his mother's warrior on guard even in peacetime.

By declaring open war with each other, Mike and Lucy re-created the behind-the-scenes hostilities of their original families. In her marriage Lucy played her original role by provoking hostilities and then trying to smooth everything over. Mike, sensitive to the slightest provocation, prepared his weapons and tensed for attack. Each re-created the roles they had perfected in their families.

One difference was that they had replaced the secret cold wars of their families with a hot war of their own.[35] Battle was the order of the day for these two experienced warriors, and violence was only a short step away.

Original families influence the style and pattern of our new love. How we relate to people, and how we expect people to relate to us, is laid out in our family of origin. A child who learns to be accommodating to please his or her parents goes through life playing the same passive role. But it goes deeper than that.

Families are powerful shapers of all the relationships we create. In the new family we try to master original family traumas. Unknowingly, we duplicate family dramas that tormented us as children; but we also can solve them in our new situation.[36]

A young bride may be "passive and accommodating" because of a problem in the relationship between her mother and father. Her mother was overpowered by her father and compensated by dominating her daughter. In this way the daughter was used by her parents to stabilize their relationship.

When she grows up, she may marry a man who appears strong (like her father) but eventually reveals himself as weak and impotent. She repeats the original family drama by uncovering and exposing weakness in men. She makes *very obvious* in her new family what was *not obvious* in her original family. She tries to undo what was done to her.

I know a twenty-one-year-old woman whose mother had so many children that she was forced to put this woman and another child in foster homes when they were small. The girl grew up, married twice, and had three children by the time she was nineteen. Now, having left her second husband, she is destitute and unemployable. "I'll never give up my kids," she says. "I'd die first."

The best way to overcome this kind of old family trauma is to try to become more complete yourself. A strong personal identity is the key. It means being able to make choices based on self-knowledge rather than compulsion.

Another example of the way original family dramas haunt children and carry over into their new families is the story of Ken Walker. His situation offered the opportunity to uncover and overcome a family conflict that had been hidden.

Ken's parents separated when he was three years old. "I never knew why," Ken said, "but my father left and I never saw him again." Ken grew up, married, and had a son of his own. He is presently separated from his wife but cannot decide what to do about his marriage.

Ken and his wife were barely twenty when they married, too young to know whom they were marrying or why. As they matured, they grew in separate directions until they were so far apart that nothing was left of their early love. Ken was miserably unhappy at home and dreaded returning, yet he felt that he must go back. It was the voice of conscience, not heart. He feared he would lose his relationship with his young son.

In the last several months Ken had formed a deep attachment to another woman. Now his decision was complicated by choosing between "responsibility" and "selfishness."

In painful moments he chose his family, especially his son, over his lover.

"I don't want to leave my son the way my father had to leave me," he would say.

In his struggle for happiness Ken "accidentally" had re-created his original family trauma. By putting himself in the same spot he imagined his father was in he duplicated the drama of his own childhood.

It was inconceivable to Ken that he could be a responsible and loving father if he left home. "If it's possible to divorce and still be a good father to your child, then what about my father? He must not have cared anything about me."

Ken suffered tremendous grief facing this truth about himself and his father. But by re-creating and reliving the experience with his absent father, he resolved the problem that had troubled him all his life and rewrote a better ending for his own child.

Ken eventually made the break; he fought hard and won frequent and extended visiting rights with his son. "It's ironic," he said, "but I think divorce made me a better parent."

These are some of the ways family problems repeat themselves from one generation to the next. Unknowingly we duplicate family patterns in an effort to master our original family traumas.

Chapter 5

REMARRIAGE AND THE COUPLING PROCESS

Blended families are a unique social form. Four-fifths of all divorced people remarry.[37] Forty percent of these remarriages will not survive.[38] In these new marriages, two families with different histories, beliefs, patterns, and rules merge into one. Long after they blend, original family loyalties continue.

Blended families are the most complex family form. They place members at several stages of the life cycle at once, and these people must cope with all of them simultaneously, like juggling oranges and orange crates together. The couple scarcely has time to work out their intimate relationship before they have to create cohesiveness among disparate family units.

Beverly Grant and Fred Jenner had a lot in common when they began seeing each other. Both were divorced. Fred had three teenage children who lived with his wife. Beverly's three young children lived with her.

Divorce involves two separate processes: the legal, paperwork divorce, and the emotional divorce. Even after the legal divorce is accomplished, the emotional divorce may drag on.

Bev, who had been divorced longer than Fred, was further along in mourning the loss of her nuclear family. Her bitterness toward her former husband had been muted by his willingness to maintain a compatible relationship in terms of their child-rearing responsibilities.

Fred's divorce had been far less amicable. He was still trying to protect his children from its aftermath. Also, like most divorced men, he was the one to move out of the family home and lived *ad hoc* in a small apartment. Through divorce he had lost both home and children, and had less sense of wholeness than Bev. So that although they had a lot in common, they were in two different emotional places.

After they had been going out together for a while, Bev wanted to share more of her life with Fred. She was interested in his work and his children, but he seemed to lock her out of these areas of his life. "I feel like a plaything," she told him. "Someone you sleep with sometimes and trot out for parties."

Fred was astonished by her feelings. "I love you," he said. "You're an important part of my life. But I can only give so much."

Fred felt he had more responsibility than ever before, and less support. He tried to juggle his several incompatible lives by dividing his job, children, alimony payments, and his affair with Bev into compartments.

"I'm in over my head already," he said. "I can barely keep up with my obligations." For this reason he resisted involvement with Bev's children. He liked them but didn't want a larger role in their lives.

Fred was trying to protect himself and still fulfill his responsibilities. He had a strong loyalty to his family and tried to shelter his children from any upset or distress. "If my wife remarries," he said, "I will take the children. It would be unfair for them to share their lives and home with a stranger." Fred assumed his children wouldn't want to stay with a remade family.

Bev was offended by this comment. What were the implications for her? Was she, too, an intruder? Was Fred saying she would never be allowed to have a place in his family?

"When I was married," Bev said, "I used to sweep all my problems under the rug, and accommodate my husband. I don't want to do that anymore. I want to be more open, and risk more. That's why we're here." To open up the issues, they came for one therapy session, then continued to work through their problems alone, occasionally telephoning or coming in for a consultation.

Beverly and Fred struggled to define their romance. Coping with four separate groups of intimate relationships was chaos. "Fred and his family are one unit," Bev said. "My children and I are another. Fred and I as a couple are a third; and all of us together are a fourth. It's totally insane." All four groups were separated by past and current experiences and loyalties.

Bev wanted to ask, "What are we doing this summer?" but couldn't bring herself to say it. Was there a "we" or was it "me, you, your kids, my kids?"

Amid the confusion of so many competing loyalties, Bev and Fred were in love. But there was almost no room for their relationship. They were forced to stretch the fresh boundaries of their intimate "we" to include family obligations.

Bev told us, "I want to be closer to Fred. I feel this urgency to integrate all these far-flung outposts of our lives. If we don't, I don't think we'll make it."

"I just don't think I can handle it," Fred said. "I need more time."

They both knew that they couldn't afford the luxury of an exclusive attachment. Boundaries had to be established at the same time that doors were left open.[39]

After several months they made their first attempt to blend the two families. Bev and Fred and all their children took a joint vacation. The trip was a disaster. Beverly described a typical scene: after a day of swimming and sunbathing, together the family(ies) met for dinner at a beautiful garden restaurant. The children were sullen and pouty throughout dinner, particularly Fred's teenagers. Beverly and Fred tried to make jokes and liven up the nonexistent conversation, but their efforts to amuse were greeted by silence and long faces.

Under the best of circumstances teenagers are less than ideal companions on a family vacation. Beverly described Fred's fourteen-year-old son as withdrawn, sulky, arrogant, and self-interested—a typical description of an average teenager.

Although they continued to maintain separate households, Bev struggled to define her role in this new "family." She wanted to get something more going with Fred's children, but couldn't find an appropriate role. In an attempt to connect with them, she fell into the trap of lecturing them. If she wasn't a teacher or an instructor, then what role did she have?

Together, Fred and Bev were doing fine in their personal relationship. Bev had mixed feelings about remarrying, because she had learned to enjoy the luxury of being single. "It would be easy for me to fall right back into the wife role, and I'd miss out on doing more for myself," she said.

For the time being she and Fred agreed not to take positions of authority over each other's children. And also they decided to forgo vacations as a group. For the following year they planned three vacations: Bev and her children; Fred and his kids; Bev and Fred alone.

It seemed important for them to continue building their intimate relationship together, and also to allow each other time alone with his or her children. But they also had to take steps consistently to integrate the families and not fall into a pattern of separating them because it was easier.

For instance, Fred and Beverly went together to Fred's daughter's graduation from high school. Bev had to accept the fact of Fred and his ex-wife's parental tie on this occasion. Her place was somewhat peripheral, but these are the kinds of things parents in blended families have to do. On winter weekends Fred and his kids and Bev and her kids went skiing together. But the full integration of their two families was a slow process.[40]

They were willing to give it time. "I've learned that divorced people sometimes try to put failed marriages behind them too fast," Bev said. "They gloss over their children's reaction to the marital difficulties and subsequent divorce. Fred needs time and we can't push the children too fast." Bev thought it was important to talk to children about what's happening to their lives and to keep the connection between natural parents alive. She was right. It takes time—as long as two or three years—for children to recover from a divorce.[41]

Over the next year and a half, Fred and Bev developed their personal relationship and consistently worked at blending their two families. They were married last summer.

Kenneth N. Walker and Lillian Messinger, both of whom are family researchers, think of blended families as two countries that permit dual citizenship. The new family fully acknowledges

> the prior allegiance and affection that may exist between parents and children, whether living together or not, but also expects some sense of membership in the remarriage household. The two memberships overlap and need not conflict if neither "family" demands exclusive loyalty from its members.[42]

Ideally, children can enjoy the benefits of both memberships and widen their network of affectionate relations with adults and other children, thereby increasing their social support system. Members of blended families have to learn to live with two sets of families of permeable boundaries, rather than the single, more rigid boundary of the nuclear family.

This ideal result is extremely difficult to achieve. With so many people involved, the main goal must be to make the situation as easy on the children as possible without causing too much pain to the adults involved.

The meeting and mating of two people is no accident. We seek partners who provide something that we are missing. And in the process we often choose people who share our deepest insecurities and fears, even though they appear opposite in behavior. Couples frequently get caught in the trap of trying to make the other person do what they can't do themselves.

A major turning point occurs when we abandon the one-sided picture we have of our loved ones and encounter them as whole people. By doing so we discover ourselves. The family has overcome its first hurdle.

But in Stage 2 the recently intimate twosome must now be willing to make room for another person. Having a child, no matter how many other children are already in the family, throws marriage off balance, and the family with young children at home becomes an emotional pressure cooker.

Stage 2
COPING WITH PARENTHOOD

Turning Point: To be a "me first" family or put the family first

Chapter 6

READY FOR PARENTHOOD?

A new father said of his ten-minute-old son, "He looked like a little rat—but in a couple of days, oh, he was beautiful." Babies are loving and lovable. We count their amazing miniature fingers and toes over and over again. They laugh, and make us laugh, too. Babies are so small that they need help to turn over in their cribs, and they can't find their toys if they drop them. The pure helplessness of an infant is perhaps its most endearing quality.

Yet the miracle of childbirth signals the most hazardous and upsetting stage of family life for young couples. Suddenly married life centers around the most demanding, helpless human being alive.

"Why," contemplates a career woman thinking about motherhood, "should a baby be so much trouble? It sleeps all the time, it can't talk, it's confined to a crib, and it doesn't take up much room." Obviously the voice of one who has never lived with an infant.

A new parent will tell you that, on the contrary, a baby never sleeps at all; that it cries all the time, interrupting civilized conversation with its own pagan outbursts; and that baby accouterments—bassinet, bath, clothes, toys—totally dominate any household.

A new baby is fed at least every three or four hours around the clock, and each feeding time lasts about thirty minutes. In between, parents have a few hours to take care of personal and work obligations, not to mention all other aspects of baby care.

Any parent can describe the feeling of frustration at the end of a long day, when the smell of diaper-rash ointment hangs in the air and baby formula fills the refrigerator to capacity. Or when a toddler, newly accustomed to standing on two feet, clamors for attention, pulls your ear, and wrecks any thought of an evening of peaceful regeneration.

How different is this stage from early marriage, when a man and woman first begin to share their lives, and each still retains a certain amount of independence. The loss of some personal freedom was made up for by the pleasure of that exclusive-couple feeling. Having a baby forever alters the nature of this hard-won relationship: marriage never again will be the same.

Children are not added onto a marriage like a baby seat to a bicycle. Having a baby requires a shift from a relationship that caters to two adults to a relationship that nurtures a child. In Stage 2 a genuine sense of family begins.

This transformation from twosome to threesome is so little anticipated that many marriages suffer irreparable damage when a baby is born. Even those most prepared and forewarned are caught flat-footed.

Among the classic social documents of the 1950s is a study which anticipated some of the issues family therapists would expand over the next three decades. A group of young couples who recently had become parents were interviewed. They were like many middle-class couples of that decade: urban or suburban residents, between twenty-five and thirty-five years old, the husband a college graduate, the wife unemployed after the birth of their first child. The research interview included both husband and wife; discussions were informal. Couples talked about the changes they were experiencing and dealing with in their personal adjustments, their marriages, and in relationships with their young children. In this decade of relative social tranquillity, 83 percent of these couples said they went through an extensive or severe crisis when they had their first child.[1]

Today, no less than in the 1950s, parenthood is still a major life crisis in which positions are shifted, values changed, and new roles assumed. Not only are adults turned into parents, but out of the crisis a *family* is born, and the family evolves a personality of its own.

THE CRISIS IN STAGE 2

The continuing struggle throughout family life is how to balance the needs of adults with the needs of children. In Stage 2 this juggling act requires skill plus knowledge. This is the most dangerous stage in any marriage. And perhaps the most important bit of information that helps new parents is that infancy doesn't last forever.

For the next few years, however, husband and wife must turn inward and shape their lives around the needs and demands of this new thing, "the family." For now the family comes first, and all other obligations are second. Parents begin to make sacrifices in terms of time, money, and attention. Pressure is put on the couple. They give up some of the pleasures that enriched their marriage—time together alone, deep consciousness of each other's needs, moments devoted to the desires and needs of one another. Most of these pleasures are put aside.

We say that new families have to turn inward to nurture the very young child. Yet all relationships in the family have to be considered all the time, and this nurturing must also include parents. To meet the needs of all its members at this stage of family life, the family must temporarily close ranks. Parents who neglect to nurture one another as well as their child grow apart. And I believe this is the cause of the high divorce rate for this stage of family life.[2]

As with all stages of family life, the transition period from one stage to another is the most difficult. The rough passage into Stage 2 can be smoothed. Couples start to build a sense of family during the months of pregnancy, taking childbirth classes together, planning the baby's wardrobe, reading books on diet and child rearing, bracing themselves for the moment of birth. These activities in anticipation of change help ease the transition, but most couples still retain the illusion that parenthood is joyous and even romantic. The reality, when it finally occurs, is like a cold shower.

A few couples begin the transition months—even years—before pregnancy by examining their lives to decide if they are ready to have children. This kind of close self-examination, however, is still unusual. Having babies is considered a natural, healthy instinct and every person's right. But it is becoming increasingly common for couples to choose to remain child-free. (The term *child-free* is beginning to replace the negative-sounding *childless*.)[3]

FREE TO CHOOSE

A hundred years ago newly married couples had little choice about whether or when they would have children. Birth-control methods were almost unknown. In the 1920s Margaret Sanger went to jail several times for counseling women about contraceptives. An outspoken advocate of birth control and women's rights, she eventually succeeded in making contraceptive devices available to women who came to her family-planning clinics and, as a result, made "birth control" almost respectable. When "the pill" became generally available, coincidentally with a fear of overpopulation, the practice of birth control became the norm rather than the exception. Now, after more than two decades of the widespread availability of several contraceptive strategies, couples can easily plan their families.

Implicit in the promise of birth control was the idea that couples could decide not only when, but if, they would have children. Changes in modern society have made the choice to remain child-free an option that is unique to our time.

Men and women have begun to question whether they want to disrupt happy marriages with the stress that comes with children. Career-oriented wives wonder if they need to prove that they are superwomen by having children. In the past people with a profound cynicism about living often avoided family life. Now couples have begun openly to express darker fears and secrets they have kept to themselves. Some men and women review past hurts and sins out of their own childhoods and believe they will perpetrate the same transgressions upon their children.

Other questions are more general but no less stirring. Modern society itself creates an environment dangerous to children. Some people worry that regardless of how much love and protection they give their children, a drug-laden, disintegrating culture will destroy their children in the vulnerable bloom of adolescence. Others ask if it is right to bring more children into the world when so many are homeless and in need. And on a more intimate, personal level, both men and women question themselves: "Will I be a good parent? Can I rear a happy child? Can I be a better parent than my mother and father?" These questions are not easily answered.[4]

The freedom to choose has brought its burdens, and most people still prefer to avoid, at least overtly, making a choice. They would rather take life as it comes.

Certainly overpopulation and the cost of living have made smaller families the trend today.[5] Large families, even among the rich, are considered against the greater good. The family with six children playing in the front yard is no longer seen as the American dream. This down-scale trend has almost made the child-free marriage socially acceptable.

Yet despite the trend toward smaller families, remaining child-free is still a deep-seated social taboo. Couples who do not have children are accused of being selfish. A woman who rejects motherhood is "not a woman." She has missed out on life's primary purpose and reward. For hundreds of years women without children were considered failures not only as wives but as human beings. Men, too, are accustomed to measuring their virility by offspring. For some of us, having babies calms deeply hidden anxieties about not being good enough. Children prove to the world that we're normal, that even if you lose your job, don't make enough money, seem to do everything wrong—there is one thing you can do right.

For decades the mental-health community has fully supported the concept that sex, marriage, and children are irrevocably linked. Most therapists still hold that having children is a strong, natural human instinct and not having babies is deviant. The goal of the "The Parenthood Prescription" described by social commentator J. E. Veevers is to lead all couples to parenthood.[6] This traditional approach views parenthood as normal and healthy and nonparenthood as negative and pathological.

In spite of all these social, religious, and philosophical prejudices, child-free couples in recent history have become more common, more vocal, and more visible. In response, at least some therapists are reviewing their biases.

I think people who want babies and who are emotionally ready to have babies should have babies. Those who feel unsure should wait until they are sure. And those who know they don't want children should have the freedom to remain child-free without feeling guilty or suffering slings and arrows from relatives, friends, and therapists whose rhetoric includes statements such as, "You don't know what you're missing," "Isn't it too bad; they're such a nice couple," or "All they care about is themselves." People should think carefully about what having a child will mean—to themselves and to the child—before bringing a new life into the world. Too many lonely people have babies in a desperate—unsuccessful—effort to solve their own personal miseries.

Choosing to remain child-free will not become a major trend, I am sure. Most happily married couples will probably continue to have children. Since the turn of the century, the number of women who marry has increased.[7] And although there has been a decline in the number of children per family, the proportion of couples who have children has increased.[8] This last is apparently due to medical advances in combating infertility, which have more than compensated for birth control.

Even those who recognize that they have a choice are often paralyzed by the idea of making a decision. Some decide by refusing to confront the issue. One woman who says she really wants to have babies never allows her relationships with men to develop. Although she says she wants a family, she takes no steps toward family life. She manages to make it look as if the decision is out of her hands: "I just never met the right man."

Others delay the decision until it's too late. At thirty-eight Glinda Rodgers underwent surgery to remove a cystic ovary. Her surgeon told her that during the procedure he could cut the fallopian tube to the remaining ovary, assuring her permanent freedom from pregnancy. She had been happily married for ten years and diligently used a diaphragm. She had no children. "I'm not ready to decide yet," she told her doctor. Five years later she still couldn't decide.

In my experience the decision to have children still rests primarily with women. Should their marriages fail for any reason, women feel that the major responsibility for bringing up the children will rest with them. For most couples, women are seen as the force behind parenthood, and men go along because it's expected of them. Men have even less room than women to reject parenthood. For every man who walks away from his pregnant girl friend, a thousand take up the responsibilities of parenthood without question. For every man and woman who decide together that they want to be parents, ten thousand men have fatherhood foisted upon them. It is a shortsighted woman who believes that whatever she decides will make her husband happy, or, if not happy, at least acquiescent.

But the decision to have a baby is a genuine choice that a couple should share. The choice to remain child-free is neither more nor less healthy than the choice to have a family.

The family therapist can help couples evaluate both options and then support whatever decision they make. But—and this is a crucial point—

making a rational choice means being able to consider both possibilities objectively. And this is where—and why—couples become paralyzed.

COUPLE TROUBLE

Jack Newkirk and Lily Rosen had been living together for five years when Lily decided that she wanted a baby. She was thirty years old, and Jack was thirty-one. They were both entering a time of life when a shift takes place, a resettling and reevaluation of life's goals.

Their unspoken contract was that he was free to come and go pretty much as he pleased. And as Jack was adventure loving and spontaneous by nature, he treasured this freedom.

"I like the excitement he generates," Lily said. "He's always stretching the limits, defying the odds. I'm much more conventional." Jack, on the other hand, loved Lily for her stability. She was his rock, his center, the place where he could always come home. The relationship was complementary in the most positive sense.

There were some minor problems. Jack was a Don Juan who proclaimed a need for sexual freedom. Lily was a one-man woman, faithful even in her thoughts. Somewhere along the line she realized that his supposed philandering was a harmless weak spot. He wasn't quite "grown-up," as she put it. "If you're going to have affairs," she said, "don't tell me about them." That was all right with Jack. He was free to pursue other women, and it remained his secret that he didn't. On occasion he tested the boundaries. One rainy night at a hotel in Seattle he picked up a young woman at the bar and invited her to his room. He was surprised the following morning that he didn't feel particularly pleased with himself.

The arrangement may not seem ideal, and it spoke loudly of Jack's reticence, but it was, nevertheless, a pretty successful relationship. Then Lily said she wanted to have a child.

She knew a child would alter the way they lived. They couldn't run off climbing mountains for weeks at a time. There would be no more Saturdays racing motorcycles at top speed over unknown country roads, and no more jumping from one whim to another. But she believed the baby would bring them closer together and make Jack more the sort of mature man she wanted.

Since they had never discussed having a family before, she didn't suspect the kind of feelings the idea would generate. Jack's response was a shock to them both. He wasn't merely against it, he actively despised the idea. He had an almost physical revulsion toward family life. His reaction was so violent that it frightened them both.

It was now clear that the gentle transition to fatherhood envisioned by Lily would never take place. She thought of the future: "Years from now," she said, "I'll be nagging and complaining and Jack will be kicking and screaming. Or he might leave."

Yet she still wanted the baby, still felt it would bring them closer to the things she felt were important to her: family, home, constancy. Jack and Lily were at a genuine standoff.

When we met, they were at a complete impasse. Suddenly these two people, who until now had managed to find a satisfactory formula for their lives together, were threatening each other and giving ultimatums. "I'm not getting any younger," Lily said. "If I want children I have to do something about it." And if Jack didn't want what she wanted, she implied, maybe she should find somebody who did.

Jack felt she was pulling the rug from under him. He counted on her but took her for granted. She was the one person who would always be on his side, always want and need him. Now his Lily was making a demand that he couldn't possibly meet.

I was the second counselor they had seen. The first therapist who worked with them had felt the goal was to bring Jack around to the idea of parenthood. Jack and Lily both rejected this approach, but, although laden with suspicion, they still wanted someone to help work out the problem. They were firm about the idea that the issue was not to achieve a preconceived goal but to be free to make a rational decision. I made it clear to them that I had no stake, one way or the other, in their ultimate choice.

Too many people assume that having children is a magical experience that will transform their basic feelings about families. It's true that you can't know what it will be like to have a child until you've done it. But exploring your feelings about families can give you strong clues about your readiness to have children.

The decision to create a family is related to the experience of growing up: how we feel now and how we felt in the past about our own parents. Images of family life are important. They tell us about our feelings, fantasies, and memories. Lily remembered the security she still feels with her parents, the trusting relationship with her brothers, the fun she has when her extended family gets together.

What did families mean to Jack? He didn't hesitate: "Families are boring and suffocating. Families are traps." There was vehemence in his words. Families were obviously dangerous stuff.

The situation with Lily forced him to explore his family background. I don't think anything else could have prompted him to delve into the past, and the reason was soon painfully clear.

The transformation that men and women often make out of their past is a constant source of amazement. Jack was tall and lean, almost spare. His hair was fair, his eyes gray, his features regular. When he wore a suit, it was well tailored and subdued. To our meetings he usually wore faded jeans, a sweater, a well-worn leather jacket, and sneakers. He seemed the kind of person for whom jeans invariably fade to just the right color. He was articulate and well spoken; confident in himself and what he had to say, the kind of confidence usually enjoyed by New England Brahmins. He was a lawyer who took his responsibilities seriously, defending the poor, the indigent, and the radical. There was no trace of darkness behind the golden facade. At least there didn't seem to be. Jack didn't want to explore the reality.

In fact, Jack grew up in one of those small towns in southern California put together with stucco, screen doors, and scraggly palm trees. His parents were middle-aged when he was born, their first and only child. His father was a quiet man whose life revolved around his managerial position in a small local bank.

While he was growing up, Jack was very close to his mother. She was an energetic woman who generated the liveliness in the household, while her husband reduced his own life to a stale but comfortable routine. "When I was a child," Jack said, "I don't think I ever saw either of my parents take a drink. But when I left home to live in the dorm at college, my mother began to drink. She had a part-time job in the mornings, but every afternoon she drank."

Their house was a small shingled cottage behind a larger apartment building. Jack remembered coming through the alleyway one afternoon, feeling apprehensive about seeing the blinds drawn over closed windows in the heat of a California day. The door was ajar. "The smell of gin was so heavy in that stale air that I gagged. My mother was passed out on the living room floor. I picked her up and tried to make her sit upright in the chair, but she kept slumping forward; then she grabbed me and hung on to me, crying. She always called me 'Sonny.' 'Sonny,' she said, 'where have you been?' It happened a lot after that."

Jack's father seemed not to notice the change in his wife, and the predictable rhythms of his life continued uninterrupted. Jack moved back into his room at home. For a while things would improve. Then there would be some regression. Whenever he left the house, she headed for the bottle. The longer he was away, the drunker she became. Slouched in the same chair in the darkened living room, she began barely to notice his return.

"I couldn't stand seeing her like that. I began to stay away, first for days, and then weeks at a time. Finally, I went on the road with one of my friends from school, and hitchhiked to the Mexican border. I just needed to be on my own for awhile. But I couldn't get her off my mind. I came back about a month later, and she was in the hospital. She died a few days later."

Jack's father bought a good-quality casket and decorated his wife's grave with roses. "After the funeral, my dad and I cleaned out the house, discarded a lot of the old furniture and all my mother's personal things. We never mentioned details of her life. We never talked about her the way you do after someone dies. Dad just talked as if she had been ill, but he never said anything about her drinking or anything. I just wanted out. I took off that same day and headed East. And that was the end of it. I see my dad once in a while, but well, it's not much."

We were sitting together in front of windows overlooking the reservoir in Central Park. Snow was falling against the window. Jack's eyes were full of tears, and Lily took his hand. She brought him back to the present.

Jack loved Lily for her loyalty, but he was suspicious of belonging to anybody. And being responsible for any human life panicked him.

"Jack, what do you think I'd do if you left tomorrow?" she asked.

"Why—you might miss a day at work," he said and tried to smile.

"Well, maybe. I'd miss you like hell, of course. But I don't think I'd jump out of a window or anything."

Jack laughed. The prospect of Lily killing herself over a man was ridiculous.

Before he could make a free choice about fatherhood, Jack needed to separate what was rational from the irrational parts of his feelings. Clearly what he said and what he did were two different things. He demanded freedom but had lived happily in the same apartment with the same person for more than five years. He stated in his slightly aristocratic, intellectual manner that he needed many women sexually, yet he was more faithful than most married men.

Three important issues divided Jack and Lily, issues which only slightly interfered with their present intimate relationship but which would create hard problems in a family situation: sex, money, and children. Lily saved, Jack spent; Lily wanted monogamy, Jack wanted open sex; Lily wanted a family, Jack didn't. There was no casuistry here, only different points of view. They both agreed, however, that they wanted each other.

Jack chose to continue therapy to reach the darker areas of his past. He did this willingly because, once on the track, he had the courage to pursue the mystery. He became aware of feeling constant pressure to prove that he was free, alive, and unrestrained. He had always sought new challenges, pushing himself to the limits. Always on the move, partying late at night, smoking dope to reduce his anxiety, competing in swim meets, squash tournaments, motorcycle races—he seemed to be running in a private marathon to see how much he could stand and how long he could last. Underneath, death haunted him as he raced against his own mortality.

I don't know what Jack and Lily will decide. My guess is that eventually they will have children. As Jack levels out his major objections to family life, Lily's strong desire for children will probably sway him toward her point of view. On the other hand, if she is neutral, they probably will not have children. Even if they do have a baby, family life with Jack will never fulfill Lily's fantasy. And when she thinks it over, she wouldn't want it to. One of the reasons she loves Jack is because he's not like everyone else.

A decision about parenthood should never be based on panic, repulsion, or fear. Nor should it involve living up to social obligations, trying to please our families or spouses, or just doing the right thing. Making a rational choice means we can consider both possibilities, weigh one against the other, and decide. It's a far cry from being programmed in one direction or repelled by the other.

My friend Kaye Howden says I go too far. "If everyone had to go through all that before having a child, they'd never do it. There's always something better to do than have a baby—a trip to Europe, a new job—you could put it off forever. Choosing makes it almost impossible."

Kaye isn't the only one who has mentioned this. I am told that I am naive. "Deciding is too difficult," they say. Most couples take for granted that when they marry, they will have a family. "Why else would we get married?" Most young couples I know, but not all, use some method of birth control until they feel secure enough to start adding new lives to their household. And most often their accidental pregnancies are unconsciously planned, as in Kaye's own situation.

"My first pregnancy wasn't planned," she said. "It was an accident. But we took a look at ourselves. We had been married three years, we were both working, and while we weren't rich by any means, we were okay. And I was thirty-three years old. Well, why not? That's what we were there for. After Jake was born, we didn't want to wait too long for a second child. We already knew we wanted two children and thought it would be easier on all of us to have another child right away, so we did. But if I had to consciously decide, I'd still be lying in the sun on Barbados."

If you've got the right stuff going in your marriage, and you're comfortable with the idea of family life, the decision to have children is like an automatic response. But many people would be better off facing what a baby means to their marriage. Not every marriage can support a baby. And regardless of the stability of the relationship, having a baby is a turning point—a shift into family life that is a genuine crisis.

Chapter 7

HAVING A BABY

Family therapists are often in the Dark Ages when it comes to understanding how a family organizes itself after the birth of a first child. We can find volumes that describe the subtleties of the mother/child relationship, on the other hand, and it's common to see this relationship as central to family life. Feminists declare this view to be damaging to the identity and growth of women. From a man's standpoint, also, the exclusive mother/child relationship is no less damaging, since it deprives fathers of a place in the family and robs them of their emotional center.

MOTHER AND FATHER

In the past, husbands were applauded for their masculine achievement (impregnation) and assigned a backseat or, at best, a supporting role to the real drama enacted by wife and obstetrician, and later by mother and newborn.

This estrangement is slowly fading as fathers take part in childbirth and parenthood-preparation classes and are present at the actual birth of their children. How different they are from our own fathers, who first nervously paced waiting rooms and subsequently felt awkward and uncomfortable with their infants.

The trend toward having babies at home is a response to the loss of humanness and family focus in hospitals. The birth of a child is a family experience. Participating in the delivery and holding a new baby immediately after it's born imprints an intense feeling of family on mother and father and older siblings. A family, not a baby, is born.

TYRANNY OF NATURAL CHILDBIRTH

Unfortunately, sharing in the birth of a baby is not always a positive experience. For some couples, the idea of "natural" childbirth is a tyranny that divides parents. I know one woman who became troubled because in the last stages of labor, she needed medication to mute the pain and help conserve strength for the pushing phase of the delivery. Another woman developed a complication during labor and had a cesarian section. Both were convinced that their husbands were disappointed because they had failed to live up to the ideal of natural childbirth. An unpleasant rift developed between the new parents; they avoided talking about the birth experience, because to them the episode was a failure—although both infants were thriving. The whole family experience got off to a poor start.

For the most part, though, the close involvement of a father in the childbirth experience is a happy event with long-range implications for the future generation.[9] A new father who is comfortable holding his infant is likely to feel a more immediate attachment to the child, which should affect the nature of their entire relationship.

Men are discovering their nurturing selves, showing more interest in childbearing decisions, and desiring more influence in child rearing. *Kramer vs. Kramer* was a hit movie because in it Dad pinch-hits for Mom and discovers parental love.

Big business, in response to pressure from both men and women, is also getting involved in child care, and some farsighted companies provide paternity leave for prospective fathers. The trend toward a shared work load is not only bringing women into the work force, but also brings men into the home.[10]

Social science continues to lag behind with respect to the complex mother-child-father unit (or triad, as family therapists call it). Three-person relationships are more complicated than two-person relationships. All three relationships are intertwined, and the survival of the family depends on how well all of these relationships are nurtured.

Few couples make the transition into Stage 2 of family life smoothly; most find having babies and raising preschool children the most difficult time of their lives. Even the happiest and best adjusted married couples can be stunned by parenthood. The event of childbirth sends shock waves through their lives and sets in motion a process of adjustment that takes years to complete. The results of marital-satisfaction studies made at different stages of family life will startle anyone who holds a romantic view of parenthood.

MARITAL VS. FAMILY SATISFACTION: OPPOSED OR BLENDED

Several independent research studies uncovered this interesting information: after a baby is born, marital satisfaction sharply decreases. According to the studies, the quality of the relationship between husband and wife begins to diminish when their first child is born and declines steadily throughout the active parenting years. Marriage does not improve again until children have grown up and left home.[11]

This research data is bad news for those of us who hope to combine a good marriage with a happy family life. But when we take a closer look at the backbone of the research, the picture isn't quite so dismal. The problem with the validity of these studies is the criteria they use for "satisfaction."

Investigators measured marital satisfaction by asking couples how often they went out together, socialized with other couples, enjoyed (uninterrupted) sex, and talked together privately about personal problems. A majority of the couples interviewed said these activities declined after children were born. But the researchers did not find out if they were replaced by other satisfactions associated with family life: the pleasure of reading a story to a child, seeing children grow and develop, having family outings, and the like.

Once couples have children they lead a different life, and it is unfair to say that they are less happily married because they seldom enjoy the pleasure of being alone together. After eight years of married life, my intimate relationship with my husband became inextricably tied with the kind of parent he was to our children. The happiness of our marriage depended more on sharing parental responsibilities and less on being alone together. Our children were in turn affected by our marriage; how good we were as parents depended on how much we helped each other. If I neglected him or he neglected me, all our relationships were thrown out of kilter.

The young mother who complains that her husband neglects their child usually feels neglected herself. The father who competes with his son for his wife's affection feels displaced. When we become parents, we can't expect the same loving devotion from our spouses that we once received; husbands and wives need to build new connections to each other.

Catherine Chilman's research among families selected from two middle-class suburbs in Wisconsin confirms that satisfaction as parents goes hand in hand with marital satisfaction. Adults who were "mostly happy" with parenthood rated their marriages better than adults who were unhappy as parents. The majority of all parents interviewed were not only "mostly happy" as parents, but claimed that their families were the most important aspect of their lives.[12]

VULNERABLE TO DIVORCE

Most people marry in their early to mid-twenties and have a baby within the first three years of married life.[13] About 40 percent of all marriages currently end in divorce.[14] The majority of these involve couples between twenty-five and thirty-nine years of age.[15] Fifty-six percent of divorcing couples have one or two children.[16] The divorce statistics peak among newly married people, and there is statistical evidence that couples who have been married between fifteen and twenty years may be a second high-risk group.[17] Looking at these trends from the family's standpoint, divorce threatens when children are very young, and again when children leave home.

Playing the Odds

Why are married couples between their second and fourth anniversaries, often with a new baby, more vulnerable to divorce than any other group? The cycles of adult life described by Gail Sheehy, Roger Gould, and Daniel Levinson offer a partial explanation.[18] These investigators define the age between twenty-two and twenty-eight as a period when young adults try to get into the established adult world. Couples who marry while they are still in their twenties often are trying to imitate and satisfy their parents. Sheehy calls this the "I should" period of the life cycle. Marriage and parenthood may be key symbols of adult status, but they don't replace the real thing.

Husbands and wives often find themselves distant from each other as they make the transition into their thirties.[19] As full-fledged adults, they become more inner directed and begin to think about what they really want from life and how they can fulfill the promises they made to themselves in their youth.

This personal life crisis is difficult to manage successfully with the unexpected stress of having children. After children are born, the changes adults need and want are not so easily achieved. They find it difficult to serve themselves and also satisfy other people who depend on them.

Yet once they are past the transition, their thirties are a time for settling down and extending roots.[20] At age thirty most men and women have achieved separation from their families of origin. They know more about themselves and what they want out of life. They are on the track of individual pursuits. This is the time when it would seem that lasting relationships can be formed, the time to get married and start a family.

But this is also a time when careers become important. If the decade between twenty and thirty is the time for making mistakes, the following decade is the time to get things done. The thirty-year-old has some life experience, a sense of identity, and a sense of purpose. Is there time and energy left over to have children? Can babies be added to all the demands of the thirties?

Statistically, couples who defer family life until after the jolting personal transitions into the thirties have been weathered are more likely to have lasting marriages.[21] The older a man and woman are when they marry, the better the chances that the marriage will last.[22] The longer couples remain married before having children, the greater the odds that they'll stay married.[23]

Combining family responsibilities with work—for both men and women—is the challenge of the 1980s. More and more couples are delaying childbirth until their thirties. Nearly 100,000 first babies were born in 1979 to women over the age of thirty, making that group the only one for which the birth rate is increasing.[24]

Older parents may better understand their children's problems, they may have more patience and sympathy, and certainly they have more experience in life. They are likely to have a stronger sense of their own identity and worth, so that their own growing pains, which are still awesome through the twenties, are not tied up with their children's.

The stronger the relationship between husband and wife before they have a baby, the more likely the family will survive. This sounds so obvious as to be ridiculous. But it's surprising how many couples still believe they can solve their marital problems by having children.

MYTHICAL SOLUTION FOR A TROUBLED MARRIAGE

Having a Baby Will Bring Us Together

We know from overwhelming and bitter experience that having a baby doesn't solve marital problems, but couples continue to insist on having children in order to save threatened marriages. Babies are used to provide a common ground: they will bring husband and wife together over the bassinet. She hopes a baby will bring her husband closer to her and stimulate his interest in home life. He believes a baby will make her fully committed to him and their home and so unable to pursue a career, go to school, or meet other people (other men). Or he thinks he will have more freedom if his wife has someone else to occupy her affections. Babies are used for all sorts of marital machinations.

Throughout her childhood Vanessa Galin's father adored her. Even after she was grown up, she was still Daddy's girl. He selected her college, suggested that she major in political science, and offered ready appraisal of her friends. Dad had an uncanny sense of what was right and set high standards for his daughter. He showered Vanessa with praise, but she sensed that he loved her conditionally, the condition being that she conform to his standards. She did everything she could to live up to his expectations. Until she fell in love.

When Vanessa met Stephen Fitzgerald, she took one look and fell hard. Interestingly, although she didn't notice it at the time, Stephen never showered her with attention and set no special standards to which she should aspire. In fact, he was primarily committed to himself, and although he was in love with Vanessa, he never sacrificed his own wishes for hers.

Stephen was a sportswriter for a newspaper chain, who took things as they came. He was shy and charming. Vanessa felt completely relaxed in his company, and his nonjudgmental attitude let her release the outgoing, eccentric personality that she usually held in check. They were both aware that they were a good match. "He's tall and skinny and adorable," she said. "She's crazy," he said.

Predictably, Vanessa's father objected to the relationship. "It's either Stephen or me," he told his daughter. "If you choose him, don't expect me to be so available to you."

Vanessa surprised everyone when she chose Stephen. Although she continued to see her father, there was a strained formality in their meetings.

"I felt bad," she later admitted. "But I thought he might come around later. And I also thought that being married to Stephen would be so fabulous that it didn't really make any difference if Daddy and I weren't so close anymore. Looking back, it seemed like a good way to kind of get out from under his thumb."

Vanessa and Stephen were married. But Stephen didn't seem to appreciate that Vanessa had made a sacrifice for his sake. He didn't try to make up for her loss or try to prove his devotion. Vanessa was disappointed. She had lost something, and her new husband wasn't compensating her fully for that loss. Now Stephen seemed distant from her.

Stephen loved Vanessa, was fascinated by her and attracted to her humor, which was so different from his own reserved style. But she began to get on his nerves. She seemed to want something from him that he wasn't prepared to give. They began to fall into two separate roles: Vanessa was disappointed; Stephen was aloof. She was always hurt; he was always distant.

Vanessa began to wonder why she had exchanged a doting father for an uncaring husband. Why didn't Stephen love her in the same way her father had? Over the next three years she became steadily obsessed with this question, until she grew desperate. But Stephen's distant manner continued to frustrate her desire for greater intimacy.

"It seemed like a deadlock that would go on forever. I desperately wanted to change the pattern of our marriage. I thought that if we had a baby we would feel closer to each other, that a baby would make Stephen a devoted father and therefore a more devoted husband."

However, Vanessa didn't express this idea to Stephen. When she became pregnant, Stephen was pleased because he thought a baby would satisfy Vanessa's constant desire for affection and closeness.

A year and a half later, Stephen was still distant, Vanessa still felt hurt. "Now," she said, "I don't care about myself, but I can't stand what he's doing to the baby."

Theirs was a classic example of a vulnerable couple who, hoping a baby would solve their marital problems, quickly involved the child in their conflict. Both Stephen and Vanessa realized that in some mysterious way the baby was solidifying their problems and making the situation worse.

After Nicky was born, Vanessa assumed all the responsibility for the baby's care. Stephen didn't help her care for the baby and never offered to watch him, and when Vanessa asked him to keep an eye on the baby while she did the laundry or went grocery shopping, he was casual and irresponsible.

Vanessa was angry. Nicky, now fourteen months, was old enough to get into all kinds of mischief. Vanessa came home one afternoon to find the baby, his diaper wet, powdering the kitchen floor with cleanser while Stephen watched the ball game.

Vanessa and Stephen were on the threshold of divorce. Each wanted to change, but neither one could seem to break the pattern.

"He's so cool," Vanessa said. "I can't reach him. I don't know what he's thinking—or even if he is thinking. I know I'm not the only one who's unhappy, but he never says what's on his mind. He's either silent or chats away about trivia. I can be thoroughly depressed and miserable about our situation, and he'll start talking about a new restaurant he read about in the *Times*."

Vanessa retaliated by withdrawing sexually. Stephen was fed up with her coldness. If she couldn't be more responsive, he announced one morning, he would look elsewhere. "How can I be loving in bed," Vanessa asked, "when we're not together out of bed?"

The situation was serious. Unless Vanessa and Stephen could resolve their problems, they would either divorce or permanently detour their conflict through their child.

They both wanted to make their family work. They both said that sharing parental responsibility was their desire, but they didn't do it. In this instance the strong bond of family life applied pressure in a positive way to make them try to solve their difficulties. This sense of themselves as a *family*, and the desire to pull together, brought them into therapy.

The timing of their therapy (Stage 2) was best for change. The way new parents relate to their baby not only defines their marital problems but says something about the unresolved conflicts each has with her or his own parents.

In one early session Vanessa detailed a situation that especially bothered her, in her opinion a supreme example of Stephen's insensitivity: one Saturday morning, as they were getting ready to visit Vanessa's parents, Stephen, on his wife's instructions, went to fill a baby bottle with apple juice for the trip. But there was no apple juice in the refrigerator, so he filled the bottle with milk.

"Do you believe that!" Vanessa said.

"Is that it?" I asked.

"Are you kidding?" Stephen said. "When I came back with the bottle of milk, she accused me of unprecedented brutality."

"You knew I'd never let Nicky have bottled milk," Vanessa cried. "I've been nursing him for fourteen months; I even express milk when I'm at work and save it for him." Tears were welling up in Vanessa's eyes. "And *you* filled his bottle with milk from a carton! You don't care anything about him—or me!"

"That's the craziest thing I've ever heard," Stephen told her. "Sometimes you are really a flake."

Stephen tried to treat Vanessa's outburst as a joke, but he finally got the picture: Vanessa wanted him to join in family life—as long as he followed her rules. In this case the rule he broke was that Vanessa was the most important person in their son's life because she was the *only one* who could make milk.

Vanessa interpreted the apple juice/milk caper as direct hostility against her, a negation of her role as milk-maker and controller of her son's life. As far as caretakers were concerned, Stephen was in the minor leagues.

Vanessa and Nicky were developing a coalition, and Stephen would soon be the odd man out. Both parents were horrified by this idea.

"That isn't what I want," Vanessa said. "Honestly it isn't."

I agreed that switching from apple juice to bottled milk was a protest on Stephen's part. Asked why he had never before objected to Vanessa's obsession with nursing, Stephen answered that he "enjoyed watching the beauty of mother and child together."

"Oh, come on. Now who's kidding?" I said.

"Really, it's wonderful."

"The more Vanessa is involved with Nicky, the less responsibility you have. Doesn't it take you off the hook?"

Vanessa seemed surprised. Stephen looked uncomfortable. Clearly this was a new idea.

Although it was dangerous for Vanessa to prolong Nicky's exclusive dependence on her, we switched away from this problem and focused on the marriage. If the marital problem could be resolved, the overly strong tie between mother and child would lessen of its own accord.

When we spoke of issues unrelated to parenting, the conversation almost immediately turned to sex. Vanessa admitted that she felt "sexually inhibited" with Stephen. Months would pass without any attempt at sexual intercourse. And yet when they first met, she had been extremely attracted to him. "I still think he's gorgeous," she said. "It's just that when we go to bed, I feel all tense and I don't want him to touch me."

One night when they tried to "cooperate," as they put it, Vanessa was tense and resentful over past hurts. But she "tried." Stephen didn't have a condom and Vanessa couldn't find her diaphragm. On the brink of sexual ecstasy, Stephen had to withdraw to stop himself from ejaculating. Vanessa once again felt abandoned, and Stephen felt guilty.

Stephen and Vanessa played out all the nuances of their relationship in bed. Vanessa desired emotional closeness but refused responsibility for sex.

Stephen held himself back emotionally but was too responsible for sex. (Sex was *his* idea; their sexual failure, they agreed, was *his* fault.) Each partner held out on the other: it was a perfect way to maintain balance. Instead of the emotional closeness Vanessa wanted, Stephen offered sex. She gave herself to him emotionally, but held out on him sexually, depriving him of his primary mode of expression. At cross purposes, they complemented each other perfectly and kept the distance between them intact.

Their marital difficulties suggested that there were problems that had never been worked out in their original families. A glimmer of this surfaced when Stephen mentioned that while Vanessa was pregnant, he had been turned off sexually. This is fairly typical for a young husband who closely identifies his wife with his mother; she becomes even more like "a mother" when she is pregnant. It may be all right to have sex with your wife, but it's not all right to have sex with your mother.

Yet Stephen maintained that his childhood was happy and problem free. What then was the reason for his unusual detachment? Over several sessions we continued to focus on his youth, and the picture of an insecure child began to emerge. Stephen's mother had been impossible to please. His good grades in school, his polished manners, and his outstanding athletic ability gave his parents some pleasure, but his mother let him know in a thousand ways that it was never enough.

He tried to shield himself from the unhappiness this caused him by adopting an attitude of complete indifference. He grew arrogant and seemed interested only in himself.

"Even when I was still in my teens," Stephen said, "I kept people from getting too close. I had friends, but it was always superficial." Behind his facade of arrogance, his inability to please his mother continued to erode his self-esteem. "I trained myself not to think about it, but I always had a nagging sense that there was something wrong with me."

Stephen had created his aloof stance to protect himself from getting hurt and being controlled. If he opened up to Vanessa, she would have the power to hurt him as his mother had.

Vanessa's relationship with her father almost mirrored Stephen's dilemma. As she unraveled her past, she saw that if she ever gave herself completely to her husband—both emotionally *and* sexually—he could wield power over her as her father had done. She would lose her independence and once again become the puppet-child she had been in her youth.

"Maybe that's why I fell in love with Stephen," she said. "Maybe I sensed he would never get close enough to control me." As much as she demanded attention from her husband, she avoided deep intimacy with him by cutting him off sexually.

For both Stephen and Vanessa, closeness means being controlled. Neither had discovered how to accept love and still feel free. For both, being loved meant being dominated. Unresolved in youth, the problem was carried into adulthood and marriage. Stephen holds out emotionally; Vanessa holds out sexually. Closeness for them equals surrender.

After five months of therapy their relationship began to shift in several important ways. Most important of all, they gave up the game of Vanessa being hurt and Stephen being guilty. Stephen began to consider Vanessa more in everyday things. If she had been with Nicky all day, he tried to relieve her. Taking Vanessa's emotional state into consideration meant he was including her in his private thoughts and responding to her on a deeper level. Stephen became more considerate, more loving, less detached. It was clear that he was losing some of his fear.

Vanessa had more trouble with her sexual inhibitions. She had no history of so-called frigidity; before she married she had passionate affairs with other lovers. But she was still afraid to let go with Stephen. She couldn't seem to get past this, and it was making all three of us crazy.

"Let's talk about something else for a while," I said one afternoon after we had discussed the issue for the umpteenth time. "What's happening with your folks?"

This was another chronic problem. All new parents have to decide how much and to what extent they will visit the grandparents. For Vanessa and Stephen, both sets of Nicky's grandparents lived out of town, so that visiting in either direction meant devoting the whole weekend. It seemed to me that they were always either being invaded by parents or planning a trip to visit them. Stephen mentioned that his parents were coming to town for the weekend. "We'll take them to the theater with us," he said.

Vanessa agreed, and added, "Next weekend I told my parents we'd come up to the country."

I interrupted and asked, "When do you spend time together?"

"Well, Monday and Wednesday I teach in the evening," Vanessa replied. "And Tuesday and Thursday Stephen has his photography class and poker. But we always spend our weekends together. It's a rule. The weekend is family time."

"But this weekend and next weekend you're visiting your parents."

"Ummm, yes. It's a bore, but it wouldn't be fair to deprive our parents of their grandchild. After all . . ."

"I don't get it. You're always saying you don't spend enough time together, yet you book your weekends solid. Of course, it makes a certain amount of sense. If you visit your parents every weekend, there's not much chance you'll get romantic with each other."

"Why do you say that?" Vanessa asked.

Stephen interrupted, "We do spend a lot of time with our folks. They expect it, and we just fall into it."

"And besides, Nicky does need to know his grandparents," Vanessa said.

"Definitely," I agreed. "If you two split up, he'll need his grandparents to fall back on."

Vanessa challenged me in her best Tallulah tones: "Do you *seriously* believe I'd go through all those *wretched* family weekends just to avoid *sex*?"

There was an extremely weighty pause. Vanessa began to laugh. "Oh, God. When we go to Stephen's family, I resent his mother so much that I don't speak to him all weekend. When we go to my family, my father never lets us alone. It's fabulous!"

"I'm glad you think it's funny," Stephen said. "I'm walking around with my knees pressed together, and you're laughing it up. I'm going to call my folks and tell them not to come down this weekend. Then I'm going to lock you in the bedroom and show you a skin flick."

"You wouldn't dare!" Vanessa said.

"Well, I think I will. What are you going to do?"

"Stephen, I really do want to solve this sex thing . . . at this rate I'll reach my sexual peak and not even know I had it."

Whatever the Fitzgeralds did that weekend, their sex life began to improve. They were thrilled and declared that they were ready to leave therapy with all their problems solved. Then, predictably, it was Stephen's turn. He started to pick fights with Vanessa and fell back into his old pattern of aloof indifference. He stopped helping with the baby and grew distant. Vanessa was back to doing all the family chores, and she was furious.

This time, however, Stephen quickly recognized the pattern. "Now that sex is good," he said, "it's my turn to hold back and keep us apart. But I can't help it. It's too much closeness."

In the ensuing months of therapy, they went back and forth, each taking a turn to keep the distance intact and protect them from too much closeness. But each time they switched roles, the distance between them became a little less. It's possible that Vanessa and Stephen, like many couples, will need to preserve a certain amount of distance in their marriage to accommodate their special natures. But ultimately I believe they will be able to achieve a satisfying balance where they can be close to each other without feeling they have lost their freedom.

Chapter 8

BIRTH OF A FAMILY:
SOME CLASSIC FAMILY STRUCTURES

Forming a family is a unique process for each family. As the initial marital pattern dissolves, a new *family* pattern emerges. There are several family structures, each with its own advantages and hazards. Whatever kind of family structure we choose, or is thrust upon us, the stages of family life are the same—although some family structures can weather certain stages more easily than others. But in general, traditional nuclear families, dual-career families, blended families, and single-parent families all make similar journeys through the family life cycle, and the transitions affect them all.

The structure of the family does play some part in the way families stand up to the crises. The critical transition of Stage 2 is from a couple to a family. Traditional nuclear families, where fathers work and mothers stay home with young children, have a strong potential for creating distance between parents. Single parents find it almost impossible to meet the demands of children, work, and also find time for personal life. They run the risk of burning out, literally starving to death emotionally, in this stage. Families where both parents work are also in danger of being overloaded with responsibilities.

It is possible for any form of family to successfully navigate the rough passage into Stage 2, and it is also possible for any family—regardless of structure—to falter.

THE TRADITIONAL NUCLEAR FAMILY HANGS ON

Although the trend toward smaller families continues to point away from the traditional nuclear family (TNF) as a practical, rewarding family system, it persists as an American ideal. "What's wrong with it?" demand men and women who have built their lives around the system. Well, nothing is necessarily wrong with it. In past generations families were larger; while teenagers were growing up and leaving, there were still young children at home. The TNF (father at work, mother at home with the children) was a simple way of dividing responsibility, serving the economy, and raising children.

For over a hundred years the traditional nuclear family was the most popular family structure in America, diminishing only during the war years, when women joined the labor force in large numbers. But in the last decade, as families have grown smaller, the TNF has declined radically: only 23 percent of American families fit the traditional form, and only 7 percent of these reflect the "perfect" family of father at work and mother at home with *two* children.[25]

The classic example of the TNF is the "Father Knows Best" family, that idealized TV sit-com that in simpler times showed us all that was good about TNFs. My generation grew up believing that most families shared this structure, and those that didn't aspired to it. The spiraling divorce rate of the last two decades is ascribed to a degeneration of values in modern society. Yet thirty years ago, before divorce became a widespread option, sociologists already knew that marital dissatisfaction was rampant in the ideal American family.

Sociologist Jan E. Dizard studied four hundred traditional middle-class couples in the Chicago area in the 1950s and discovered that "it was among those couples in which the husband had been most successful in his occupational pursuits that spouses were most likely to report deterioration in the marital relationship."[26]

Another large-scale research effort launched by Robert O. Blood and Donald M. Wolf during the 1960s involved nine hundred middle-class urban and suburban TNF couples.[27] Blood and Wolf also noticed that "high income husbands had conspicuously dissatisfied wives."

Apparently emotional distance develops between the ambitious, successful husband and the woman at home. Underneath the harmonious and peaceful exterior of these traditional families, all sorts of problems were brewing. Since divorce became more socially acceptable in the mid-1960s, the rate jumped over 115 percent (from 17% in 1960 to 40% in 1979).[28]

Because of its basic structure the traditional nuclear family has built-in danger zones in almost every stage of family life. The biggest danger is that husband and wife grow apart while the children are still young, and this rift continues to affect the family throughout its life cycle.

The relationship between mother and children naturally tends to deepen, and the father is left out. This pattern can develop in any family structure, but the TNF is especially vulnerable. Once this system is established, it is difficult to shift. Within the TNF, parents are often starved for closeness and affection. When mothers overinvest in children and fathers overinvest in work, they cease to invest in each other.

It's an easy trap to fall into. A mother forms strong ties with her helpless infant. Her life revolves around the baby's feeding times, doing the laundry, shopping. She works around the house, shops with the baby in its stroller, and devotes her conversation to the child. The house and its feeble little despot who cannot even talk are her whole world.

Mother assumes this responsibility, sometimes with relish, sometimes with resentment. But when given the opportunity to relinquish it to her husband in the evenings or on weekends, she may grow stubborn and push him aside. After all, this is her domain. One overburdened young mother said, "I don't want my husband to help me, because if he takes over some responsibility, he'll want a say in how I handle things. He's so used to having authority. This is *my* job, not his." This is a tough spot for mothers, and an even tougher one for fathers. While mother clings to baby and all baby things, father is denied a strong emotional center. The result is that the odd man is out.

In contemporary society a mother's isolation in the home creates serious problems for her as the children grow older and develop their own lives. In small families the mother is out of the family business early (usually by her early forties),[29] with little to do and no work experience outside the home. And she has a long life ahead of her.[30] She has trouble finding her way back into the outside world.[31] Depression among women in their forties and fifties is a common emotional problem stemming from the TNF dilemma.[32]

Fathers cut off from family life at the crucial time when familial relationships are being formed become almost mythical figures to their children. Caught between family and work, men are convinced that progress in their careers depends upon sacrificing their home lives. The supposed formula for success in the top echelons of corporations says if you're not a workaholic, you'll be passed over.

What was a practical and even efficient way of handling the family during a different social era has become a quagmire in modern society. This does not mean that the structure by definition is unhealthy. Family *structures* in themselves are not unhealthy, but the way families adjust to their form can create problems. The way the family copes with this potentially—but not necessarily—divisive structure is crucial.

It is possible for parents to successfully sidestep the danger zones of the TNF and keep the family balanced. Couples who elect in Stage 1 to structure their families in the TNF mold need to negotiate with each other so that both participate in baby care. The new father, even if he is the only breadwinner, can reduce some of his outside obligations and devote more time to his family. If he doesn't, he is in danger of missing all that's good in family life, and experiencing only the hard part, like Philip Ostler.

Philip gets up at five-thirty, commutes to his job as a dispatcher, works till six-thirty, and commutes back home. He feels trapped in a job he hates. He says he does it for his family, but he feels that if he continues this way, his family will survive and he will not (emotionally and perhaps literally, he believes he will stop living). Philip feels that there is a free spirit in him, and he longs to be expressive and creative. He is pressured to support a young family, and at thirty-two he's starving to death nurturing it.

If Philip didn't have a family, he might still feel trapped and respond to some inner pull for self-expression. But his personal crisis clashes with family obligations and is too much for him. He needs career and family counseling to find his way out of the maze.

A few years ago another young father found himself in a similar spot, although he enjoyed his work. "I was wrapped up in my career," he recalled, "and the life my wife and kids led didn't have much to do with me. I realized this, but thought it was the way things were supposed to be. Most couples we knew handled family life the same way."

A crisis suddenly altered the life of the family when the youngest daughter became seriously ill. Lingering like a shadow in her hospital room, the father was painfully aware that he had lost touch with his family.

"I realized how important she was to me, and knew I'd missed out on her childhood. We had four children between the ages of two and nine years, and I didn't really know any of them. I didn't belong. My wife and I decided together to change our style of living. I cut back on the extra office hours that I had taken for granted. When evening and weekend meetings were called, I just said I couldn't make it, that I was expected at home. Business travel was kept to a bare minimum. It was surprisingly easy, and as far as I know, it didn't hurt my career. But it certainly helped our home life. I joined the family for the first time."

Today, with the youngest child in school, the mother has begun a career of her own. The father is comfortable sharing household and child-care responsibilities, and enjoys spending time with the kids alone. "I sometimes wonder," he said, "where we'd be today if we hadn't changed."

Some parents automatically make these adjustments without even discussing it. Others talk about even the smallest details and carefully structure their lives to create some equality in the family hierarchy. Systems can become rigid, and unless a family is in trouble, I don't think you need hard and fast rules to schedule family time. Rules are necessary when a family has gone too far overboard and needs to shift back into balance. A father who works a sixty-hour week and feels that one hour a day with the children is too much has to find a way to cut back on his work time.

Leeway and *flexibility* are the key words, and good intentions count. One mother says, "If we talked about everything we do, we'd go crazy and decide it wasn't possible. But when things get out of hand, one of us—usually me—starts to complain.

"I'm surprised; even though I'm the one who stays home with the supposedly soft job, I'm also the one who feels overburdened a lot of the time. Everything is piled on Mom because she's there."

Mothers who choose to stay home in these demanding years need to put aside bottles and diapers sometimes and do something just for themselves—classes for self-development or career training, community interests, hobbies, leisure—anything, even in a small way, that helps establish an identity beyond the home.

The TNF family is blending with the two-career family these days. The same people develop different family structures for different phases of their lives. They weave family and career cycles together, make tradeoffs with their time and energy, and see life as a series of transitions. For instance, the working wife who drops out to take care of her preschool children chooses a TNF structure for specific reasons and for a specific period. But it's not a choice for a lifetime. This is what some of the shifts, role changes, and options are about for many families today.

TWO PAYCHECKS, TWO CAREERS

Not so long ago most women worked outside the home only if they had to. Even those educated for professional careers readily abandoned the working world in favor of family, once given the opportunity. The suburbs of America were full of forty-year-old housewives and mothers with B.A.s and masters degrees who had never held a job outside the home.

In 1963 Betty Freidan wrote a book that almost single-handedly launched the women's movement. *The Feminine Mystique* exposed the plight of the American housewife.[33] Women consciously began to move away from traditional roles and campaigned to gain an equal foothold in the working world. Today, more than fifteen years later, although women still experience discrimination in business, they have made tremendous gains, and in the decade of the 1980s many strive to develop lives which can encompass careers as well as marriage and motherhood.

In 1970, 51 percent of American families had two working parents. In 1978, that figure had risen to 65 percent; and researchers predict that by 1990, 75 percent of all mothers with children under ten will work outside the home.[34]

THE MOTHERING MYTH

Even though women are rapidly gaining equality in their professions, they continue to be the primary homemakers. Mothering, meaning the care of young children, is still a woman's domain.

Professional literature on child development often begins with the premise that the emotional needs of a young child are best met through its mother. For decades this bias for mothers doing the "mothering" has guided child-development research. The bias works against the situation most families find themselves in (namely, the need and desire of both parents to work outside the home) and suggests that if mother does not fulfill the primary nurturing role, children will suffer. The premise is grossly impractical. Over 60 percent of all mothers work, and almost half of these working mothers have children under the age of six.[35] The concept not only is impractical, it cannot be substantiated.

When I tried to trace the background of the nearly sanctified mother-child relationship in our culture, I was surprised to find virtually no fundamental research to justify the claim that mothers are the best caretakers. There is no empirical evidence that young children suffer when their mothers work, no evidence that daily, routine separations from mother blunts a child's development, and no evidence that one-to-one care in the home is the only healthy way to raise a child.[36] On the contrary.

The research strongly indicates that stable, caring relationships with *adults*—the mother, father, or any responsible adult—is vital for children, and that an optimal environment can be achieved in numerous ways. The crucial variable is not *who* but what kind of care is provided for children.[37]

There is no special reason, from the available evidence, to think that mothers are the only, or even the best, caretakers. Fathers make equally good caretakers. Babies need responsible, caring adults to provide for their needs.

Unfortunately, most literature about child rearing continues to extol the virtues of motherhood rather than parenthood in the early stages of a child's life. Confronted with major discrepancies between the reality of the working mother and the "ideal" mother/child focus a leading child psychologist said, "I'm an advocate for children, not mothers and fathers." This careless remark reflects a shocking disregard for families.

I believe any advocate for children should also be an advocate for parents. The rights of children and parents are intricately intertwined. To protect children, we need also to understand and support parents. I am an advocate for families. Current approaches to child development show little understanding of how the family as a whole operates during the crucial years when children are young.

The reason I think parents should personally provide most of the care is because infancy is the time when parents, by performing even menial child care tasks, develop emotional bonds with their children. Even if they wake up tired the next day, it's better for parents to get up in the night to feed and walk the floor with their baby. Better for mommy and daddy to wipe baby's bottom and change diapers. This doesn't mean they shouldn't get help, but both parents need to participate in nurturing little children. This is where the real "mothering instinct" emerges for both men and women. I don't think it always happens automatically at the moment a baby is born. It didn't for me. But it did happen in the day-to-day drivel of babyhood.

Caretakers make an impression on children, sending subtle messages through their fingertips, and by their very presence influencing a baby's nature. Although we were lucky enough always to have some help in the house, we wanted to be the ones who shaped the character of our children, even—perhaps especially—when they were infants.

In some ways parents who both work outside the home are in a good position to plan together. They have outside responsibilities, would like to sleep through the night, and are tired at the end of the week. They are in similar positions with similar needs and demands on their time. But it's not surprising, given the long tradition of mother myths, that mothers still assume the major responsibility for children.

HERE COMES SUPERMOM

A career woman I know gets up at dawn to clean her suburban house before catching the 8:03 into town. She races home after work to cook dinner for her husband and the kids, attends PTA meetings, plans family outings and vacations, and jogs around the track, without fail, every other night before she goes to bed. It may be a joke, but she wears a blue sweat shirt with a red *S* in a yellow triangle. It's surprising she doesn't have the matching cape.

She is exhausting herself, throwing herself like Sisyphus against the hill in her abiding conviction that to be fulfilled, to be a *woman*, she must do everything.

All of us, finding ourselves in the midst of change, cling to old habits learned early. It's hard to give up familiar responses that have been passed on for generations. Women particularly hang onto wifely service, perhaps because they are so frequently accused of losing their femininity when they step into the wider world of men. But I am convinced that a woman who wants to have it all—a demanding career and family life—has to shift some of the responsibility or she will either drop from exhaustion or wind up at the funny farm. Hopefully, you can *have* it all, but you can't *do* it all.

One interesting aspect of the dual-career effort is the marital and family issues that surface as couples try to work out their household arrangements. Who stays home when the baby-sitter is late or when the kids are sick? Who goes to school conferences, buys birthday presents, and takes the kids to the dentist? No matter what kind of child-care arrangements you can afford, you cannot pay someone to be a psychological parent. Parenting is a passionate career—a career that demands a major investment of time, energy, and commitment for at least the first five years of a child's life. It is an investment that pays off in family solidarity and children's vitality. Babies and young children can seduce even the most ardent careerists into cutting back on their professional responsibilities in order to structure their work around the parameters of family life.

In this sense family life does serve to bring independent husbands and wives closer together. Because so much time is spent away from home, family time is cherished and there's less tendency to take the family for granted.

An amazing variety of arrangements support the dual-career effort. Far too few communities have high-quality day-care centers, but family day care (small groups in a neighbor's home) is becoming increasingly available, as are small cooperative child-care groups. If the family can afford it, nurse-housekeepers can be hired.

Both the difficulty and the strength of these new patterns is that there is no special formula. Young working parents have to depart from traditional family styles to search for their own patterns. The most refreshing part of their search is that they can experiment with different solutions and keep the ones that work. They aren't boxed into rigid patterns. These couples are persistent pioneers. Because they have to be inventive and flexible, they should adjust more easily to later transitions that typify the family life cycle.

Even simple values such as family dinners, once religiously embedded in family life, are being discarded. Many two-career families don't share a meal from Monday to Friday, because work schedules have to be juggled with child care. Housekeeping, too, will probably never be the same.

The common feature among two-career families is that the husband-and-wife relationship departs from the traditional ideal in significant ways. Women who combine careers with motherhood make personal changes that reverberate through the family, and this has its most profound impact on the relationship between husband and wife. The traditional role of wives, even if they also worked outside the home, was to serve, support, and nurture husbands. What's new about working mothers today is that they are cutting back on their wifely duties. At least some of this shifting is due to the availability of better jobs and more money. Husbands of working women have had to give up the comforts of wife-endowed homes to go into the partnership business.

Wives and mothers who are serious about their work outside the home have to fight for their integrity all the time, and usually their most ardent enemy, no matter how enlightened they may be, will be their husbands. I think I'm a good mother, and I have a time-consuming and difficult but successful professional career, but I am by some standards a terrible wife. Until we had children, it was possible for me to fulfill my own interests and still be my husband's household helper. I cooked dinner, bought those family gifts that have to be "right," and sent condolence and thank-you notes. I entertained business associates, made sure that clothes got to the cleaners and laundry was done. I did the day-to-day cleaning and picking up. It never occurred to me to question these activities. I provided all these services before we had children and provide almost none of them now. It's possible, in view of a decade's worth of consciousness raising, that I would no longer provide them even if we didn't have children. In any case, fighting resistance every step of the way (both my own and my husband's), I have discontinued these wifely duties. Feeling uneasy about making these changes, I first blamed my husband for exploiting me. Later I came to face the contradictions in myself rather than place the responsibility on him.

Today we parcel out these personal chores of family life between us. Along the way to transition, my husband offered perfunctory protest but made each adjustment and was much more flexible and adaptable than either of us ever imagined. (He complains, though, that he no sooner changes one thing, than he has to change another. True. The rules keep changing.)

A NEW BREED

The central issue for all families, regardless of their structure, is how the family can nurture and care for *all* of its members. Dr. Jerry Lewis described a healthy family as one that does two things well: (a) it encourages the psychological growth of the parents or, at least, preserves their sanity, and (b) it produces autonomous children.[38]

In the midst of all the shifting and sliding in family life, an unexpected trend has developed. For a particular slice of the life cycle, women—and some men—are giving up careers to raise families.

I'm not sure how many women opt for motherhood alone because the heat of a big-time career breaks them down. I think women as a group still feel conflict about sustaining power positions at work and also being wives and mothers. But many women, and men, too, are questioning their lives. They are going against trends, movements, and social obligations and trying to decide what they find personally valuable.

A highly respected scientist had her first child at forty, and I was surprised when she told me she was giving up her work, at least for the time being. She was in a perfect position to reduce her hours and work part-time, but instead she was dropping out. I couldn't believe that she would give up her work, even temporarily. She tried to describe her feelings about it: "I've been working all my life," she said. "I was a superachiever even as a child. I liked it, most of the time. I've been happy. But I feel that I'd like to change my life in some ways—mid-life crisis, I suppose— but I want to stand back for a while and look at life, enjoy being with people, especially my husband and our baby. I want to think things over. I don't feel as though I'm giving anything up. I'm reaching out to something new, feeling something new. It's like going on a trip around the world."

A friend writing a magazine article about career women who become mothers for the first time in their thirties discovered that many women she spoke with chose not to work after their children were born.[39] These women, often with high-powered professional careers, felt they couldn't do two demanding jobs simultaneously. They wanted to give their babies a good start and closely guide their children's development. They felt that staying home was an affirmation of family life and solidarity. Many believed that they would return to work when the children were old enough for school, and some had decided to create new careers that would blend more with family life.

These are a new breed of mothers,[40] women who have already established careers and achieved a good sense of their capabilities. They do not see motherhood as a social role; nor do they see themselves locked into mothering for a lifetime. They make different choices for different periods of their lives. Instead of one role, they choose a series of roles, allowing themselves maximum flexibility. They say, "Now I'm concentrating on parenting. Three years from now I'll still be a mother, but I may concentrate on something else."

If women can take time off to raise children, why can't men? Men who would like to take six months or a year away from their careers to reevaluate their lives may have to suffer the opinion of their friends and family who think they're cute, but some men have done it.

The danger in the arrangement, according to one man who tried it, is thinking that time spent at home with children is time off. A newspaperman married to a lawyer elected to take a year off to stay home with their new baby and write a novel at the same time.

"It was the hoax of the century," he says now, almost eight months later. "I don't know what I was thinking about. If it was possible to take care of a family and write a book at the same time, half the women in America would be pounding away at their typewriters. Staying home with a baby is full of so much crap that you just piddle the day away—shopping, washing, cleaning, playing, bathing, bottling, and feeding. And because I was at home, working friends asked me to do them little favors. Would I let the telephone-repair man into their apartment while they were at work? Could I wait for the furniture delivery—or could I just get across town and pick up theater tickets? That takes half a day. I think women should run screaming in droves to get out of the house and into the work force.

"The person who decides to stay home with a baby should know he's not going to get anything else done. It's okay if you want to do something different for a while, change your perspective on things. But don't count on doing something in your spare time, because you don't have any spare time."

The hazard of two careers in families with young children is that there is never enough time for everything. Parents have to function well at work without being hindered by fatigue and worry about children. They need time for children, time for work, time to be alone together, time for themselves as individuals. The demands are enormous. Over the long view of the family's life cycle, working parents have certain advantages. But in Stage 2, they tend to be overloaded. Parents need to plan their careers so that during this stage the family can come first.

THE SINGLE-PARENT FAMILY

My seven-year-old son and I were watching a TV movie. The story was about a single woman who was thinking about having a child. My son was thoughtful. "Of course she could do it," he said, "but it's not a good idea because it's better if you have two parents to take turns doing all the work."

The single-parent family is ordinarily not formed by choice. It comes about through marital disruption, desertion, death, or unplanned (and generally unwanted) pregnancy.

A young couple with babies underfoot is at the most vulnerable stage in the family life cycle. Thirty percent of all marriages dissolve while a couple is still in their twenties, and many already have started families.[41]

Of all family structures, the single-parent family has the toughest time in Stage 2. In later stages, when children have some measure of independence and protection in school, single-parent families adjust in much the same way as any other family, with, of course, problems specific to the single parent. But in Stage 2 these families are in serious trouble almost by definition.

The single parent, who is usually the mother, is often isolated. Her life usually has been disrupted by marriage and divorce; she is lonely. She's financially vulnerable. Her need for love and attention clash with the endless demands of a small child or children. She's depleted, overburdened, and needy herself. I say "she" because few fathers head single-parent households, although those who do face similar, although not identical, problems.

Although today men more frequently pitch for custody than in the past, single men head only 3 percent of American families, while single women (separated, divorced, or widowed) provide homes for 13 percent of the families in the USA.[42] The financial picture of these female-headed families is grim: they represent the single largest subgroup of the population that lives below the poverty level.[43]

Barbara Blum, New York State's commissioner of social services, has observed that cases of child neglect have increased sharply in New York State in the last two years. More than 85 percent of all cases of child abuse were described as "neglect," instances where children were unsupervised, left alone at night, were undernourished, or had unattended medical problems. She attributes the unprecedented numbers of neglected children to single parents trying to raise children alone. "Very often a single parent has sole responsibility," she said in an interview with the *New York Times.*

> We don't have as many related persons living together. There is no buffering or relief from grandmother or aunt. . . . The

extent of such problems is not likely to diminish in the 1980's, with some forecasts of as many as 45 percent of the nation's children residing in single parent households.[44]

Mrs. Blum feels children of single parents are suffering from a "cumulative kind of neglect." Single parents need help. These are not cases of deliberate child abuse but of parents without resources. The point she made was that new ways need to be found to help single parents cope with rearing young children. Financing for day-care centers to alleviate the problem of child neglect is crucial. According to Mrs. Blum: "We absolutely need to increase services to the working mother instead of cutting back."

Single-parent families with preschool children are at a distinct disadvantage in our society in every respect. It's simply that they're understaffed. And there is no strong support system, either in the extended family or the community, to help. I don't think it's possible for single parents of infants and toddlers to do all the things that families are supposed to do without exceptional community support services, which are not now generally available (such as good child care at a low cost). Sometimes the extended family comes to the rescue. A communal family, several single parents sharing a household, works better than the isolation of separate single-parent households.

María Ramirez got pregnant when she was sixteen and married Johnnie, her eighteen-year-old boyfriend. By the time the baby was born, Johnnie had left town and Maria and her baby were abandoned. She moved in with her mother, where they shared a one-room light-housekeeping apartment. "My mother couldn't support me, and there wasn't really any room for us, but we stayed there. I stayed all day in the room and nursed the baby and took care of him. But I needed to get a job. I was going crazy. My mom worked days, so I had to look for something at night. I finally got a job in a coffee shop and that helps, but we just make out. The worst is I don't have a personal life. If I don't come home right from work, my mom really gets upset. She remembers what happened before. Lots of times somebody comes in and asks me out after work or something and I say, I got to go home. I don't meet anybody. I just go from the rooming house to the coffee shop and back again. I don't know what's going to happen. I thought about joining the army or something, and just leaving it all behind me."

The continuing deprivation among single-parent families who are poor and disadvantaged is a problem that does not stand still or just go away but intensifies by its very nature. With little outside help and child care, any sort of career training or amibiton for mothers is an exercise in futility, a futility that is passed on to the children.

But the problems of single parenthood increasingly are not restricted to the poor. Ellen and Marty Katz thought that a piece of the American dream was guaranteed. Marty, the son of a successful dress manufacturer, grew up in a comfortable Tudor-style house on a tree-lined street in Great Neck, Long

Island. Ellen's father owned a store in suburban Connecticut. They met in college and married after Marty graduated and Ellen completed her junior year. Marty went into his father's business. A little more than a year after their wedding, Jeffrey was born. A year later Dawn became part of the family. The grandparents chipped in and gave Ellen and Marty the down payment on a house in Chappaqua, about an hour and a half by train from New York.

Marty wasn't home for Dawn's third birthday party. He was swamped with work, he said. It was a year later that Marty moved out of the house and into town.

He hadn't had a chance to find himself, he said, and he needed some time alone to think. He moved into a floor-through apartment with high ceilings in a restored West Side brownstone and began to take the walls down to the old brick. Then Marcia, who had been a model at the factory, moved in with him.

"He said he'd always take care of us," Ellen said, "and I believed him. I still believe he would if he could."

The divorce agreement gave Ellen just enough money to take care of the house and children. But business at the dress factory fell off. Marty wasn't able to take care of his own bills on what he could draw out of the business. He got a job as a salesman in New Jersey and moved to an apartment in Fort Lee. He sent what he could, he said, but it wasn't enough to take care of Ellen and Jeffrey and Dawn. Ellen's parents had retired to Florida on an income that was just enough to take care of themselves. They couldn't afford to help. And Marty's father was as strapped as Marty.

Ellen had been taking college courses while Marty was still paying the bills, and she was a semester away from her degree, but she had to drop out to take a job—any job to bring in some money. She got work as a waitress in a coffee shop in White Plains, because it paid better than office work.

"I never dreamed I'd be working like this," she mused. "You know, I made Phi Beta at Cornell. But I'm glad to have the job. I can get the kids off to school and then be home soon after they get there. But I don't know where I'm going. I can't get started with a career. There's just no room. I'm living on the edge right now. The house is mortgaged right up to its value. I just can't move the kids from their school, anyway. And the kids feel so bad all the time. Their father never comes to see them; he's afraid if he sets foot in the state, I'll have him thrown in jail. I always felt sorry for Marty, but now I'm not so sure I wouldn't. At least he's got some sort of social life. I couldn't possibly meet anybody else. I'm always working or taking care of the kids, and a divorced woman in this community is a pariah. Everybody's coupled up. I'd like to chuck it all in. I wonder if I could still join the Peace Corps?"

Chapter 9

PARENTHOOD AS CRISIS

A new family requires a delicate balancing act. Three relationships need nurturing: husband and wife, mother and child, father and child. In healthy families all three relationships are homologous and all three are open to the others.

Should the intensity of any one attachment shift, the family will be out of sync. Quick adjustments automatically take place to stabilize the imbalanced family structure. For example, a new mother becomes so wrapped up in the baby that she neglects her relationship with her husband. His tie to both his wife and child weakens as the mother/child attachment grows more intense. He may turn to work, his parents, or another woman to compensate. These compensations are the way hazardous family patterns get started early in family life.

Family problems tend to develop around three major themes that reverberate throughout all stages of family life: sex, dependency, and power.

Children are pleasure-oriented, loving beings. Their warm responses to parents temporarily can fill a sexual void between husband and wife. An overly close attachment between one parent and child can displace a husband or wife. When a family is in trouble, the first thing to look for is where and what kind of special attachments exist within the family.

The second theme is related to dependency. Who are the nurturers in the family? Who is dependent? How are giving and taking distributed?

Finally, how is power distributed? In healthy families, power is shared between parents when children are young. When there is an imbalance in the power structure, the weaker parent often uses the children to strengthen his or her position.

These themes are constant tunes through the life cycle of all families. How the new family uses them to build attachments inside the family makes a pattern. Some patterns are positive and ensure survival, and some patterns are dangerous.

Unhealthy patterns are at their most malleable—and dangerous—in

Stage 2, where they are innocently set out for the first time amid new, developing relationships between parents and children. When they are anticipated or discovered early, these distortions are relatively easy to readjust. If they go unrecognized, the patterns become fixed as family relationships solidify and inevitably cause problems when the family moves from one stage to another.

DANGEROUS FAMILY PATTERNS IN STAGE 2

When family relationships shift so that one deepens as others grow weak, some classic problems emerge around major family themes. In any one of these problem areas, the survival of the family is at stake.

These dangerous patterns frequently are born in Stage 2, when babies are helpless bystanders to their parents' troubles. There are many ways that husbands and wives use babies to avoid facing their problems with each other. By Stage 3, when children are a few years older, the patterns are firmly entrenched and the children become active participants in a full family drama originally created by their parents. By then they are thoroughly trained and expected to take up their roles in the full-scale war.

Hazardous styles seem to develop out of two extremes: *families that are too distant* and *families that are too close.*

DISENGAGED FAMILIES[45]

Most family problems in Stage 2 arise out of a schism or profound distance between parents. A schism is like emotional divorce, but husband and wife remain together.[46] A schism may be deeply buried and extremely subtle, or in blatant situations, sustained, open conflict lacerates married life. There is a sense of hopelessness and no prospect for improvement; divorce is threatened but never actively sought until children and parents have suffered tremendous emotional abuse, and sometimes not even then. Children of warring parents may be ignored or left to fend for themselves; at worst, they are tossed back and forth in marital battles, figuratively torn to pieces in the throes of their parents' conflict.

Sometimes the conflict is completely silent—a deep, brooding bitterness that both parents understand but neither will speak of. In this grim, unrelenting situation, children may be used brutally to express the couple's profound unhappiness with each other.

When a serious rift exists between parents, several different family patterns develop.

The Me-First Family

Me-first couples are usually independent, self-interested people who, even after they marry, place careers and personal interests first and spouses second or even third. They may be adamant about maintaining their freedom, carefully parceling out financial and household responsibilities, traveling and going out with friends rather than each other, assigning ownership to each new piece of furniture so there will be no confusion should they decide to separate. Their system of marriage runs into trouble when they decide to have a baby without shifting gears. To remain child-free would be a valid choice. Instead, due to family or social pressure, or thoughtlessness, they have a baby. They find themselves in Stage 2 with preschoolers, totally unprepared for the sacrifices in time and energy that children require.

Both parents struggle against being tied down. They sense that the career and personal commitments that could be fulfilled in marriage are now in jeopardy. They refuse to give up staying late at the office, dining out with clients at the last minute, going on the road for business, sleeping late when they can manage a day off. Both husband and wife shy away from family obligations. They have what Dr. Salvador Minuchin, a leading family therapist, calls a disengaged family style, meaning that they are out of touch with each other. If disengaged families make it through Stage 2, they tend to dissolve in later years.

The couple may try to solve their problem by hiring a nurse or housekeeper. This isn't a bad idea. Babies respond to loving care from any adult. But if parents completely abrogate the caretaking to an outsider, they lose the most valuable aspect of Stage 2: the formation of a strong bond between themselves and their child. It's the mundane things such as comforting and feeding and bathing and diapering that make parents and baby a family. Whoever supplies baby's essential needs at this stage will form a close, influential attachment with the child. But the me-first couple thinks of baby as someone else who lives in the house and needs special attention.

Ginny and Tom Dixon, a married couple in their early thirties, found themselves in this situation. Faced with an unexpected pregnancy, they decided to have the baby and negotiated a sort of compromise on the way to cope with this change. Genuine negotiation means fully discussing an issue until you come up with an idea that satisfies all parties involved. But negotiation requires time, a willingness to work together, and an ability to express your troubles and examine your own life. Ginny and Tom were in the habit of solving their problems independently: she looked out for herself, he for himself. They were not accustomed to working things out together.

Looking back, Ginny recalled their situation at the time: "We couldn't see any satisfactory solution, so I gave up my job—temporarily, I thought—to stay home. I had this idea that I had to take care of everything, that if I didn't, everything would just go to hell. I knew Tom wouldn't help unless I nagged him to death. I tried to get my boss to keep me on part-time, but he couldn't; he said he needed someone all the time. It never entered my mind that Tom might put off some of his work obligations to help take care of the baby. It was either get a full-time, live-in baby nurse—which would cost almost as much as I made—or stay home.

"But I remember thinking even then that I was making a noble sacrifice. For the first few months after the baby came, I played at being the mommy and enjoyed the novelty of keeping house. After a while I started to resent it. I felt used, that I had nothing for myself—no time, no money of my own, no way to show who I was. If I met someone who asked me what I did for a living, I cringed and said, 'Nothing, I'm just a housewife.' Then I felt obliged to explain that I was really an administrative assistant to a top executive and that I was only staying home temporarily while the baby was little. I would actually apologize for having a child.

"I got so mad about being the baby keeper that I shut Tom out. Since I made all the sacrifices, I wanted all the authority. Every time he made a suggestion, I snapped at him. When I needed help, I ordered him around and expected him to follow my instructions. If he didn't do it exactly as I wanted it done, I flew into a rage. All the time I hated myself, but I felt I had the right."

The best answer, from Tom's point of view, was to stay out of the family. When he came in at night, he would tweak the baby under the chin and occasionally feed her in the evenings if he was early enough. But he treated these father-daughter events as strictly novelty acts in the main performance of his life. He had never wanted to be involved in the first place, and offered small resistance as Ginny pushed him outside the boundaries of the family. He tried to take her nagging and irritable temper in stride but began to dread being with her and the baby.

Ginny grew more bitter daily until she lost all pleasure in motherhood. Unable to integrate her personal needs with family life, she was completely without options. All she wanted was out. After months of trying to suppress her unhappiness, she was thoroughly sick of her sacrificial role.

The break came on a hot Saturday morning at the tennis club. Ginny sat under an umbrella and tried to quiet the baby, who was uncomfortable in the warm weather.

Tom felt like he was at Forest Hills. His cream-colored, pleated flannel shorts were sharply pressed, and two bleached sweatbands emphasized the tan of his arms. From under the shadow of the umbrella, Ginny watched him play. His shots were coming together. Sliding into a forehand, he flicked his wrist at the ball and sent a flat overspin skidding off the tape; a cross-court backhand practically whistled. He approached a desperate short lob with the exultation of the hunter drawing a bead on the big kill; the overhead smash scattered doubles partners on the next court. "Game, set, match," he shouted with a laugh.

Ginny almost choked on the gall rising in her throat. She lifted the whining baby girl in her arms, walked onto the court, and placed the child at her husband's feet. She cried, "Now I want some free time," and turned around and walked out of the club. Tom, embarrassed and enraged, shouted after her, "I'm sick of all this family shit and your lousy temper tantrums." And he stalked off the court, leaving the child behind. Another couple, friends of Tom and Ginny, picked up the squalling infant and took her home for the afternoon.

Six months later Ginny and Tom divorced. She left, taking the baby with her, to live her own life.

The me-first style of living cannot work in Stage 2, when parenthood, at least temporarily, means family first. Commitment to self, albeit vital in many other stages of family life, is anathema in the second stage. But even in Stage 2, both individual and family needs count.

It is by no means impossible for a couple with two careers to raise a family, but it takes thoughtfulness and negotiation from both partners. Negotiation considers the needs and wishes and troubles of everyone in the family. Parents who cherish independence can work together to find more flexible child-care arrangements, learn to share responsibilities, and balance their obligations to one another and the family with their own personal needs. But one basic assumption is required: they must agree that the family is important enough for both to make real sacrifices.

Triangling [47]

When children are asked to line up with one parent against the other, a family triangle is formed. Parents fight their personal battles through this small third person. They may quarrel over whose approach to child rearing is best, who gives the baby the right kind of attention, who chooses baby's diet or clothes. Children drawn into prolonged custody suits are also used in this way. All triangles are harmful to children and to the survival of the family. If parents continue to disguise their intimate grief with each other by fighting over the baby, the child eventually begins to suffer from the strain.

When a child is bed-wetting at age nine, failing in school, or unable to make friends, a family therapist assumes he is carrying the burden of some problem for the family that isn't being resolved directly. The child's symptoms hide the real problem. As long as the child requires attention, there is no pressure to discover the genuine difficulty between the parents. A child's suffering is a smoke screen to hide the parents' personal problems.

Instead of confronting each other, parents agree or argue that their child is spoiled, or unhappy, or difficult. If they agree they have something in common. If they argue they have an outlet for their intimate hostility. It doesn't matter whether they harmonize or clash; the focus is put on the child, to make him or her the major part of their marital relationship.

When parent-designated "problem children" grow up, they usually have enormous difficulty leaving home because they sense that their parents need them in some mysterious way. Their development may be so retarded that they haven't enough confidence to separate from the family. They may try to leave home, only to return periodically because they fail in school or lose a job or get sick. If they manage to separate from the family, the parents may subsequently divorce. These triangles are often laid down in Stage 2 when a child is still in the cradle.

Scapegoating [48]

Scapegoating is a special, advanced version of the triangle. The term *scapegoating* is used when the triangle situation worsens until the child's normal development is blocked. No longer an innocent bystander in parental wars over baby food, the older child contributes actively to the triangle by developing a serious behavioral problem for her parents to focus on. She may behave outrageously, get in trouble at school, start stealing, or deal dope or drink heavily.

Parents and siblings attack or blame the scapegoat who is "bad" or "sick." Everyone else in the family may appear normal and healthy, because they permanently detour all family conflict through the one person. The elected scapegoat is usually a child, although an adult can also be designated as the problem by the family.

In young families, parents may unknowingly encourage deviant behavior: they label a high-spirited child difficult, a sensitive child shy or insecure, a physically active child uncontrollable. Children—and adults—tend to live up to the labels applied to them. In time the child achieves his reputation in the family.

The problem child actually holds the family together. But families can make their scapegoats totally dependent and unable to exist in the outside world, and may even drive them to suicide. Triangling usually develops in Stage 2, but the more serious scapegoating situation takes time to develop and often does not appear in its severe form until Stages 3 or 4 of family life.

Coalitions [49]

When a family is in trouble, family therapists always look for coalitions. Who gangs up on whom? Who sides with whom? Who does Mom/Dad/Jr. look to for support?

In healthy families, parents share leadership, although each may be a specialist in a different area.[50] This doesn't mean they agree on everything or that their leadership is exercised in the same style. But when they disagree, they work things out between them without bringing the child into it. Each parent respects the other's right to discipline and guide their child.

Parents in families that survive work together to maintain an effective parental coalition. Children can't play one parent against the other, although most kids try this regularly.

The most positive aspect of having more than one child is that the children have a chance to form an impressive coalition of their own against Mom and Dad. Acting as a team, they can negotiate for bigger allowances, later curfews, more privileges. The sibling axis is strong only when children are independent of the husband/wife system. When one child gets hooked into a triangle between the parents, jealousy and competition among sisters and brothers is usually intense, grossly disrupting a positive sibling coalition.

Healthy coalitions are set up within the same generation: children's coalitions, Mom-and-Dad coalitions, grandparents' coalitions. When coalitions cross generational lines, they are red flags of danger and often the beginnings of family triangles.

Robert Trayner told his five-year-old son Bobby to stop making so much noise when he ran his train across the living-room floor. Robert was trying to read, and the whistles and toot-toots were driving him nuts. The more he complained, the louder Bobby whistled and tooted, until his father picked him up from the floor and sat him on the sofa. Robert turned off all the switches on the train. "If you can't be quiet," he said sternly, "you can sit there by yourself. And don't you dare move." Big tears began to slide down Bobby's cheeks.

Laura Trayner, conscious of the sudden silence in the living room, came in from the kitchen, saw Bobby crying on the sofa and Robert's back, stiff with anger, turned toward his son. Laura put her arms around Bobby and comforted him. "Daddy's just a tired old grouch," she said. Even if she had only signaled Bobby with a shrug of her shoulders or a crosswise glance at Robert's back, Laura let her son know that she sympathized with him and they would both have to bear up—and unite—against an unreasonable father.

Family therapists would call this little scene a cross-generational coalition between mother and son. Even such a small exchange shows that something's up between Robert and Laura. Laura could have stayed out of the exchange or made some neutral joke to ease the tension, but instead she sympathized with Bobby and, perhaps inadvertently, took his side against his father. By doing so she negated Robert's right to be angry with his son; and more important, by placing herself between them, she prevented Robert from making up with Bobby on his own.

Naturally, family life is full of these little dramas. Little children are naturally on the alert, and when scolded by one parent, try to align themselves with the other. Parents fall into the trap when they are out of sync with each other.

A family maintains its balance by shifting its coalitions. This particular cross-generational coalition temporarily balanced some unresolved tension between Robert and Laura. If it becomes permanent, the cross-generational coalition can be dangerous. A permanent pattern is called a *stable* cross-generational coalition.

Cross-generational coalitions frequently involve grandparents. Husbands and wives tied more closely to their own parents than to each other are in serious trouble when they have children. When a young wife complains to her mother about her husband, she has established a cross-generational coalition against him. If her mother makes even the most subtle comment in a discussion of this kind, the daughter is tempted to use it as ammunition later ("Do you know what Mom said about you the other day?"), creating even more trouble in the family. She can use her friends in the same way. Any situation that sets up husband against wife or vice versa is a potential trouble spot.

When couples are still tied to their own parents, the nuclear family—husband, wife, and child—cannot insulate itself; the temporary wall new families must erect around themselves is constantly battered by outsiders with powerful influence. In place of the nuclear family, a stronger relationship exists between grandparent/parent/child, commonly grandmother/mother/child. But a young husband also may be tied to his parents. He can ignore his wife, loyally insist on visiting his parents every Sunday, idealize his mother as the perfect parent, or lean on his father for advice and financial assistance.

Grandparents who side with a child against parents or with a wife against a husband can cause enormous trouble in families. The stereotypical interfering grandmother is not acting strictly on her own, however. She is only one player in a family drama that encourages her role and supports the divisions in the family.

These dangerous family styles can interplay, and infinite variations of the themes are possible. The odd-man-out families count on cross-generational alliances to keep the family pattern going.

ENMESHED FAMILIES[51]

If the disengaged family is too distant, the enmeshed family is too close, or symbiotic. The enmeshed family literally sticks together.

Usually the enmeshed husband and wife have built a relationship based on their insecurities; they cling together and retreat from the world, depending on each other to an extreme degree, even forgoing separate identities. Family therapists often see husbands and wives whose individual identities coalesce until they are almost impossible to distinguish. They seem to melt together, blending fully for mutual survival.

A fused couple creates a fused family.[52] The symbiotic family can look ideal in Stage 2, when an introverted style of living is required to nurture the young family. If the family maintains this style, however, flaws may begin to show up when children start school or when grown-ups, on the threshold of personal crisis, feel a need to break out of the nest. But the most severe crises or turning points for these enmeshed families occur in Stages 4 and 5, when children begin to leave home.

Dr. Lyman Wynne first noted the unusual symbiotic pattern when he observed families of children who became emotionally ill in adolescence.[53] He studied a group of hospitalized adolescents diagnosed as schizophrenics and discovered that their families were remarkably similar. The families typically were so glued together that no one could be a separate individual or think for himself. They were overprotective, and in exchange for their protection, demanded extreme loyalty. All social life outside the family was carefully discouraged. Children grew up to be dependent and insecure. Buried in their families, they found it impossible to discover their own identities. Dr. Wynne called these families pseudo-mutual, because their closeness disguises weakness and tyranny.

(There is a further discussion about symbiotic families is Stages 4 and 5, when the long-range effects of this enmeshed style begin to cause real trouble for families.)

These are some of the hazardous patterns families can slip into during Stage 2 of family life. Problems may erupt into divorce at this stage, but they often become softly established patterns that develop into major conflicts in the coming years as children grow up, and then frequently emerge full-blown when children are in late adolescence.

Unless the distorted patterns are worked out in some phase of the family life cycle, they will deepen until there is serious malfunction in one family member. Family problems become more and more difficult to resolve as dangerous patterns harden. Year after year the aggravation, grievances, and conflicts pile up. Children become deeply saturated with family traits until the pattern is almost literally in their blood, to be passed on from one generation to the next.

The sooner trouble spots are dealt with, the easier it is for the family to rebalance itself healthfully. To be aware of these hazardous patterns in early stages is to set the family on a survival path.

PORTRAIT OF A STARVING FAMILY

Jonathan Griffin was twenty-one years old when he met Kitty Bouchard. He mowed the shaggy lawn in front of her little bungalow, trimmed the overgrown hedges, and cast an inexperienced eye over the faded surface of the house. "I think the house could use a little paint, don't you?" he asked.

"Jon, the whole place is falling down; it would take you the rest of your life to fix it up."

"Then maybe I should get started," he replied. And in those few words their future together was established.

At the time of their meeting, Kitty was a thirty-year-old divorcée with weekend custody of her three small children. She was lonely, her life moving regularly between a routine office job at a local college and weekends spent alone with the kids.

Jonathan, an art student at the college, moved into her life like a rescue team, helping her with the kids, supporting her in her battles against her ex-husband, filling up the empty spaces of her life.

Standing barefoot in his jeans and T-shirt, he flipped pancakes on Saturday mornings, teased and roughhoused with the children, fitted into family life in a dreamlike aura that filled his whole being with happiness. During the week he had Kitty to himself, and her bed became his. Slowly his belongings seemed to become part of her house—his easel and paints standing in a corner of the living room they now called the studio, his sandals wedged under the threshold of the back porch because he hated wearing shoes in the house, his shirts drying on the line in the sunny backyard along with Kitty's lingerie and the kids' play clothes.

At first Kitty hesitated to get involved with a man so much younger than she, but Jon brought so much gaiety and pleasure into her life and relieved her of so much daily wear and tear that she quickly surrendered to his ardent courtship. A slender, graceful woman with a face like a Renaissance maiden, Kitty brought Jon into his manhood. She represented what he longed for in life—security and a sense of belonging in the adult world.

He gave up his little apartment and permanently moved into her house. After he graduated he continued his studies and joined the faculty as an instructor in art history. For the next few years their lives were easy and content. Jon put any thoughts of a painter's life to one side and happily devoted himself to family life. He felt needed and appreciated; Kitty, too, was satisfied with the private world they had created.

They seemed to live for each other, their intimacy so deeply satisfying that neither thought much about the world around them. They continued to spend weekends and vacations with Kitty's children and enjoyed these pleasurable times.

When Jon turned twenty-five, they decided to get married. A year later they had a baby of their own, something they both wanted. Two years later, when they entered family therapy, their home life was in shambles.

Kitty had developed insomnia and was totally exhausted. Chronic migraines combined with lack of sleep made her continually uncomfortable and sometimes almost hysterical.

Their problem, as they described it, was that they just couldn't get along anymore. Arguments constantly flared up, usually over the care of their two-year-old daughter, Kim. Recently the situation had worsened because Kim began waking at 5 A.M. and wouldn't go back to sleep. They tried everything to get her to sleep through the night, but nothing worked. Both parents were overwhelmed and perpetually exhausted.

The family portrait had changed. Kim ran gaily about my office, climbing on furniture. She clapped her hands gleefully with each new discovery. Kitty and Jon were collapsed in chairs at either end of the room, done in by a two-year-old. Kim was thriving; they were falling apart.

As Jon and Kitty tried to describe their situation, a fight erupted:

KITTY: Jon lets her cry too long in her room. By the time he goes in to her, the baby is so upset she can't go back to sleep.

JON: She has to learn that she can't wake up the whole house just because she's awake, and we can't go running every time she whimpers. It just makes it worse when you bring her into bed with us.

KITTY: It's the only way to quiet her down.

JON: I can't sleep when she's in the bed. That's why you do it. You bring her in because you know it keeps me awake.

KITTY: Well, it keeps *me* awake when she cries in her room. She could cry forever and you'd sleep right through it. You don't care what happens to me.

JON: I'm telling you, if you keep bringing Kim into bed, I'll sleep in the basement.

By this time Kitty was sobbing as Jon paced menacingly. Their most heated arguments erupted like this, and always revolved around Kim. They accused each other and argued over whose parenting style was right. Literally and figuratively, Kim came between them.

Each parent pulled Kim into his or her corner. They played tug-of-war with her. When she is old enough to talk, she will be forced to choose sides, and if she sides with one parent, she will automatically be defined as attacking the other.

A family triangle was forming, with Kim at the apex. Jon and Kitty fought about who made the better parent, who was right, who cared most. The arguments went on endlessly, and the tension drained them both of energy. If the situation continued, the family would disintegrate and Kim would probably develop serious difficulties. She might become overly fearful, develop learning disabilities, or become asthmatic.

How did Kitty and Jon, two intelligent and resourceful people, arrive at this point? What was happening in this family?

We looked back to the time Kim was born. Kitty and Jon had approached parenthood with the understanding that they would be partners. From Kim's early infancy, they alternated their work schedules so that one parent could work while the other stayed home. Because they shared parental responsibilities, each maintained a strong relationship with their child. What went wrong?

When Kim was born, Jon and Kitty absorbed the infant into their relationship and made her part of their marriage. There was no Jon or Kitty or Kim—there was only "us." On their evenings out they took Kim along, supposedly to save money on a baby-sitter. When they visited friends, Kim refused to sleep on the sofa and spoiled parties by crying or throwing a tantrum.

This entanglement with Kim was an extension of their overly close marriage. Jon and Kitty never had lives as individuals; together they existed as one person. When Kim came along, they tried to absorb her into their marriage, but the marriage couldn't take another weak person. At this point the family was a glob, missing a clear differentiation between the parts: three separate individuals, a couple,[54] and the parent-child unit.

This was the guts of the problem as it appeared in those early sessions. There were other pressing issues that plague many young families. Although Kitty and Jon made extra money by juggling their work schedules, money was still tight for them. They always were short of three vital commodities—money, time, and energy—and they all felt shortchanged, including Kim, who expressed her neediness with her tantrums, sleeplessness, and constant demands.

Their complicated routines of sharing child care and work left husband and wife little time or energy for each other.

Sex was just another chore. Kitty wanted to be courted, to have Jon's complete attention. But after working all day, fixing dinner, and putting the baby to bed, he wanted to put his feet up and watch TV. Kitty expressed her sense of deprivation: "My relationship with Kim is the closest relationship I have. At least she hugs and kisses me."

The Rx Process

At this time it seemed the immediate problem was to curtail the erosion of the marriage. We agreed to meet on a weekly basis, and one requirement was that they leave Kim with a baby-sitter when they came to sessions. It was urgent to get Kim out of therapy and start Kitty and Jon thinking of themselves as a twosome. It was also important for them to find some time alone together. Having dinner out one night a week didn't seem impossible, but the idea met with instant resistance because they had no money for baby-sitters.

Like many other isolated, overly close families, Jon and Kitty had no close friends to call on for help. I suggested they join a baby-sitting co-op with some other parents from a local nursery school. This would give them baby-sitting privileges and also introduce them to other young families in the community. Sharing experiences with other couples facing similar problems would help them feel less harassed and less isolated.

Once some of the immediate pressure weighing on the family was eased, we tried to see what Kitty and Jon were doing to each other. They seemed to lock horns most often over disciplining Kim. Jon's style had changed over the years as his responsibilities increased, and he had become a disciplinarian. Jon set rigid limits, while Kitty was gentle and permissive. They represented two extreme styles of parenting.

Jon said they had different ideas of what family life was about. "Kitty has this fantasy that we should all be cheerful in the morning, and have friendly conversations over the dinner table, like that. This TV-family idea of hers is totally unrealistic. I mean, eating with little kids is pure chaos."

Kitty wanted them to eat together at all meals; Jon felt Kim should be fed separately. Kitty wanted Kim to have a ritual bedtime story each evening; Jon felt Kim should be placed in her crib with a few toys, so that she could play until she fell asleep.

Underneath these different parenting styles they both had a large capacity to love and nurture their child. Their styles could work together if each could acquire something of the other's. They had two tasks: first, when they were all together as a family—at dinner or in the yard or out visiting— Kitty was to set limits on Kim's behavior; second, when one parent was dealing with Kim alone, even if both parents were at home, that parent was in charge and the other wasn't to come in and interfere.

The primary purpose of this arrangement was to end the bickering between parents and let them learn from each other. If Jon wasn't interfering, Kitty, given the position of disciplinarian, might see the necessity of imposing a firmer hand. If Kitty wasn't continually complaining about his rigidity, Jon could ease up on his rules. The assignment went smoothly, and there was a brief easing of tension. Jon and Kitty started to negotiate child-care schedules.

Jon kept his end of the agreement. He got up at 6 A.M., dressed Kim, made breakfast, and when it was his turn to watch Kim, kept the child with him while he worked at his easel. He was never able to accomplish as much as he wanted, since Kim interrupted incessantly, but he accepted this as reality, at least for the time being.

Kitty, though, continued to be chronically dissatisfied. According to her complaints, Jon was never responsive enough or giving enough. She was still swamped by Kim's needs and her fits of crying in the middle of the night. She saw herself as overburdened and felt victimized by Jon's callousness.

In spite of attempts to find time for the two of them to be alone, Kitty wasn't feeling any better. She still cried throughout sessions. The only improvement I could see—and it was an important change—was that Kitty and Jon were now fighting directly with each other. Since some of their practical problems were no longer pressing, I could get a clearer picture of the intense anger and rage between them. But I still didn't know what it was about.

I thought that now the only way to get at the core of the problem was to pressure Kitty. One difficulty was that she might see my intervention as another deprivation and walk out, but it was a necessary risk. They were at a critical point. I felt her escalating demands were spiraling toward an explosion that would end the marriage. By making it impossible for Jon to satisfy her, Kitty was forcing him to leave her.

I told Kitty that she was powerfully and effectively destroying her family. The session was heated, but Jon reaffirmed his love for her and told her that he wanted to make things work between them. Kitty walked out, saying she didn't know if she'd be back.

A week passed. When I didn't hear from Kitty, I called, and she agreed to return to therapy. In the following session, for the first time, Kitty seemed calm. She said, "When I feel weak and overstressed—the way I've felt ever since Kim was born—I'm terrified Jon won't stick by me, that he'll leave me. I'm filled with panic. I remember how my father stood by my mother and took care of her, and I want Jon to do that for me."

"Kitty, is this all a test? Are you doing all this to find out if Jon loves you?"

"I don't know."

According to Kitty, Jon had changed toward her soon after Kim was born. He began to talk about concentrating more on his painting and spoke of how he might have a gallery show if he knew more people in the art world. His attention seemed to shift away from Kitty, who was used to being the center of his life. At one time Kitty was all Jon professed to need; now he seemed to be pulling away, dreaming of a life outside the special world they had built together.

Why did this frighten Kitty so much? Here, again, one family's history was emerging and floating onto the next generation. Often it's possible for families to meet a crisis without delving into the past, but sometimes looking backward is the only way to learn what's going on in the present family because from generation to generation, families replay unsolved problems.

Kitty came from a large family in which, as the oldest, she was what therapists call a "parental child."[55] "My mother was the director," Kitty told us, "but I carried out all her orders. She was an invalid and spent most of her days in bed. We had a sofa bed fixed up for her in the living room and she would lie there all day and tell me what she wanted done. She was always nice, but tense. If I didn't do something just right, she would make me do it all over again."

Dr. Salvador Minuchin describes the predicament of the parental child:

> The allocation of parental power to a child is a natural arrange-
> ment in large families, in single parent families or in families
> where both parents work. The system can function well. The
> younger children are cared for, and the parental child can devel-
> op responsibility, competence, and autonomy beyond his years. A
> family with a parental child structure may run into difficulty if
> the delegation of authority is not explicit or if the parents
> abdicate, leaving the child to become the main source of guid-
> ance, control and decisions. *In such a case, the demands of the
> parental child can clash with his own childhood needs and exceed his
> ability to cope with them.*[56]

Minuchin might have been describing Kitty. The girl grew into a highly
competent adult with a tremendous wish to be taken care of. One could
almost predict that nurturing a child of her own would stir up conflict for
Kitty, and that her own neediness would compete with the child's until she
felt overwhelmed. If a mother must give too much from her own meager
supplies, she may starve emotionally.

Although Jon was more fortunate in his childhood, he too had a demanding mother. "To get away from her," Jon said, "I used to hide in my room
with my sketch pad and draw for hours." Though he was harassed by his
mother, he fought back, shouted her down, and, when things got too hot,
retreated to his room. His father quietly supported Jon's rebellion. Jon came
into marriage with a tendency to overreact to demanding women who made
claims on him.

In marriage Jon and Kitty managed to achieve a balance. As long as she
had Jon to herself, Kitty felt satisfied and didn't pressure him. They could
be together exclusively and play at family life on the weekends when they
entertained her children. Jon felt he had a full life, and Kitty felt taken care
of.

Kim tilted the balance. Suddenly Kitty was no longer the sole focus of
Jon's attention, and she panicked and began to make excessive demands on
him. At the same time Kim—an innocent bystander—was also making
demands.

Kim cried all night, threw tantrums, and created scenes. Kitty complained that Jon didn't care about her and cried that she was worn out and
used up.

Jon responded badly. He tried to win his battles with Kitty by shouting
her down; he no longer knew how to discuss problems with her. The more
Kitty clung, the more Jon pulled back to protect himself.

As the situation approached a climax, Jon increased the stress by trying to develop his artistic and professional life. At twenty-one Jon had bypassed his own growth to become an instant adult; he had walked into a family situation before he had developed himself as an independent person. Now his desire for a career and a life outside the family conflicted mightily with the reality of Stage 2. These two simultaneous crises—the unusual need of wife and child and his own need for growth—could now destroy the family.

Kitty was seriously threatened by any move that took Jon beyond the family. She didn't want more freedom, she wanted less. From her position—at age thirty-eight, with one failed marriage behind her and four children—she was afraid of the future.

Kitty was reaching a major life crisis. Who, precisely, was she? And what was her life all about? Could she cope with this personal turmoil and still live up to her family obligations? Kitty wanted to hide from it; she was frightened by change.

Some of the tension in the family will automatically ease when Kim starts school and becomes more independent. But as long as Jon insists on having a life of his own, family life will never again be the way it was before the baby was born. Jon realized that at least for the time being he would be up to his neck in fatherhood. But he knew there was a time limit on this, and that he could start to plan how to develop himself when Kim goes to school.

It was absolutely essential, if the family was to survive, that Kitty make a life for herself also. It was an extremely difficult situation. Both Kitty and Jon had to be more self-sufficient so that caring for their child didn't threaten them, and so they can grow into Stage 3 of family life.

I was sure that a natural, positive complementarity could exist between Kitty and Jon as parents: Jon's firmness and his willingness to stand up for his rights could balance Kitty's tendency to comply and surrender. Her intelligence and logical mind could help him learn to discuss problems instead of debating and arguing.

But the central task for both—especially Kitty—was to learn about themselves as individuals and find ways to grow beyond the family.

In Stage 2 adults are required to do things for children that children cannot do for themselves—which in this stage of family life is almost everything.

Parents of small children readily acknowledge that the unrelenting pressure to care for, soothe, serve, protect, and fulfill is draining. There is the additional psychological pressure to do everything right, the feeling that any false move will create a neurotic human being. In the midst of all this caring and giving, parents can begin to feel empty. The giving is all going one way—out. Parents forget to take care of each other.

In the healthy family, parents nurture children and they nurture each other. As their children's capacities and personalities unfold, they feel rewarded and rejuvenated. But it is only a few brief years until the young family faces a new turning point, and another difficult transition. One curl of the pattern is nearly finished and another is about to spring out.

Stage 3
WHEN CHILDREN GO TO SCHOOL

*Turning Point: To be lost in the family
or create a personal identity.*

Chapter 10

A FAMILY CRISIS

Joanne remembers clearly the morning, in fact the very moment, that changed her life and catapulted her family into a full-blown crisis.

Prompted by an inner clock, she awakened before the others and padded downstairs, careful not to disturb the deep silence of the sleeping house. She made coffee for herself and stood at the window to watch the winter sky lighten through the branches of a dogwood, the tree's dim shape growing more distinct until the branches were black against the whitening sky.

Then, without thinking, from the habit of a thousand mornings, she began to make orange juice from syrupy concentrate and set aside the better part of a Pullman loaf for the day's toast.

The quiet was suddenly dispelled by a muted alarm buzzing somewhere upstairs. A few minutes later another clock shrilled, followed by the sound of thumping footsteps and doors slamming.

"Mom, where're my socks?" shouted Tom from the upstairs hall.

"Mom, who took my blue sweater?" yelled Kevin from his bedroom.

"Mom," wailed David, "I can't find my shoes."

"Honey, did you do the laundry this week? I'm out of underwear."

"Mom," demanded Sarah from all the way up on the third floor, "make extra coffee—I want to take a Thermos to school."

"Mom," cried Jimmy, "my baseball fell in the toilet!"

Joanne McCarty (a/k/a Mom and Honey), running late for the 8:13 train, tried to ignore the commotion upstairs as she stirred orange juice and fed bread into the toaster. A dull ache throbbed in her left shoulder. The pain had started a few weeks earlier, and now, although it had steadily worsened, Joanne was almost used to it. A drop of water splashed on her nose. She looked up anxiously and saw water seeping through the ceiling from the second-floor bathroom. Visions of baseballs clogging toilet bowls swam before her eyes.

Five children and their father appeared in the kitchen. Framed by the doorway, their disgruntled faces made an unpleasant family portrait as they raised their voices in a loud chorus: "Mom!"

"Something clicked," Joanne says. "I felt hypnotized—as if I had no control over my body. I poured the orange juice into the sink, dropped the toast in the garbage, took off my apron, and walked out of the kitchen. I remember announcing out loud, 'I quit.' "

For the second time that morning, there was silence.

Joanne caught the train to her job at a metropolitan corporation, where she went through the day with the same deliberate concentration that had marked the morning. She lingered in the office after everyone else had gone and didn't return home until after eight that evening. Then she took her clothes from the dresser and right-hand closet in the master bedroom and moved them into a small spare bedroom. "I decided to be a roomer, and Dan and the kids could fend for themselves. I felt absolutely cold-hearted."

For the next three weeks Joanne left for work before breakfast each morning and didn't return until after dinner. She slept in the little room at the back of the house. Passionate entreaties by Dan and the children failed to arouse her familial emotions, and on the heels of her defection, family life rapidly deteriorated. Dinner at home now was mainly sandwiches. Dan's organizational efforts included assigning each child a personal jar of peanut butter with her or his name inked on the label. He did the laundry in a single large batch, and the children rummaged through the basket every morning looking for clean clothes. Without their mother to discipline them, the children came and went at odd hours. There was no family gathering at dinner, no family discussions, no sense of unity. It was every man for himself, each child a separate little nomad. The McCartys without Joanne were leaderless and floundering.

Three weeks after Joanne resigned, a disheveled family group straggled into my office. Dan herded the children together while Joanne sat apart, her attractive face drawn into a delicate mask that couldn't hide her unhappiness. Dan McCarty was a robust, handsome Irishman who even in that moment looked ten years younger than his wife. Their five children appeared as sad and deprived as Dickensian orphans.

Joanne's voice as she described the brief details of the morning that she quit was without expression. Dan took up the story and related the ensuing events that had brought them to this day. He was full of resolve and determination. His objective was clear: somehow, Joanne must resume her duties as head of the family and bring them all back into balance. They were falling apart without her. As Dan talked, Jimmy, the youngest child, began to cry.

Crises are extremely sensitive periods when family life can go either way, toward further deterioration or growth. In the best sense a crisis is an optimal time for families to get unstuck, to move themselves out of unrewarding and stifling situations. Up to this point only one member of the McCarty family—Joanne—was unhappy with the way the family operated. Everyone else was satisfied. Joanne's move had effectively upset the family system; and now everyone was in the throes of crisis.

The McCartys viewed the situation as the ragged edge of catastrophe; I agreed, but thought if they could get through this together, they could achieve a viable family life that was rewarding to all of its members. But it was important to learn why, on that particular morning in January, "something had clicked."

The pressure had begun to build up for Joanne six months earlier, when she decided to find a job. "After I went to work, I learned that I had raised a generation of incompetents. They couldn't do anything for themselves; I was mother, wife, housekeeper, cook, bookkeeper—and something more. I realized that I always told them what to do and when to do it. I think being in complete command was the only way I could keep order, so I was like a full support system. I started to get this picture after I was working full-time. I tried to get them to help around the house, but I got tired of nagging after a while and it was easier just to do everything myself. I was overwhelmed."

Faced with the choice between quitting her job or her family, Joanne, apparently quite suddenly, quit the family. "I couldn't change them," she said, "and I couldn't go on. I was simply worn out."

"That's what I don't understand," Dan said. "If it's too much, and God knows I can see how it would be, I think you should give up the job. We've managed all these years on one paycheck. We still can. I just don't see what the problem is."

"The problem is, Dan, that I don't want to."

"But everything was fine before . . ."

Joanne stopped talking again and returned to the stony silence that had marked the beginning of this session. Silence would prove to be her most effective weapon throughout family therapy. I think Joanne felt it was useless to try to explain her feelings to the family, and that also she wasn't certain she was justified in her radical stance.

Family therapists look for two things when a family is in crisis: what went on in the families of origin, and what happened in earlier stages of family life. We all needed to understand what had brought Joanne to this dramatic switch. "Tell me how you two got together," I asked, directing the question to Joanne. The children seemed fascinated by the question. Joanne was willing to turn away from the immediate situation and look at the past.

"When I met Dan," she recalled, "I was just starting college and he was a junior. I still lived at home. I had six younger brothers and sisters, and I had been sort of an extra parent in the house from the time I was a youngster. Dan was so carefree and so much fun, he did things I'd never dream of doing. It was as if he opened a door and let me out. When I was with him, I had fun all the time. I was a different person."

"We used to go out," said Dan, "and everything struck us as hysterical. We'd laugh at anything. Joanne has a devastating sense of humor—she's very witty and clever. She was also level and honest. I'm a joker, but she had real humor. I loved being around her."

Joanne and Dan were a natural combination, different from each other yet well balanced as a couple. When Dan graduated in 1956, they married. Their first child, Andrea (now married and away from home), was born a year later. Soon after they encountered their first serious crisis, but didn't seem to notice it.

"I became a real mommy. Dan worked most of the time, and he loved having a family of his own to come home to. He was the daddy going off to work, and I kept the home fires burning."

The balancing act that works in marriage doesn't always succeed after children are born. (Any extra stress can throw the balance out of whack; weak spots grow more pronounced, minor problems intensify.) In this instance Dan and Joanne split themselves up into two distinct roles. It looked like an efficient way to handle the family, but in fact they were growing apart, and the gap widened as the family grew.

Sarah, now sixteen, was born in 1959, followed by Tom (age fourteen), and then by Kevin (twelve), David (nine), and finally Jimmy (age six). The entire family rattled around in a suburban relic, a shambling barn of a house that Dan said always needed a coat of paint. "That house is like the Golden Gate Bridge—you start painting the front and by the time you get to the back it's time to start all over again." Mostly they let the outside of the house and the yard go. Joanne took charge of the inside.

Joanne's strongest point, the single characteristic for which she was most admired by her friends and family, was her outstanding competency. Joanne could do everything—usually better than anyone else. She became the foundation upon which the family was built. She handled everything involved with the house.

Dan, a sales executive, traveled a lot and spent long hours with clients, sometimes not getting home till late at night. He loved his work and had many business acquaintances, whom he entertained. When he was home, sometimes only on weekends, he showed the kids a good time and created the sense of unity that is the great joy of big family life. Dan had been an only child himself and clearly enjoyed family life. Saturday ball games and outings with Dad were routine. He was the clown, the buddy who joked with his kids and took them all out to breakfast on Sunday mornings.

"Where were you during these forays?" I asked Joanne.

"Cleaning house," she replied. "Haven't you noticed that people get stuck with the jobs they're good at? Well, I'm good at cleaning house—and that's where I was. Dan's good at having fun." Dan looked as if she had slapped him, but she continued. "Actually, I cherished the moments when they were all gone so I could get things done. When he took them out, it was really a respite for me."

After nineteen years of this arrangement, the separation between Dan and Joanne was almost complete. They faced a loaded situation. Joanne said openly that she was thinking of moving out of the house. The children were filled with panic. They had never known there was the slightest problem between their parents, and the present situation terrified them. All of them, from the oldest to the youngest, broke into tears throughout the family sessions.

Divorce can threaten in any stage of the family life cycle. The McCartys, well past the early, unstable years of marriage, still had young children and continually had to relive certain problems over again. They were in several stages of family life at once, all of them grating on a basic flaw: the family's overwhelming reliance on Joanne to provide its cohesiveness. The present crisis was deeply rooted in the McCartys' relationship, a flaw upon which past crises were heaped and buried.

Everyone in the family was blind to one important fact: everything that happens to an individual has repercussions in her or his family. A change in anyone's age, status, job, school, or behavior requires some sort ot adjustment by every member of the family.

Three people in the McCarty family had made major changes in their lives in the last six months, and the family had failed to accommodate or even notice any of them. They tried to continue family life as if no change had occurred. Andrea, the oldest child, had married and left. Dan and Joanne, with five children still at home, made little fuss over Andrea's departure.

"We miss her, of course," Dan said. "We've known her for so long." He smiled. I knew he was thinking of the special relationship parents have with their firstborn, but didn't want to say so in front of his other children. Not only had Andrea married, but she had moved to Chicago, so her family didn't see her at all. "One day she was there, a part of the family, and the next she was just gone."

But Dan insisted they hadn't felt upset about this. I asked how Andrea's leaving had changed their lives. They all said it hadn't.

Sixteen-year-old Sarah was willing to add dimension to the discussion. "At first I was glad she was leaving. Andrea was always first. She got everything first, she did everything first. . . . By the time it got around to me, it was old hat. I thought it would be good to be on top for a change. But I got really scared when she was actually gone. Andrea sort of paved the way for me. She was the only other girl—she was pretty neat, you know. But nobody asked me, so I didn't say anything."

When family members leave, the family has to back and fill, slip and slide, and reshape itself around the remaining members. All relationships change, some imperceptibly, others dramatically. With Andrea gone, Sarah, Joanne and Dan sustained the most severe loss. Sarah, however, had the opening to form another, stronger alliance with her brother Tom, who was closest to her age. She could move into a more effective role vis-à-vis the younger children, as she was now "the oldest." Joanne and Dan avoided the shock of losing one child by making a deliberate effort not to change anything in the family.

The second member of the family to change his status was six-year-old Jimmy, who started kindergarten full-time. In all the years Joanne and Dan had been married, there always had been at least one baby in the house. Jimmy was the last, and now his going marked the beginning of a passage that would culminate eventually in all the children's permanent departure from home.

Joanne registered these changes to some degree when, at the age of forty, she took her first job. Dan had always made a good living, but with six children there was no chance to put much aside and little for luxurious extras. When Joanne decided to get a job, Dan said it was fine with him. Of course no one in the family, least of all Joanne, expected Mom to ease up on her family duties.

Although all these changes affected the family, Joanne's move was the most radical because there was no established social convention to ease the family over the change. Society marks major life changes with ritual and celebration. Birthdays and graduations, confirmations and bar mitzvahs, weddings and baptisms and funerals are society's way of spreading shock— children growing up, babies being born, parents dying—through the larger community. No ritual exists to help a forty-year-old mother leave her family and begin a career.

The McCarty family failed completely to realize that a change in Mom's life would affect the way they lived. They made absolutely no concession for her increased work load and responsibility. But the blame was not all theirs.

Joanne had accustomed them all, including her husband, to depend on her. And now, after all these years, she suddenly removed her support. "No fair!" they cried. And in a way they were right. The family could not readily reshape itself overnight simply because Joanne demanded it. She had spent years training them otherwise.

It was a stalemate. The ultimate goal was to get Dan and Joanne on the same side. But the immediate problem was to put the household back into some kind of working order. Given these two aims, a good way to get started was to bring Dan into the arena of household responsibility. Joanne refused any sort of joint effort and would have nothing to do with organizing the family. She felt that if she gave an inch she quickly would return to her old situation. Isolating herself from the family had brought them into therapy, and she figured that only by sticking to her position would the family change. I didn't argue with her.

I suggested that Dan take charge and delegate household chores to the children. He agreed to plan the meals and do the shopping; he would assign various responsibilities to the children, and they agreed to cooperate. Joanne continued her exile within the house.

When the family returned a week later, it was clear that this was not a winning system. "Daddy can't do anything right," complained Sarah. "I have to do everything." Sarah was in danger of being indoctrinated into Joanne's old role, and she was fighting it every inch of the way. The boys added their complaints. "Dad forgot to pick me up Friday night after basketball practice. I waited for him and everyone else left and the pay phone didn't work, so I finally had to hitch a ride home." This was Tom speaking. "It's really crazy around there. Nobody knows where anybody is."

As agreed, Dan had assigned them tasks, but then had sabotaged all their efforts to carry out their assignments. "He told Tom and me to make a decent dinner for a change," Sarah said, "then he criticized everything we did. I mean, he can't boil water, and suddenly he thinks he's Julia Child." The night of the failed gourmet dinner, Sarah went to her room in tears, Tom stormed out of the house to "see the guys," and everyone else had peanut-butter sandwiches. Kevin said, "Dad sits around and talks about how we're going to run the house, and makes lists of errands and shopping and stuff—then he forgets all about it. He never does any of it."

"It's an admirable effort, Dan," I said, "but I don't think it's going to work." We all sat for a few minutes without speaking. Dan had packed enough trouble into one week to effectively destroy a half-dozen defense plants. As a saboteur, he could have won the Second World War with one hand tied behind his back. From then on we called Dan the king saboteur because he always threw a monkey wrench into the machinery of family life.

Dan had a mischievous nature. In the past, when he committed what Joanne called Daddy's shenanigans, Joanne had overcompensated and doubled her efforts to keep the family on an even keel. But with Joanne out of the picture, Dan's idiosyncrasy stood out as a truly destructive impulse.

At first Dan denied he was deliberately screwing up the family's efforts to take care of itself. "I'm just kidding around with the kids. It doesn't mean anything. Besides, I have a lot to take care of. It's not as though I can spend all my time worrying about the house and kids. I've got a job."

"And if the family continues to foul up," I said, "it might put enough pressure on Joanne to force her into taking a hand. I think that's what this is all about."

"I'm getting pretty tired of all this," he said. "I can't handle everything at home and be expected to meet my commitments at work, too. It's just too damn much to ask."

"That's the point. The children aren't babies—you're making it much harder than it should be by preventing them from helping you."

Dan finally began to accept that family life was never going to return to its previous condition. He seemed depressed and had little confidence that the family's problems could ever be resolved. He said little for the rest of the session.

In spite of this setback I persisted. From professional and personal experience I know that families cling to old patterns and resist change.

It was still necessary to keep Dan in the center of things. I suggested that he think of himself as the administrator of an unwieldy corporation and try to organize his staff into effective teams. Dan wasn't the only one who had trouble taking responsibility. The kids had leaned so heavily on Mom that they hadn't learned how to support each other and work together.

In spite of their efforts to change, old habits continued to create havoc for the next several weeks. Dan was already training Jimmy, terror of the toilet bowl, to be the second biggest joker in the family and Junior Saboteur. The two oldest children were asked to keep an eye on Jimmy.

Joanne was absolutely adamant about staying out of the family. The kids were equally determined to keep Dan on the hook. When he fooled around too much or messed up too much, they were ravishingly quick to remind him. In the ensuing weeks Dan, although sticking to his defense of just being a fun guy, tried to keep his pranks under control.

One of the dangers in any family therapy is that once things get rolling, family members try to find someone to blame for their troubles. It is the task of the therapist to keep shifting points of view and keep the family focused on change. If one member is on the hot seat for too long, there is the danger of that person being scapegoated to avoid the genuine family problem.

Family therapists don't take sides, because allocating blame is not the point. Problems develop when family relationships aren't working. The therapist tries to help families shape these relationships so they work better. In this way family therapists are advocates of the family as a whole. We lose perspective if we get locked into being the advocate of one person or one position.

Originally the kids viewed their mother as a traitor; now they made Dan the bad guy. Everything that went wrong was Dad's fault. I was looking for a way to shift the focus when Joanne suddenly spoke up and addressed the children: "I think you should take care of some of these things yourself. Why should Daddy do all your dirty work?"

Dan gave a sigh of relief. He was caught off guard a moment later when Joanne added, looking straight at him, "Not that I think you're doing such a swell job."

There was a lot of pulling and tugging in the next few weeks, but Dan and the kids got some kind of cooperation going, although how they managed from day to day was anybody's guess. It's not easy for six people unaccustomed to working together to devise efficient methods of running a household the size of a small business. It took them a week of high-powered negotiating just to decide who would make the oatmeal in the morning.

Negotiating is like a game or a puzzle, and it can be fun to work out efficient and equitable ways to achieve your objective. It's a challenge, and the kids were fascinated by this approach. Could they pull it off? Could they run a household where each person pulled his or her weight but no one had to do more than his or her share?

The McCartys' scheduling of household events rivaled a general session of the United Nations. But they did it, and as they grew more adept, their plans grew more efficient in design and execution.

They finally worked out a weekly schedule, rotating the dishwashing, cooking, laundry, and housecleaning chores among all members of the family. The two youngest children set and cleared the table and emptied the garbage. "We get all the jobs for short people," David complained, but he staunchly drew the line when Sarah suggested that with the aid of a stool he and Jimmy would be eligible for dishwashing.

Each person was responsible for cleaning his own room, and a weekly monitor was assigned to make sure everyone complied. Things did not always run smoothly, and there were sibling arguments about who had done the most dishes in any given week, or was it fair for Sarah, even though it was her turn, to have to clean a bathroom after Jimmy had meticulously lined the bottom of the tub with Silly Putty. Most of these fights wound up with someone in hysterics, and in no instance was everyone completely satisfied. But in fits and starts, the family was functioning without Mom.

The McCartys' biggest asset as a family was their sense of humor and their affection for each other. As sessions continued, although the children would often break into tears when things got rough between Dan and Joanne, they were just as likely to laugh at themselves. Although Joanne continued to live apart, her room became central headquarters for the family. After dinner the children drifted there, sat on her bed, read with her or watched her television. In a twelve-room house, all seven McCartys congregated in one tiny back bedroom.

The kids teased Joanne about being a "career woman" and "Gee, Mom, you must get tired of eating in restaurants when we're all such great cooks." And Joanne expressed her amazement and admiration for their skills at running the house. This was a unique time between mother and children. The children's lifelong relationship with Joanne was based on her taking care of them. They loved her because she was Mom. In this new situation they confronted her for the first time as a person separate from themselves. There was no underlying responsibility or dependency to interfere with the relationship. Each person in the family had the opportunity to be known and liked for who she or he was. This was a novel wrinkle in the family system, one that most families don't encounter until long after children have left home and established themselves separately from the family.

After about six weeks all five kids came into the session grinning and looking conspiratorial. "What's up?" I asked. Joanne and Dan looked puzzled. Tom looked at his shoes, David giggled. "Come on, you guys, what's going on?"

Sarah, glancing sidewise at her parents, who I noticed were sitting together on the same side of the room for the first time since the family began therapy, opened up: "Daddy spent the night in Mom's room," she said. All five children collapsed laughing. The expression on Joanne's and Dan's faces—complete dismay—seemed to give Jimmy and David an uncontrollable fit of giggling. It's very hard to keep a straight face when five people are laughing uproariously. I started to laugh. Dan broke out a smile. Joanne just shook her head, the barest gleam of amusement crossing her face.

"You kids have been seeing too many old movies," she said. "Sex is not cause for rioting and dancing in the streets."

"It is at our house," chortled Kevin.

That almost ended any kind of serious conversation for that session. For the better part of the hour, none of the McCartys could even look at each other without laughing. Things only quieted down when I asked Joanne if she would like to get back into the family. The silence was so swift and final it was as though someone had switched off a blaring radio.

Expectedly, Joanne did not leap at the opportunity. She said she would like to try but was still worried that when she did, the family pattern would shift back to mom-dependency. There is a standard reminder I give to myself and my clients when we reach the point where we're aware of the problem but they have not changed a behavior pattern: it doesn't have to be that way.

I gave Joanne a prescription: when she took up a share of the household responsibility, she also must assume a share in family fun. She had to join the family in games, going out, anything they all did together as a group—whether she wanted to or not. Anytime the family acted as a group and had good times together, Joanne had to participate. The rest of the balancing act, the parceling out of chores and responsibilities, would have to be worked out among them.

Dan and the children were enthusiastic. At this point they no longer considered Joanne's position outrageous. Thanks to her determination, they were taking care of themselves and had learned that, while it was nice to have someone else do all the work, it was grossly unfair to expect it. They grumbled but at the same time took pride in the fact that they could clean their rooms, cook, do dishes, vacuum—all the hundreds of chores that go into keeping a large house without help.

Joanne came back under very specific conditions. The children would continue to parcel out the chores according to their system of rotation. Joanne and Dan would supervise the shopping and cooking, Joanne minimally during the week and Dan on weekends, but they would always have at least one chef–helper-in-training. Since Dan's hours at work were erratic, Joanne agreed they could be flexible about assuming household responsibility—because they had a watchdog committee of five to see that they stayed relatively balanced. Their balancing was complicated, but the kids enjoyed the complexity and considered it a challenge to create equality in the family.

Joanne eased back into family life. She looked years younger, more relaxed, happier. The McCarty family is one of the successes of family therapy. They were a basically happy family with one serious, deeply rooted flaw. Their immediate crisis was resolved within three months, and the family was stronger and more viable than before.

All the McCartys had become fascinated with the process of therapy and the way changes had come about in their lives. They decided that even though they had resolved the immediate crisis, they would like to work on other problems in the family that they were beginning to recognize. Because the family was so large, several children were in different stages of development, presenting the family with a myriad of conflicting relationships. Sarah, now the only girl in a family of four brothers, had special problems coping with adolescence. She also faced a temporary, predictable conflict with her mother as she established her own strong personality. All three teenagers faced new problems with sexuality, drugs, and gaining independence. Dan also had predictable difficulties as he changed from clown and pal to father and husband.

I became more of a group leader as the McCartys took over their own therapy, working on different relationships within the family as well as individual growth and fulfillment.

The McCarty family problems were very similar to the problems most families face at one time or another. Many families respond to crises in such a way that they automatically straighten themselves out. But any family, in or out of therapy, can get stuck in a pattern that worked at one point but is now outdated.

The McCartys, even though they had a lot going for them, were so stuck that they needed the extra help of therapy to put them back on the track. Joanne, by keeping her children dependent, had trapped herself. The McCartys overrelied on her and buried her in the family.

Some changes just creep up on us. We expect to take them in stride but can't seem to make the transition easily. We are unprepared for the havoc connected with the inevitability of children growing independent. This brings the family to a new stage in the family life cycle.

Chapter 11

FINDING AN IDENTITY BEYOND THE FAMILY

As the first child in a family prepares for school, the family begins to shift into a new stage. Latency,[1] the period in a child's life between six and puberty, is a blossoming time, a time when children offer their most astounding pleasures to their parents as they make dazzling intellectual leaps, learn to read, and master arithmetic. Theoretically at least, a child has achieved, some ability to get along with other people and, in latter phases of this period, is supposed to be pliable and calm.

It's no accident that formal education, compulsory from age six, takes advantage of the child's industriousness.[2] Emotionally and intellectually, children are now ready to be away from parents for a substantial part of the day.

The community beyond the family becomes the child's world. Classrooms, playgrounds, afterschool clubs, and children's camps are places where he begins to test his mettle and find his place in a larger world. These moves are ingrained in our society, and the parent who resists the new activities bucks both the child's natural instincts and the community.

There also are more subtle signs that a fledgling has exchanged the nest for wings into a wider world. One day, as I walked my seven-year-old son to the pickup spot for his afterschool baseball group, he shyly asked me not to kiss him good-bye. A new era in our relationship had begun. He no longer wanted to be kissed in public. The days of smooching and hugging were over. He wanted our relationship to be more remote, more grown-up. I exercise restraint, but I don't like it much.

In another stage, only a few years earlier, family life depended on self-sacrifice. Survival in this stage now depends on self-development beyond the walls of the family. Children, no longer bound to parents out of helplessness, experience their first taste of freedom, and for many families the separation is wrenching. It is a time for the family to change again. Mothers, fathers, and children need to look at themselves as individuals.

124

As children grow more self-sufficient and capable, they need space and time and friends of their own. Parents, too, have to move out on their own. The family's ability to encourage independence for all its members and still maintain family cohesion is the crucial task in Stage 3. Both men and women need to redefine themselves with regard to family, work, and the quest for personal gratification. Individuation is the foundation of a healthy family. The family that survives supports its members and helps launch them into the larger world.

I remember other routine events that actually signaled important changes in our home. After the children were born I began to take a long break in the middle of the day so I could lunch at home. Since my office is near home, this was convenient, and soon the afternoon break became a ritual. My arrival was an event. Toys were put aside at the sound of my key in the door. There was a rush of kisses, hugs, and demands. My children and I shared lunch, and I read stories, pushed strollers to the park, and played peek-a-boo. As the children grew older, our afternoon respite corresponded with their return from school, but it dwindled from several hours to one or two. Now I turn the key to silence. I am affronted by the undeniable fact that high-decibel squeals no longer greet my arrival. I lunch alone, and when I return to work, I don't have milk and jam stains on my clothes. Everyone has someplace to go, and I am thankful that I do, too.

ADULT VS. FAMILY LIFE CYCLE

If children take huge leaps into the world during latency, how does this jibe with parents' personal development? If we match the adult life cycle with the family life cycle, do we have a "fit" or a collision in Stage 3? How does the lessening of active parenting affect parents as people?

According to Dr. Roger Gould, adults between the ages of twenty-nine and thirty-four have an inner drive to search for self-knowledge. "Marriage and career lines have been established and young children are growing, but some inner aspect is striving to be accounted for."[3]

Levinson, Gould, and Sheehy, chroniclers of the adult life cycle, all describe the struggle to find ourselves in the transition into our thirties. The transition is marked by the need to express those parts of ourselves that we suppressed in our twenties. As Sheehy asks, "What do I want out of this life now that I'm doing what I ought to do?"[4]

As they move into their early thirties, couples who wed and bred in their twenties have an opportunity to expand their private world at the same time that their children learn to be more independent. As family pressures ease, adults have more freedom to develop themselves in new ways. The family has to struggle to create new rules and patterns to accommodate this increased need for independence.

Some married people don't survive the transition. Instead of changing *with* their partners, they end up changing partners. Sheehy calls this the Catch-30 couple crisis.[5] But from the family perspective, if husbands and wives view their individual changes as natural, the restructuring in Stage 3 can be compatible with adult growth.

Trouble starts if we sidestep our own development and try to live through our children. Pliable and energetic, school-age children seem natural extensions of our unexpressed dreams. This detour of self-discovery is dangerous to individuals and to families.

It's easy to confuse our own needs with the development of our children. Unrealized dreams are brought to fruition by children. Little League tryouts make the World Series a pale event by comparison; piano lessons with the best teacher for potential Horowitzes and only the School of American Ballet for young Gelsey Kirklands. Our own dreams and ambitions are reborn in our progeny. Anecdotes about our children get so mixed up with our own memories that it's hard to sort them out.[6] A mother who bullies her daughter into playing the flute instead of the guitar that the child desperately wants undermines, rather than nurtures, her daughter's confidence.

Tempting as it may be, the search for validation as an adult person cannot really be achieved through our children. By denying ourselves personal growth, we also deny our children the right to be themselves.

Stage 3 of family life begins as children make their first forays into the world as independent people. Everybody can grow and change while family relationships are restructured to accommodate these changes.

FAMILY BOUNDARIES[7]

Making the transition into Stage 3 involves changing the family's boundaries. The notion of boundaries is a central concept in family theory. The boundaries in a family define who participates in the family and how. The key to understanding family crises in this stage is to understand how boundaries work.

An *external* boundary distinguishes the family from the outside world. *Internal* boundaries define and separate the different relationships inside the family—parents, parent-child, and brothers and sisters. Both sets of boundaries can be open or closed, clear or murky, rigid or flexible.

In Stage 2 the internal boundaries of the couple stretched to embrace children. The surviving family created a style in which everyone felt secure and nourished. Now in Stage 3 the family must open itself to outside life. It must stretch its outer boundary to give its members more freedom, opportunity, and confidence to venture into the wider community. At the same time members still need the family for support.

As the family increases its contact with the world, it must also intensify its internal life. Couples have to reaffirm their marriage so that the family remains closely knit when it opens its outer boundaries. This balance between freedom and commitment will shape the family for the rest of its life.

All family styles fall somewhere along a continuum whose poles are at two extremes: at one end, rigid and impenetrable boundaries within the family separate individuals in the disengaged family; at the other end, murky, weak boundaries fuse members in the enmeshed, overly close family. It's interesting that families with rigid internal boundaries are usually excessively open to the outside. And families with weak internal boundaries are usually closed to the outside world. In healthy families, both inner and outer boundaries are clear and flexible.

Most families fall somewhere between these extremes, with some relationships too close and others overly distant. When family relationships consistently reflect either extreme, the family is headed for a major crisis.

THE DISENGAGED FAMILY IN STAGE 3

If the "me-first" family survives Stage 2, it tends to grow into an "every man for himself" family. There is practically no family unity in the disengaged family. Disengaged families are excessively open to the outside world, and within the family, relationships do not exist.

Boundaries are wide open between family and nonfamily. Family members are excessively independent, never eat meals together or join in any family activities. Since so much time is spent away from home, there is little feeling of family cohesion. Relationships within the family are bland, and members seldom talk to each other about personal feelings or problems. There are no strong friendships or alliances inside the family. The McCartys' family style, for example, was disengaged—except for individual relationships with Joanne, who overworked to keep the family together. As soon as she withdrew her support, the family fell apart.

THE ENMESHED FAMILY IN STAGE 3

The enmeshed family is the opposite of the disengaged family. Family members spend all their time together, and there is no privacy. Everyone is into everyone else's business. If Mom and Dad argue, the kids get in the act. Mom and Dad don't define a separate relationship, and all sorts of parent-child coalitions exist. The family is closed to the outside world and sticks together like glue. This is the family that talks in *wes*. Individual freedom is forbidden, and dependency is approved. Enmeshed families have rigid boundaries against the nonfamily world, but their internal relationships are too close.

Extreme styles are dangerous both to the survival of the family and the well-being of individual members. Less extreme patterns work better in some stages of family life and worse in others. Families need to modify these patterns as they move through the life cycle.

During Stage 3 families that are overly close must offer their members greater freedom and independence. Disengaged families such as the McCartys, who were held together by one central member, will disintegrate if this person seeks greater freedom. If the others are to survive, this major release from the family must be accompanied by a strengthening of internal boundaries.

The primary danger in Stage 3 is the unspoken agreement that it's acceptable for some family members to be confined in the family while others are free.

Some marriages—and families—are based on the covert understanding that one person's freedom is ensured by another's confinement. This unhealthy arrangement can exist in exaggerated or mild forms, but is characterized by the husband or wife who does not live life fully because of a flaw in the relationship.

Because family cohesion diminishes in Stage 3, families struggle to find new ways to be close. Family time and work time may have to be negotiated and then renegotiated. Children may complain more about their chores, reminding everyone that family cooperation is still important. Or Dad may need his working wife to help him prepare a presentation, reminding her that *his* work is important, too. Or Billy gets into trouble at school, reminding parents that he also needs attention.

The surviving family is in the throes of adjusting its inner relationships to redistribute power and create a new closeness. The family that short-circuits this process and tries to cling to old patterns can self-destruct.

Chapter 12

POWER, MONEY, AND SEX

When her youngest child started school, Leah Parker welcomed the chance to look for a job. She found a place as a secretary in a rapidly growing advertising agency at a time when better positions were opening up for women. She was a fast learner and advanced quickly, becoming first an assistant account executive and then account executive. Her achievement in the business world was so sudden that it was hard for Leah and her family to absorb the change. She was both excited and a little scared. Her career soared.

Oddly, with all her ability Leah couldn't drive a car, and Richard, her husband, drove her to work in the morning and picked her up from appointments. This chink in her competence reassured both husband and wife that they needed each other.

I think any agreement between husband and wife, no matter how eccentric it seems, is all right as long as it works for them. It seems that a temporary ballast can help support a family while the family adjusts to change. In this case Leah's helplessness behind the wheel of a car satisfied everyone, at least for the time being.

Then Leah said that she might take driving lessons to relieve Richard of his chauffeuring duties. He insisted that she was too old to learn to drive and they couldn't afford a second car, anyway.

She began to feel irritated by his protectiveness. But she also felt safe. Their brief spats ended predictably: Leah let off some steam about wanting to drive, to which Richard responded by not responding. Both breathed a little easier when the issue blew over.

In the early years of their marriage, Leah and Richard's relationship was rooted solidly in family life. They leaned on their roles as parents and dismissed their mutual dependency in the glow of exemplary family life. As a family in Stage 2, they were a model of togetherness, benignly emphasizing protection and closeness.

A main adjustment in Stage 3 is the renewal of the marital bond and separation of marriage from parenthood. By Stage 3 Leah and Richard were so saturated with family protection that they couldn't give it up. The marriage was stable, but dull. The "institution of parenthood" had overgrown the pleasures of marriage.[8]

Men and women who have demanding careers require emotional support from their mates. It gives them courage to take the hard knocks of the working world. Helping each other can bring couples closer as equals and partners. But in place of emotional closeness, Leah had someone to drive her to work and protect her from traffic. Instead of a wife with whom he could share his problems, Richard had someone who leaned on him superficially. They both used little crutches in place of the strong structural foundation upon which families should build.

Leah hesitated to tell Richard about work and the excitement of her job because she didn't want him to feel inferior. She never brought work home with her and never discussed her problems with him. Most of all, they never mentioned how they avoided each other sexually. She stroked his ego with her false needs: "I'm so helpless, honey, I couldn't get around without you." Once these false needs and supports get started, they are difficult to change.

A few years later, when their children were older and both Richard and Leah were approaching a mid-life crisis, Leah had an affair with a married man whom she met on a business trip. "It's perfect," she said. "We only see each other when I'm in St. Louis or he's in New York, but in between there are phone calls and love notes and things. It's just right. And I'm much happier at home since he's come into my life."

The affair was another crutch that held up the marriage. As long as passion could be sought elsewhere, the marriage would continue.

Husbands and wives in Stage 3 of family life have to consider the personal changes each is going through. We can't assume that the changes we experience will blend happily with the changes of our spouses. People who live together don't always grow in the same direction over the years, especially when each has played a distinctly different role in family life. Each partner will try to fill in those parts of life he or she has missed.

It's dangerous to act the role of parent or child to your partner in an effort to hang onto Stage 2 of family life. Leah and Richard needed to redesign their relationship to keep pace with personal changes and put vitality back into their romantic relationship. But they didn't.

This marriage may survive, but they will look for more ways to find excitement outside the family and may ultimately split up when the children leave home.

SOCIETY TAKES A CRACK AT THE FAMILY

The 1960s and 70s were times of unprecedented social change. Antiwar, civil rights, women's rights, gay rights, sex, the pill, and the war on poverty—all these movements and causes hammered away at traditional social arrangements. The family is the first institution to feel the impact of social change. Society directly influences sex roles, marriage, and relationships between children and parents.

Perhaps the most important change, as far as the family is concerned, is in the role of women. Women over thirty-five are entering college at an unprecedented rate. In 1976 the United States Department of Labor Statistics reported that during the past two years women had entered the labor force in droves. " . . . Most of the newcomers are in the twenty-four to forty-four age group, women who in the past have tended to stay home and raise children."[9]

This influx of wives and mothers into the labor force reflects numerous social currents; two of the most important are a narrowing of family life that has made exclusive child rearing too confining, and the economic necessity of having two wage earners in a family. In our society the marketplace offers power, money, and prestige as prizes for participation and success.

Women with children in school are ready to expand their lives and also contribute to the welfare of the family. Yet it's easy to see how Mom going out to work upsets the family balance. The phrase, Her husband's threatened by her success, oversimplifies this shakeup in the family.

STRUGGLE FOR POWER

The balance of power shifts when Mom also brings home the bacon. Money means power. And with two breadwinners, power is more evenly distributed between Mom and Dad. Research shows that a woman increases her power in the family in direct proportion to her cash contribution. The more money she makes, the more equal the marital relationship.[10]

Family therapists assert that the healthiest families have egalitarian marital relationships. When we say couples are healthiest when they are equal, it doesn't mean that their incomes must equal. There can be any number of financial arrangements. Money is only one way couples battle for power. But it is a powerful weapon, and many struggles in the family center around money.

Money—A Reward in Itself ?
Money does not automatically make women free, independent, and equal. Psychological dependency is obviously complex, but there's no denying that money is a major factor. A woman with no money or income of her own would need a very strong identity to overcome a gut sensation of dependence.

Theoretically it's possible to be financially dependent and still retain one's self-respect. But it's incredible how debilitating and insidious dependency is. An ex-account executive (female) comments, "I worked all my life. I was thirty-five years old when I married and had been working for sixteen years.

I quit my job to raise my kids, and this feeling started to creep up on me. Every once in a while I'd think about going back to work and I'd get scared. Or I would think about what would happen if my marriage broke up and I were left alone; how would I get along? I knew it was crazy, because I'd taken care of myself all those years, but I felt scared . . . my confidence was sapped."

This fascinating statistic has recently turned up in the press: for every $1,000 increase in salary a woman new to the job market earns, her chance of separation increases by 1 percent. Researcher Isabel V. Sawhill, examining data from a study of five thousand families in Michigan over a period of several years, found that women who achieved some degree of financial independence left unsatisfying marriages.[11]

Traditionalists interpret this information to mean that when women work, families and homes are destroyed. I am certain that it shows something else.

If you take away the economic underpinnings, what is family life all about? When husbands and wives start asking themselves this question, they often have to face up to marriages that are empty and unsatisfying, marriages based on one person's dependency instead of mutual caring and support.

Money gives women a choice. And while a woman with some financial security may be more likely to leave an unhappy marriage, a woman who is confident of her own ability to hold a good job is more likely to make a happy marriage in the first place. If the element of money is removed from the dependence-independence themes that pervade all marriages, one twist in the knotty problems of marital life is smoothed out.

In the past, only a few women saw work as personally fulfilling. Today their legion has grown. This attitude toward work transcends class lines. The fulfillment a person finds in work has to do with the match of the right person for the right job, rather than any inherent value assigned to the job itself. But even a woman who dislikes her job has the edge over the woman who doesn't make money: she's not panicked by the idea of taking care of herself. The kind of job a mother has affects the family to some extent— people with professional careers are more likely to bring work home or put in extra time outside the regular workday than nine-to-fivers. But these things in themselves are not harmful to family life.

Power struggles are everyday occurrences in marriage and seem to work both negatively and positively. In a negative struggle for power, one partner tries to dictate to or control the other. In a positive power struggle we try to define something for ourselves. It's not legitimate to try to make another person do what you want. That sort of manipulation always ends badly.

Legitimate power struggles revolve around defining what we want for ourselves and trying to achieve it by negotiation. The classic example is the woman in Stage 3 who wants to go to work for the first time or make a change in her career.

Several years ago I felt ready to make a major step forward in my career. I had finished my doctorate while our children were still small, and during that time I had stayed very close to home, scheduling school, office, and clinic hours around the children. When they were ready for school, I was also ready to move. I needed experience teaching in college, but there were no teaching jobs available in the New York metropolitan area. Finally I received an offer—not the greatest, but nevertheless a decent offer to teach as an adjunct at Adelphi College from nine to twelve on Saturday mornings. I jumped at it. The pay was insulting, the time inconvenient, and it was a hundred-mile round trip, but it was an opportunity to teach individual and family development, which made up for all the drawbacks. I was excited and enthusiastic when I told my husband about the job. Four hours later I was exhausted and depressed.

At first Bob dismissed the whole idea as ridiculous. His offhand manner infuriated me. When he realized I was serious, he was furious. He accused me of selfishness, of abandoning the family, of putting my career before him and the children. His reaction was so wild that we hammered away at each other, each angry, both trying to get our points across.

Bob's greatest personal asset is that he is fascinated by what makes people, including himself, tick. Once his initial fury was spent, he dug away at the roots. It wasn't only that I was deserting him and the family, he said, but he felt that I would join a more interesting and rewarding world. He was afraid that if he had to compete with the academic world, he would lose.

We did not resolve this problem in one night. I took the job, and we continued talking and arguing. The upset added stress to starting a new job, but I think we needed to fight in order to say all the things we felt and feared about independence. It brought us closer together. When he told me he felt I wouldn't need him anymore, that he would be superfluous to my life, I understood him and loved him more.

Admitting that we're scared doesn't have to stop us from changing. In marriage, when you know what's frightening, you know where the obstacles are and you know what you have to resolve.

One forty-year-old wife and mother told me: "You have to fight for your independence in family life. It's not given to you. My husband puts up an awful row every time I want to change anything. If I keep explaining my point of view, he eventually, sometimes suddenly, gives over. But I have to keep at it. I used to think that arguing or fighting with someone you love was horrible or that it would have a bad effect on the kids. But it isn't like that. Our so-called fights are really just talking to each other. It's enlightening—interesting. Sometimes it goes on for days. There was one problem that kept surfacing for a couple of years, then all of a sudden we understood it and it worked out."

In my own marriage this confrontation over the teaching job was a turning point. Its theme was basic to our survival as a family: balancing individual self-interest with family commitments. But there are many kinds of little and big power struggles in marriage, and they do not all involve women seeking careers.

What is important to understand in power struggles is that dominant-submissive patterns shouldn't be rigid; sometimes I win and you lose, other times I lose and you win. But there's no capitulation or surrender in a positive power struggle. Arguments should be issue oriented, and partners should seek a solution or understanding. Capitulation is not the point.

If "winning" becomes the point, everyone loses. Power struggles are the basis for reshaping relationships and marital contracts throughout the life cycle.

SEX: HOW OPEN IS OPEN?

Sex is one way couples retain their family ties while they expand their roles in the outside world. When both parents are involved in the larger community, marriages need emotional intensity and honesty.

Often when a couple opens up a marriage sexually, they weaken one of their strongest bonds. Sexual relationships outside the marriage tend to put the marriage on the same level as any other relationship. There's a difference between the sexually nonexclusive marriage advocated by the O'Neills in *Open Marriage* and the flexible marriage that keeps pace with a family's changing needs.[12]

In my clinical experience, sexually open relationships appear a lot more liberated than they really are. In some cases sex is the only dimension of freedom and autonomy allowed. In these marriages couples substitute sexual freedom for basic independence beyond the family. In one family I know the partners encouraged each other to have a variety of sexual experiences outside the marriage, but the husband stewed every time his wife went to her classes at a university.

Sexual openness profoundly interferes with the closeness between husband and wife. The truly open marriage, whose partners are busy and productive outside the family, can't afford this loss of intimacy. Marriages need the sexual tie.

WANTED: DIGNITY FOR THE HOMEMAKER

In September of 1973, on a day when the temperature soared to a record-breaking 98 degrees, I met with fifteen other women in the basement of a public school in Brooklyn. They were an attractive group, mostly in their middle to late thirties. I had run several therapy groups before, but I was at a disadvantage in this one because these women were all friends and I was a stranger. I would learn shortly that there were other reasons for the acute discomfort I felt at the initial meeting.

They were wives of local workmen—plumbers, bank tellers, electricians, telephone repairmen, factory foremen, and supermarket managers. They all lived in the same neighborhood, and their kids went to the same schools, where these mothers belonged to the PTA. A spokeswoman for the group had called the mental-health clinic where I was on staff and asked for someone to work with them. They specifically requested a female therapist, "but not a women's libber."

At this first meeting there was a clumsy silence, and a few minutes passed before a tall, beautifully coiffed blonde took the plunge: "We requested a therapist because we are all feeling dissatisfied with ourselves. We've tried pottery and sewing clubs, tennis and cards, but nothing makes us feel fulfilled." (*Fulfilled* would be an overused word that day, and nobody was sure just what it meant.)

There was a feeling of sadness in the room, very quiet, hesitant. A few other women spoke up haltingly, glancing around the room looking for support from their friends.

I listened to these bare, measured phrases and encouraged them to speak; they all made similar comments, as if they were one person.

"We feel displaced; we're not important anymore." They felt like failures when the classes or clubs they tried didn't bring them the status they sought. Sought from whom?

"Our children and husbands. We love our families and homes. We enjoy housekeeping and child care. Why is this a crime? This women's movement has ruined the reputation of mothers."

One woman cried when she recalled that her son came home from school one day and criticized her for "only being a housewife." A chorus of sighs echoed her statement. Their children were putting them down for worrying about ring around the collar. The kids suggested they get a job, get ahead in life, get a career. They were guarded talking about their husbands but acknowledged that even their men recommended work to quell their dissatisfaction.

Did they, I asked, really feel dissatisfied? Or was it just that everyone else told them they should feel dissatisfied? The answer seemed to be both. The criticism from children and husbands seemed to hurt more because somewhere deep down they knew their usefulness had run out. Their children needed them less, and as a result, they were deprived of a role they enjoyed.

I wanted them to try to separate their feelings from the social implications of the women's movement, but it always came back to the same thing. They were convinced that if it were not for the "women's libbers," they would be all right. I said that the vague dissatisfaction they felt was a normal response to children growing up and home life becoming less important. If the time had been seven years earlier, before the movement had become so visible, they would have felt the same uneasiness without a focus. They were not impressed with this explanation. The women's movement provided a ready-made target: it was society's fault that they were devalued.

For a while these women had got their lives right. They had good husbands, nice homes, their children weren't pushing dope or doing time in jail. Then, as they saw it, society pushed them out of the boat. These are the women who lobby against the ERA, the women who have never been understood by the movement. These are women caught by a social change that will benefit their children, and their children berate them for their low level of consciousness.

They were convinced that the movement had robbed them of their status. Television, newspapers, books, their children, and other working women all looked down on them. They saw women like me as their enemy, and we would find it almost impossible in the ensuing weeks to find a common ground.

This was not entirely their fault. There was a sizable gap between us about the meaning of work. Work, they said, was not for them. I had grown up thinking of work as the route to identity and self-expression. I still don't know why I was so ignorant of this aspect of their lives. To me work was rewarding. For them work meant sitting all day in a typing pool or standing at the A&P checkout counter, or selling stockings at Macy's. It meant long hours for little pay, tired feet, and headaches.

"I enjoy being a housewife; I don't want to go to work," one woman said. "I like to take care of my family."

"But you said you feel dissatisfied with your life—if you had more respect, do you think these feelings would go away?"

"I'm not sure . . . "

"Maybe your family doesn't need taking care of anymore. How about taking care of someone else?"

"What?"

"The hospital, little kids, old people in homes—if you're a caretaker, there are lots of people in this world that could use you."

"That's not what I mean."

We met together for six weeks. We drank coffee and talked, and tried to know each other better. Even though I was more of a group leader than a therapist for them, we had no sense of camaraderie. There was always a certain distance between us, a distance that even women's kinship couldn't bridge.

I had come with the thought that I'd "fix them right up"—regale them with a few truths about modern women, get them to go to college, and in four years they'd all be lawyers or psychotherapists. As it turned out, I learned more from them than they did from me.

As a group, we never were able to talk freely. This was partly because the group was so large, and also because I was an outsider. There was another element: since they knew each other socially, they were embarrassed to talk in front of each other about their intimate lives, especially their marriages. They would only share their universal, commonly felt loss of esteem. They resented the consequences of social change. "There's no dignity in being a homemaker anymore," they said. "It used to be important to be dedicated to your family."

One of the group's natural leaders, a lively, articulate mother of four, challenged me: "Can you tell me any job that's more important than raising a family? I don't care if you're a doctor or a lawyer or what—being a good mother is the most important job there is."

"But you can't be a mother forever," I said.

"Then I'll retire."

"Okay."

"Well—okay."

"So where does that leave us?" I asked.

"I don't know."

"We are for families," another woman said. Since I too was "for" family life, I didn't understand the overkill in their assertion, which was repeated over and over like a thread in a seam. But I did begin to understand. Change to them was like unraveling the stitches in fabric; once started, it never ends, and soon the whole fabric has disintegrated in your hands.

The group disbanded. I thought we had grown closer together. I also felt that I had failed them because their questions were still unanswered. But several women asked to join other therapy groups in the clinic where they would be among strangers and be more free to air their private feelings. A few applied for marital counseling. Several women in the group enrolled for courses at a local community college; others joined civic groups. The beautiful blonde got a real-estate broker's license and joined a local firm. Although we never achieved the friendship and closeness I had hoped for, I think we were all a little bit freer to add more dimension to our lives. I include myself in this statement because I know they added dimension to my life.

Chapter 13

DANGEROUS FAMILY PATTERNS IN STAGE 3

A child is often like a wild card in a marriage—he or she can be thrown into the game and played in whatever gambit the couple hasn't resolved.

Some families fail to make the transition from Stage 2 to Stage 3 of family life. They share the unspoken belief that life outside the family threatens its stability. In an unconscious pact, the family chooses a sentry (most often a child) to "stand guard" and ensure that home life remains important. By special family decree the child is endowed with problems: he is said to be fearful or suspicious, he may fail to learn in school or be a troublemaker. His problems may seem a small price to pay to keep the family together.

The family closes in and focuses on its problem child. This false attack or concern actually strangles individual growth and disguises fear of the larger world. These families are called child-centered because the otherwise-perfect family is marred by a problem child. "If only Johnny were . . ." has a familiar ring, and the child-centered family is well known to family therapists.

FROZEN TRIANGLES

The child-centered family develops a structural device to keep marital conflict hidden.[13] Chronologically, the family is in Stage 3, but it is emotionally mired in Stage 2, continuing to focus on the dependent child. Parents continue to revolve around the child, forgetting that they have any relationship other than their role as parents. A deeper study of the family usually reveals that flaws were present back in Stage 1, when the couple first established the intimate rules of the relationship. Invariably, issues of intimacy and power were not handled by husband and wife, and now these unresolved issues are put onto the child.

Focusing on a child achieves certain definite ends for the family. When two adults are dissatisfied in marriage, children give them an opportunity to fill out their lives and grow as parents. Satisfaction derived from parenting may offset their unhappiness with each other.

In Stage 2 this couple may be fighting about who is the better parent, or Mother may side with Junior when Dad disciplines him. These triangles are established in Stage 2. By Stage 3 they become entrenched patterns that keep marital problems under wraps. The child usually develops a symptom to match the problem created by his parents.

The child's symptoms develop to release tension in the family. The symptoms, in turn, support the dysfunctional pattern, proving that the parents are right. It's a no-win situation for the child.

There are two different and distinct kinds of child-centered family. These are the *detour supporting* and *detour attacking* forms.[14] In the detour-supporting family, parents band together to *overprotect* a child, who is defined as "weak" or "sick" rather than bad. Detour-supporting families often produce children who are unusually shy, insecure, and frightened, with tendencies to develop psychosomatic problems.

In detour-attacking families, even though conflict exists between parents, they unite *against* their child, who is defined as "bad" or the "family problem." Detour attacking is sometimes called scapegoating. Detour-attacking families tend to produce children who are unmanageable, with a tendency to delinquent behavior and learning difficulties.

THE CHILD-CENTERED FAMILY

Child-centered families have identifiable characteristics.[15] If the therapist blocks the topic of children, for example, parents have trouble talking to each other. They avoid mentioning any conflict between them. If the therapist keeps them talking about the definition or resolution of a problem, they seldom achieve either. Sentences usually begin with, "Yes, but . . ." An irresistible force always brings them back to the children, despite all attempts at diversion.

Children sit and sometimes even sleep between parents. They monopolize one parent and behave in other ways which show how they keep parents apart. The relationship between siblings is often fiercely competitive. "Good" vs. "bad" child roles assigned by parents are played to the hilt.

The key to putting the family back on the right track is to take the child out of the picture and try to locate the faulty mechanism in the marriage. Parents have to face each other directly and resolve conflicts without using the child.

Portrait of a Detour-Supporting Family

James James
Morrison Morrison
Weatherby George Dupree
Took great
Care of his mother,
Though he was only three.

James James
Said to his mother,
"Mother," he said, said he:
"You must never go down to the end of the town,
if you don't go down with me."

"When We Were Very Young"
A. A. Milne[16]

Nine-year-old Lisa Silver summed up her therapeutic history succinctly: "When I was five years old," she began, "I first started to feel scared whenever my mother went out. I still do. I don't feel safe with a baby-sitter, and I don't have any friends. I've been seeing a therapist, but I'm not getting any better."

Lisa's situation had worsened until she couldn't part with her mother for even an hour. As long as her mother was with her, she was relatively calm, but she had no friends of her own and hated going to school. Whenever Lisa's problem stabilized for a while, her mother tried to develop some outside life of her own, only to have the problem reescalate.

A recent, particularly painful experience had brought Lisa and her parents into family therapy. Barbara, Lisa's mother, had signed up for an evening class in gourmet cooking to "explore career possibilities." She had gone to three classes with little trouble from Lisa. About the same time Lisa's teacher at school, concerned that the little girl didn't seem to have any friends at school, arranged for Lisa to play two afternoons a week at the home of a classmate named Suzy Daniels. Suzy's mother would drive Lisa home after dinner. Lisa's fear of leaving her mother was not mentioned to Mrs. Daniels because the teacher didn't want to label Lisa as different from other children. But the general idea was that Lisa would get home before her mother went to class.

The first visit was uneventful. On the second afternoon Mrs. Daniels got involved in a long telephone conversation after dinner. Lisa put on her coat and waited by the front door. When she didn't come after five minutes, Lisa began to get nervous. Mrs. Daniels called from the kitchen, "I'll be right with you, Lisa."

Lisa looked at the clock on the mantel and watched the next five minutes tick by. It was nearly time for her mother to leave for school. Lisa began to tremble. She asked Suzy, "Please tell your mother I have to go home—my mother's waiting for me. Please, tell her." Lisa started to cry and was shaking all over.

Suzy said, "Well, all right, but she won't pay any attention."

Suzy went into the kitchen to nudge her mother off the phone. "Lisa needs to go now," she whispered into her mother's ear. "Her mom's waiting."

"Tell her to keep her shirt on for a minute. I'll be right there."

Lisa overheard Mrs. Daniels and bolted out the front door and started running down the street. She wasn't familiar with that part of town, but she knew the general direction toward home. She ran past streets and houses unfamiliar in the dark. Finally she ran almost blindly to her own street, made the turn, and kept going until she was on her block.

When Mrs. Daniels realized Lisa was gone, she immediately got in her car and tried to catch up with her, but missed the street Lisa was traveling on. She reached the Silver house before Lisa.

Gerald Silver was working late at his office that night. Barbara Silver had already left, and the baby-sitter was waiting for Lisa to come home. Lisa ran through the front door, her chest heaving, breathless and panting, tears streaming down her face. When she learned that her mother had gone, she became hysterical and sobbed uncontrollably for more than three hours, until her mother returned from school. Even then she insisted on sleeping in her mother's bed and stayed awake sobbing off and on through the night.

I asked Lisa, "What were you afraid of?"

She answered me directly. "I thought something would happen to my mother and I'd never see her again. I thought she would die."

Lisa's fear was in her very bones; it was so profound that I could feel it as we all sat together in the safety of my office.

As we talked together, I saw that Lisa was not the only scared person in the family. Barbara and Gerald were an attractive, charming couple, but they seemed unfinished as adults. They had a sweet, almost childlike manner. Barbara was a housewife who felt that she would like to develop a career but wasn't sure how to go about it. They were well off, and she knew that any income she might earn would not enhance the overall living standard of the family. Unless it was somehow personally rewarding, going to work would be superfluous for her. She was having trouble finding something to do that she cared about.

Several years ago Barbara had begun to see an analyst because she had vague feelings of dissatisfaction with her life. Whenever she made an effort to develop a life outside the family, problems with Lisa forced her to abandon them. Her analyst recommended a child therapist for Lisa. From the start Barbara did not like Lisa's therapist, but she went along with the recommendation of therapy for Lisa four times a week.

All through Lisa's therapy, Barbara had doubts, but she never had the courage to consult someone else, to discuss the problem with Lisa's therapist, or to seek alternative explanations. Gerald and Barbara did what they were told; they paid the bills.

Barbara said the analyst told her that Lisa had a serious problem because latency was the time when she should be making friends of her own, and Lisa was friendless. "I thought one reason she didn't have friends," Barbara said, "was that she had to go to see him almost every day."

"Maybe she should have gone to a friend's house and talked about not having an analyst," I said.

Barbara and Gerald laughed, but it was laughing in the dark. They were disturbed and guilt stricken about their child's suffering. But neither one of them had been able to confront the analyst's authority. Against their own judgment, they had turned Lisa over to an "expert" until they could no longer avoid the fact that in the context of her age she was getting worse. What was a vague problem when Lisa was five had become severely neurotic behavior by the time she was nine.

When children are disturbed, parents needn't abdicate to the experts. Any therapist should be willing to talk to parents and support their concerns. Parents should consider different approaches and make their own decisions. There's an idea that you go for a consultation so the therapist can analyze the situation and decide whether and how often he or she will see you. This is partially true. But the purpose of the consultation is twofold: a consultation should explore the options, and clients should also decide whether *they* want to see the therapist.

Barbara and Gerald had presented Lisa as their problem. At this point they needed to see the connection between their fears and Lisa's. Every time Barbara got interested in something outside the family, Lisa's problems flared up. Her night fears escalated, she had trouble at school, she demanded attention. Taking care of Lisa always justified Barbara's inability to get on with her life. By caring for Lisa, Barbara could be an adult without venturing outdoors. As we traced this connection, Barbara said it was she, not Lisa, who recoiled in fear every time she thought about going to work.

Gerald felt that he, too, was sheltered from the harshness of the world by being part of his family's business. Gerald was slated to take over his father's insurance business, a large, successful firm begun by his grandfather. This was the only job Gerald had ever had, and he had drawn an outstanding income from the business all his adult life. Gerald and Barbara had never been on their own in any major sense, and both sets of grandparents were heavily involved in their lives. Gerald wasn't sure that he could support his family so lavishly if he were on his own. He had never tested his judgment and competence without his father and grandfather breathing down his neck.

"If something happened—if I didn't have the business—I'd have to start from the bottom. I don't even like to think about it."

Barbara and Gerald presented a clear picture of a recycled family problem. Their difficulty in moving from Stage 2 to Stage 3 was exactly the same problem that existed in their original families when they were both growing up. Dependency and protection were central issues in both of their original families.

Barbara was the only child of an Austrian family who came to the United States in 1938, refugees from the Nazis. As a female child from an immigrant family, she was always given the message that the world beyond the family was strange, alien, and fraught with danger. Even the English language was foreign. Her family spoke only German and French.

Barbara's mother was isolated and secluded in an American suburb, where her estrangement from the American culture was profound. She kept Barbara very close to her and passed along her fears of the world. As if these insecurities had been in her genes, fear and lack of confidence were bred in Barbara.

Gerald was the youngest of two sons brought up in a wealthy suburban community in Westchester. His parents sheltered him and prepared him for a monied world of social connections. Gerald was never allowed to experience the world on his own; everything he did was through his father and grandfather. If they were not involved, neither was Gerald.

The links between the three generations was clear. Lisa's difficulties mirrored her parents' problems in making any break with their own families. Lisa's cry, "Don't leave me," was a more dramatic version of what Barbara and Gerald's parents had said to them.

It seemed that the purpose of Lisa's problem was to bring a three-generational family problem into focus. Lisa's symptoms forced Gerald and Barbara to confront the disturbing issues in their own lives and find a solution: the only way to help Lisa was to encounter their own difficulties.

Lisa was the spokesperson for her parents, her fears exactly echoing their own fears of separating and standing alone without their parents. For the family to move on, Barbara and Gerald had to separate from their own parents. Everyone had to become more independent.

Family therapists will go as far as the family is willing to make changes. In the Silvers' case, family therapy was long-term and involved several years of work: all relationships in the family were restructured, the marriage grew stronger, and Barbara and Gerald were able to separate from their families of origin.

It is fascinating that from generation to generation family problems will occur and reoccur in exactly the same stage of the family life cycle. An unsolved problem grows more intense with each succeeding generation. Some therapists believe that it takes several generations to produce a major family problem.[17] But whenever it is resolved, its impact on the next generation is reduced. The problem is less likely to perpetuate itself into future generations.

Detour Attacking: Liberated by the Bad Seed

There are many ways for one child to express trouble for the family as a whole. The Coopers appeared in my waiting room on time for our initial meeting. The contrast between them was stunning. Alan Cooper was ruddy and shining. He practically bounced as he walked. His wife, Carol, looked wan and careworn. She collapsed into a chair. Their two children, Cindy, age eight, and Scott, age six, were miniatures of their parents, the little girl serious and the boy buoyant and playful.

The Coopers had come because Cindy was bad, and her badness was getting to Carol Cooper. This mother was extremely worried about her child. But it seemed that Cindy's scandalous behavior consisted of some very minor mischief, mostly fun-loving pranks and some occasional lies. To the Coopers, bad meant climbing up on a chair to reach some homemade cookies; bad meant refusing to go to bed. They talked about her as if she were a candidate for reform school—the bad seed. I wondered what Cindy's badness was accomplishing for the Cooper family.

Alan Cooper was an assistant dean of a small private religious school in upstate New York. The family lived in a closely organized community where, as a model of family and religious life, they felt they were in a fishbowl, with all their imperfections visible to the world and magnified a million times. Carol Cooper's primary mission in life was to keep everyone in her family clean, in every sense of the word.

Alan was a respected man in the community and had a good deal of mobility and freedom. He loved outdoor sports and went sailing often on a nearby lake, rode a new BSA 950-cc motorcycle, and regularly played tennis. In contrast, Carol played the role of school wife to the hilt: she was proper, restrained, gracious, and humble to a fault. She cleaned house, entertained the wife of the headmaster, made cookies, ran school bazaars, and defined herself totally in terms of being Alan's wife.

Cindy, with her harmless antics, might be the escape valve for a repressed family situation, particularly for her mother. As soon as her "badness" was explained, I tried to take the heat off Cindy as the focus of the family's problems. I told the Coopers about some of the more memorable acts of terror my own children performed. Perhaps I spoke of them too proudly, making it clear that this was a normal part of a child's development. Mrs. Cooper sympathized with me for being burdened with such horrid children, but she was amused.

Once Cindy's behavior was no longer labeled as bad, the emphasis in our discussion shifted to the marriage. Alan complained about his wife's rigidity, her orderliness, and asceticism. She countered with complaints about his extravagance and lack of responsibility.

The children were excused from the session and asked to play with the toys in the waiting room. It was important to separate the parents' problems from the children, and the move to the playroom put the children literally outside the parents' problems.

The Coopers began to open up and talk about their dissatisfaction with each other. Their marital problems were classically tied up with money and sex, and while the two themes are often intertwined, money was the sorest issue at the moment.

Carol managed the family finances and constantly had to juggle accounts to make ends meet. "We have just enough to get by and Alan took out a loan to buy a sailboat. I couldn't even take a swimming course at the Y because I couldn't manage the seventy-five-dollar fee." Their problems over money reflected a central imbalance in their relationship: she was overresponsible, he was unconcerned. He played, she paid.

Carol Cooper's excessive self-denial bewildered me. Working with families has taught me not to buy simplistic, one-sided versions of people. I felt that Carol's self-denial (or masochism, as some therapists call it) served some important purpose in the relationship, but I wasn't sure just what it was. Why was this couple locked into extremes of self-indulgence and self-denial?

The answer started to come as Alan Cooper talked about his work. His mood shifted from high-spirited to deadly serious. He was extremely frustrated in his career; the pay was low, he had been passed over several times for promotion; he also felt confined by the authoritative nature of his school. "I don't think I'll ever get any further than I am right now. I don't have any future."

Carol looked confused and uncomfortable. "I've never heard you say anything like that before," she told Alan. "I thought you might feel disappointed about school, but you didn't seem to want to talk about it. Did you?"

The Coopers' secret deal was to protect one another. As long as Alan could play and enjoy himself, his feelings of inadequacy and failure would stay buried, and Carol's self-sacrifice made her feel in control of her life.

She does without a new coat so that he can make the down payment on the motorcycle. Her control over money seems not only natural but a necessary response to his profligacy.

This over/under pattern occurs in many marriages, but in this case the balance was extreme. Typically, one partner appears more insecure, less competent than the other. This "weak" person expresses the insecurities and doubts of the partner who overfunctions. The "strong" person expresses the more competent side of the weak partner. In such marriages the relationship is very delicately balanced so that any positive shift by the so-called weaker person is often sabotaged by both.

In this family the split between over/under was too extreme. Alan played for two people; Carol worried for both. They both did double duty. Carol was accustomed to this role; she had learned it when she was overresponsible for her younger brothers and sisters. Alan was an indulged only child from a poor family.

The goal of family therapy is not to change individual personalities; the goal is to readjust the relationships in the family, sometimes in small ways, so that basic human needs such as power and pleasure can be balanced in a better way. With the Coopers we aimed for a less rigid pattern in the distribution of playfulness and responsibility between Alan and Carol. If the parents no longer needed a safety valve, Cindy could be spunky without needing to be "bad."

Cindy's high jinks saved this family. Her rebellion against the pressure to be perfect and self-sacrificing reflected the genuine vitality of a family otherwise choking from goodness and humility. Cindy concretely expressed her mother's desire to break loose.

During the few weeks following our first meeting, Alan thought through some of the problems in his job and asked for a hearing with the director of the school to get some feedback on his status and position. As he confronted these issues, Carol got on with her own life. She got out of the house, started playing tennis, and took a sewing class.

When couples want to change an over/under relationship, they need to look for something specific that seems to represent the pattern and change *that*. Carol's reward for her self-denial had been control of the money, which made her feel in charge. Money is a powerful symbol of responsibility in most families. Carol needed another way to be in charge of her life without being overresponsible and controlling everything—and everyone—around her.

In most cases it doesn't matter who does the books, but for the Coopers, bookkeeping symbolized responsibility. I said that Carol should teach her husband everything she knew about the family's finances. They could do the books together until he was ready to assume the responsibility.

Alan didn't like the idea. He stalled, begged off, pleaded incompetency. Even with all her complaints about the financial burdens, Carol didn't insist. But they had been challenged, and it was pointed out that they were both conspiratorial about not changing. They finally sat down together over the books. Once Alan mastered the system, he felt more competent and reassured. Carol relinquished some responsibility; he assumed some.

In their sexual relationship, the Coopers had reversed their usual roles. He was sexually strong and competent; she was passive and "frigid." Instinctively Carol was again being protective. She sensed that if she warmed up and became a good sex partner, Alan would lose his potency.

The relationship wasn't working on any level. Their sex life had dwindled to nothing because sexual performance had replaced sexual enjoyment, and neither knew what to do. I thought they should forget about sex for the time being and court each other once again—take turns choosing things they could share together.

They drove to New York to see a play; she learned to ride the motorcycle. They started doing things together. I never asked about their sexual relationship again and they never brought it up, but I suspect that it didn't change much. Yet they were satisfied with the overall improvement of the quality of their relationship.

A brief period of family therapy helped the Cooper family. Alan and Carol began to see Cindy as an active, willful, and independent child who needed and could handle more freedom. Scott seemed less babyish than before, and the Coopers spoke of his moving from the block corner to the reading corner in school. For every family member the world beyond the family became more interesting and accessible.

In Stage 3 survival depends on individual development beyond the family. Children experience their first taste of independence in school, and for many families this is a harsh separation. But it's a new era for both parents and children, a time for all members of the family to begin to see themselves as individuals.

Reaching beyond the family creates major transitions in career and job decisions for men and women. The family that survives supports its members and helps launch them into the larger world.

Stage 4
FAMILIES WITH ADOLESCENTS

*Turning Point: To be on the make
or make it with each other*

Chapter 14

ADOLESCENCE TAKES THE FAMILY BY STORM

Adolescence explodes the family myths. It's a time when teenagers break the major rules established by the family and challenge their parents' reign. For the first time in the family's history, the child begins to see the world through his own lens and bombards his parents with demands for freedom and experimentation beyond the walls of the family. In the process he threatens to expose secrets he previously agreed to keep. If there are agreements that keep hidden the family's weak spots, family members should brace themselves for a betrayal. All agreements now are off. The impact of adolescence shakes family life to its foundation.

Of all the stages in life, adolescence is probably the most exasperating, for the adolescent and everyone else. Teenagers are dreamy, irritable, defiant, and contemptuous. Parents and children both dread adolescence. But there are some things that are, if not thoroughly enjoyable, at least extremely interesting. Adolescence can be survived—and with a minimum of hardship.

ANGER AND SEX: WHERE THE ACTION IS

Whether they rant and rave, whine and complain, or silently sulk in their rooms, teenagers are angry. Anger is a natural part of growing up, employed by teenagers like a weapon to blast themselves loose from the family.

Why anger?

The prime task in Stage 4 is for children to break away from parents they love and stand, shakily, on their own. Anger helps the separation process. It's easier to leave people you love when you're angry with them. The child puts his anger between himself and his parents and creates distance, so he can begin to rely on himself.

Adults use the same techniques to break up unrewarding love affairs and marriages. We can suddenly and passionately hate people we have lived with for years and dwell on all sorts of horrible offenses while we make the

151

break. In the same manner adolescents use anger to liberate themselves emotionally from the intense bonds of affection and dependency that bind them to their parents.

Conflict is inevitable in families with adolescents. Negative intensity reverberates through all the relationships in the family, exposing hidden pockets of conflict, especially in the marital relationship. Fortunately, teenage anger is not permanent. The best sign that the adolescent is making the break is that the anger begins to abate, no longer being needed to protect independence.

Many people, denied the expression of anger toward their parents in adolescence, have had to relive it in a psychiatrist's office years later. Most patients in individual therapy begin by working out their anger against their parents and then, like teenagers, are able to drop it and go on to a better understanding of their parents.

As well as anger, teenagers are bursting with sexuality. The quality and intensity of adolescent growth, combined with growing intellectual maturity and a sense of self-worth, encourage new experiments in the world outside the family.

Just at the time that children blossom sexually, feeling all the excitement of new sexual attractions, parents begin to lose confidence in their own sexual desirability. Observing the maturity of their children, parents begin to realize that they are growing older. They protest aging and often become enmeshed in extramarital affairs, trying to relive the excitement of their own youth.

Parents with adolescent children are especially vulnerable. As adolescents break away from the family and seek refuge among their friends, parents, for the first time in years, are alone together. Marriages are pressured and tested. For couples with secure but unexciting relationships, sex vibrations in the family may produce waves of disenchantment. This is one way adolescents expose family secrets: marriages dying from boredom are shown up in the light of intense adolescent sexuality.

THE THRILL PROVIDER

Adolescents experiment through action: sexual experimentation, stealing, taking drugs, and defying authority are typical, because young adolescents cannot think through or imagine experiences without trying them. Such acting out is a universal phenomenon of adolescence in our culture.

The healthy family reacts to these activities with some degree of anxiety, sets realistic limits, asserts its value system, and waits for the storm to blow over. The experts on adolescence agree that acting out is typical but emphasize that some guidelines can help tell us when such behavior reflects a more serious problem for the adolescent and his or her family. Psychoanalyst Dr. Peter Blos describes typical adolescent acting-out behavior as transient (it passes), usually benign (not destructive), and progressive (the adolescent matures).[1] In situations beyond the typical, what should be merely a phase turns into a permanent pathological condition.[2]

What dynamics within the family contribute to an impasse in an adolescent's development? For the adolescent the purpose of acting out is to sample new experiences and develop resources to meet inner urges and outside temptations. A youngster used by his family for titillation and excitement, or as a scapegoat for family tensions, is too heavily burdened to achieve this growth. Family therapists are familiar with adolescents whose "badness" is secretly promoted by their families to put some excitement in family life.

There are many kinds of "thrill provider" families. Some parents become so preoccupied with the sexual behavior of their children—obsessively worrying about their daughter's sexuality, compulsively checking for signs of sexual impropriety—that they unconsciously prod their children into premature sexual activity. Other parents listen eagerly to a litany of adolescent exploits, rationalizing that they are enlightened and not easily shocked. In truth, such parents may be vicariously excited by their children's adventures, which fill a void in their own lives.

But where do you draw the line? Teenagers are constantly testing, and it's not easy to know what they want from you. One father said his sixteen-year-old son, experimenting with photography, showed him some pictures of his girl friend in the nude. "I didn't have the faintest idea how to react," the father said. "I figured that he wanted some sort of reaction from me, but I didn't have any idea what it was. I didn't know if he wanted me to be shocked or take it in my stride and be cool or what."

These kinds of situations are impossible to read, and a parent can only try to think about how he or she genuinely feels and try to respond accordingly. I asked him what he had really thought about the scene. "To tell you the truth, I asked myself first whether I was turned on. I wondered if I had any designs on my son's girl friend. I decided I didn't. Then I wondered if I was shocked, and frankly I wasn't."

"What did you say?"

"Nothing—I just said, 'Um hum, good light values,' or something like that. I wasn't about to poke my elbow in his ribs and say, 'Nice little cutie you got there, son.' He didn't ask me for any further evaluation, and I don't know whether I passed or failed."

I think that adolescent sex is a private experience that a teenager shouldn't share with parents. When adolescents become sexually active, they are usually creating intimate relationships with other teenagers. In these relationships they struggle to differentiate between sexual titillation, romance, flirtation, sexual release of tension, physical warmth and closeness, and emotional intimacy. All have their place in adult sexuality, and the adolescent needs to sort them out.

Adolescents are uneasy with their sexual stirrings. If adults get involved in this sexual experimentation, the adolescent's needs get upstaged or diverted. The father in our story might have avoided a trap by establishing a clear generational boundary. "I'm not interested," would have been an adequate response.

Most teenage thrill providers are engaged in doing something forbidden and censored by the family. I remember one couple who were worried about their fifteen-year-old daughter, whom they described as an inch away from full-fledged delinquency: "She hangs out with bums, gambles, and smokes." A few days later we met for the first time, and indeed, the girl dangled a cigarette out of the corner of her mouth and confessed to going to the racetrack, where she pooled her resources ($2) with several friends and bet the favorite to win. A worse offense was that she ignored the nuns at her Catholic high school, and she was "antisocial." I learned that the three most sinful acts in this traditional Catholic family were smoking, gambling, and defying the Church—all of Bridget's specialties. It turned out that her mother loved to dance but kept this a secret, since *her* mother and husband disapproved of such "sexually provocative and frivolous behavior." In this family Bridget provided the excitement everyone missed.

Another family was so repressed that the adolescent's experimentation with drugs, sex, and alcohol injected the family with a liveliness they couldn't provide for themselves. If the family can't provide its own excitement, the adolescent has a mission.

As teenagers' bodies undergo radical transformations, their parents are aware on many different levels that their "children" are approaching sexual maturity. If a mother has had an overly close relationship to her son or a father to his daughter, stress in the family mounts with the increase in sexual tension.

In the healthiest families, parents are not threatened by obvious evidence of sexual blossoming. They signal their acknowledgment and also their appreciation of the profound sexual stirrings that their children are undergoing. Parents recognize the woman their teenage daughter is becoming; their approval gives her confidence. Parents respect their son's need for privacy and/or his physical preening. In a million subtle ways—by allowing them to choose their own clothes and admiring the result, no matter what; by praising and encouraging even minor athletic achievement—parents can give their children permission to be proud of and enjoy their bodies.

SETTING LIMITS: IT'S 10 P.M. DO YOU KNOW WHERE YOUR CHILDREN ARE?

In Stage 4 even the soundest family will have to shift its style of disciplining children. In Stage 2 the young child's helplessness required parents to marshal all their caretaking resources to create a physically and emotionally secure environment. Guiding little children is not terribly cerebral; parenting mostly involves legwork and a loud no to sticking a finger in the electric outlet, running into the street, hitting playmates in the sandbox, or throwing rice pudding at the dinner table.

When children go to school, they begin to learn the rules of social behavior. In Little League and Brownies, parents guide and instruct with a light touch, explaining why it's all right to compete vigorously, but that bragging about winning or making another child feel inferior is unacceptable. What Mommy and Daddy say still goes.

With the coming of adolescence, parents must face a new style of guidance, and many parents don't want to. It's a tough job to achieve a balance between permissiveness and restriction. Because teenagers stretch the limits of what is permissible, parents often experience their own crisis of values. It's not enough to tell our teenagers that they should be loyal, fair, and honest. Now we have to prove that we're living by all these standards, that our values are correct and can sustain rigorous examination.

One physician, several times a grandfather, told me that he and his wife had a code for themselves and their four children. "We always told them, 'Until you're six you do exactly what we tell you—no questions. From six to twelve, we'll try to explain why you do exactly what we tell you. From twelve to seventeen, we'll talk it over and try to reach a mutual agreement, but Mom and I have the final word. After eighteen, I hope we'll still talk it over, but you make your own decisions.' It seemed to work pretty well. At least we all knew the rules, and that was some comfort. They are always trying to get us to shave five or six months off the age limits when the time for transition was coming up, but we never would. It was the only way we could stay sane."

From a teenager's point of view, parental guidance is irrelevant, controlling, unwanted, and unnecessary. From the parent's point of view, the national slogan, It's 10 P.M., do you know where your children are? strikes terror in their hearts and reminds them that adolescents need adult supervision.

Because cohesive communities have dwindled and pockets of social deviance are now widespread, society no longer naturally protects the adolescent. The world can be a dangerous playground for the adolescent. Teenagers need parents to protect them from tempting but harmful forays into drugs and delinquency. Parents offer this protection by taking unpopular stands when necessary. And our adolescents sometimes hate us for what they perceive as a violation of their freedom.

At the same time families need to encourage the independence of all their members, and especially to support the growing maturity of teenagers. Healthy families take pleasure in a youngster going off to live his own life and returning occasionally to the family for emotional refueling.

But this is the tough part for grown-ups. We have to sustain a fairly long period of time when our children are partially independent but still more than a little dependent. They aren't children anymore, but they aren't yet adults. This is enormously frustrating. You get used to a child being gone, and all of a sudden he comes back asking for protection, behaving like a ten-year-old. It seems that the whole family has to constantly readjust just to accommodate the teenager.

Adolescents want to be free when they want to be free—and to come home and act like children when they need to. Or, as many parents say, they want all the privileges of adulthood and none of the responsibilities. That is exactly right—and exactly what adolescence is all about.

This need to move away and return is frustrating for families and may generate equally vacillating behavior from parents, who get tangled up in being too rigid and controlling on the one hand, and too permissive on the other. We have trouble reading signals from these aliens who only yesterday were children whom we understood perfectly. Says one father of a fifteen-year-old boy, "I know my kid's trying to tell me something, but I'm damned if I know what it is."

The situation is even more difficult for single parents, who tend to be overly protective of their children and who identify with them more closely. The child, too, finds it more difficult to grow up and feels more guilt because the parent is alone. The adolescent may be forced into exploits to prove his or her independence and change the loving attachment to the parent into a negatively charged one.

The key to setting limits has a lot to do with whether parents have their own lives or dread a future as retired parents. Parents strike a workable balance between permissiveness and authoritarianism when the overall goal—the adolescent's independence—is not going to weaken the family.

The major task for families in Stage 4 involves the family's ability to keep its boundaries flexible enough for adolescents to move in and out without continual trauma. Certain hazardous family styles—too free or too tight, leaderless or authoritative—keep adolescents and parents from confronting each other. Adolescents need to develop their own resources and values *against* the family system. There's no sense in trying to apply a rationale to this situation, because adolescents are not rational.

Parents have to drop some of their parental role-playing and reveal themselves to their grown-up children as whole people, even if in doing so, the faults show. Every family has a tendency to err, either on the side of authoritarianism or permissiveness. Parents seem to do best when they clearly express their expectations and set limits, and when they cannot be played off each other. At the same time they need to encourage an honest exchange of views with their kids and present information about drugs, sex, contraception, and other phenomena that plague teenagers.

Parents must continue to set and impose limits, open doors—negotiate, negotiate, negotiate—and hold their breath. Backing off, standing by, and watching children struggle with independence takes courage and patience. Husbands and wives need each other, and they need other adults in their lives to counteract being depreciated by their children.

Chapter 15

WARNING SIGNALS TO COUPLES

MID-LIFE CRUNCH

As if these dramatic changes in children weren't enough to rock a family, parents usually confront some changes in their personal lives as well. The adolescent's spurt often collides with his parents' mid-life crisis, that painful and critical time of life when adult values are questioned, dreams are reexamined, and evaluation leads to a new kind of self-awareness. This mix of adolescent arrogance encroaching on adult turf at a time when adults, in their prime, begin to feel impotent and mortal, produces family turmoil.

Marriages, careers, life pursuits, values, and priorities are questioned, turned around, and often drastically altered. Parents in Stage 4 face their own individual identity crisis—a last chance to change their lives. Mid-life concerns shake up their lives, and some parents, to avoid facing up to their own problems, concentrate on their teenagers.

Pressure increases as grandparents grow older and require more caring attention from their children. All of these changes mean that even the healthiest families will have to find new coping patterns to regain their balance in the midst of upheaval.

COUPLES IN CRISIS

A child's adolescence has a major impact on the marriage of his parents. As the adolescent shuns family activities and makes forays into the world, he offers his parents the privacy to get together for romance and renew their marriage. Couples find that for the first time in years, they have leisure time to spend together as they choose. They can get away from children and get to know one another again.

It's surprising how many parents refuse to take advantage of this opportunity. Instead they cling to their children, afraid they will lose family unity or that their growing child will leave and never return. Some parents

158

coerce teenagers, through guilt and threats, to participate in family gatherings when the youngster clearly wants to be somewhere else.

"The first time I said I wasn't coming home from school for Thanksgiving," says a college sophomore, "I thought my folks would never forgive me. My mother cried, my father said, 'If you can't come home for the holiday, don't bother coming home at all.' I mean, it was horrible. I went home and hated it. They didn't even have the grace to be embarrassed that I was there against my will. It made them happy. I mean, they won, didn't they?"

I think parents have to lose, and lose gracefully, for a while. The trick is to make the family available and let the teenager know you want him, but that his presence is not required and you won't go to pieces if he doesn't join in. Letting go is not just for the kid's sake—parents who can back off suffer less when children reject them.

Why is this so hard to do? Why do we hold on so tightly to our adolescent children? Partly because it's hard to accept change. And also because marriage has gotten lost in family life and is hard to revive when children leave. Marriages are under more strain at this stage of family life than at any time since the initial merge. In many marriages disenchantment has accumulated over the years, and for some the pleasures of marriage have completely subsided.

In Stage 2 we mentioned the accumulated research documenting the decline in marital satisfactions from the birth of the first child until the child leaves home. Many twenty-year marriages have a sad profile according to these researchers: infrequent sex, less affection, fewer shared activities, erosion of common interests, and general malaise. If the marriage is indeed in trouble, additional stress is imposed when the adolescent moves away.

Even in the healthiest families, marital pleasures are routinely replaced by parental satisfaction. When children begin the emotional leave-taking that first signals adolescent departure, parents are deprived of some of the satisfaction they had derived from family life. Marital joys, long placed in the background, are not readily revived, because over the years they have quietly faded.

This observed pattern in marriage and parenting is backed up by divorce statistics, which for the first time in history show that the divorce rate is climbing in longer-lasting marriages.[3] Historically it has been the young marriage that was most vulnerable to divorce. Now there is a hint of a second divorce peak in marriages that have lasted up to twenty years. Instead of revitalizing their marriages when children leave home, couples seem to be abandoning them. In the past the decline in satisfaction was probably the same, but older couples tended to stay married.

I don't think that modern society has wrecked family life; but it does make unhappy marriages less easy to bear because divorce is more socially acceptable today than it was twenty years ago. Today men and women are not afraid to walk away from unhappy marriages and try to find happier ways to live.

It is increasingly common for husbands to kick over the traces and leave home at this stage of family life. Life-cycle theorizers explain that husbands and traditional wives living through the adult life cycle are often out of sync. He has passed through the trying twenties; he rooted and extended in his thirties; and he is approaching the mid-life crisis of his forties.[4] His search is for tenderness and authenticity. She, although perhaps the same age, has short-circuited her own self-development by being primarily a· caretaker. If she's making a shift at all, she's becoming more confident and tougher. She may be on the threshold of an important career. Her mood is determination; her search is for strength.

It's not possible to skip stages of development and jump from an identity that was prematurely foreclosed in one's twenties to the level of emotional wrenching characteristic of the male at mid-life. Husbands and wives frequently find themselves out of sympathy with each other in Stage 4 of family life. But this is only a partial explanation. If you look at the family as a whole at this stage, you can see many other pressures coming to bear on the marriage.

Couples at this stage of family life are especially vulnerable to extramarital affairs. The mid-life crisis only partially explains it. Other powerful pressures are generated from within the family itself. Prime among them is the adolescent's burgeoning sexuality, which charges the family's batteries with sexual tension. The adolescent's sexual awakening reverberates throughout the family, and sex becomes a family theme. The adolescent is not the only family member on the make.

THE AFFAIR

Lovelady Davis described herself as "a lady who's been crying for a year and a half."

"What happened a year and half ago that's making you so sad?" I asked.

"My husband had an affair—and I've been crying ever since."

"Is he still seeing someone else?"

"He says he's not. It didn't last very long. But I can't get over it. I feel so betrayed—like I was kicked in the teeth by my best friend."

As if to prove the truth of her statement, tears cascaded down her cheeks. I sat watching her for a moment. Her green eyes full of tears were like glass, and her face had a crumpled, bruised look. She wore a long Indian-print dress and string of amber beads. She twisted the beads through her fingers. Lovelady wore her depression like a badge, a medal she had earned for years of perfect wifedom.

Lovelady's problem was not uncommon. Sexual affairs frequently occur, and they are among the most jarring episodes in married life. The faithful partner perceives the affair as a betrayal that shakes the foundation of her or his existence. Discovery of a partner's sexual dalliance makes us doubt ourselves profoundly. It seems the erring partner has deliberately humiliated us and thrown us naked to ridicule into the world.

Actually I think that's seldom the intent of the spouse who has the affair. An affair isn't a sign of moral weakness or betrayal, nor a sin that deserves unrelenting punishment. An affair is a symptom of a problem in the marriage which, for some reason, cannot be confronted directly; it gets bypassed through a third person.

An affair can be bad or it can be good.

It's bad if it destroys beyond repair the essential trust of a marriage that could work. It's bad if it fails to produce change and continues indefinitely, making the marriage a semi-permanent triangle. An affair, by providing stability for a wobbly marriage or vitality for a dull marriage, can make it possible for a couple to stay married without ever confronting their problems. This can go on for years, problems suspended, everyone living a kind of half-life.

An affair is good when it forces two ill-matched people to give up on each other, put an unhappy marriage behind them, and get on with their lives. And it's good when it creates a crisis that brings couples face to face and opens up issues between them.

My attention was drawn away from Lovelady's unhappy face when Max Davis entered the office, ten minutes late. He introduced himself, took a seat opposite his wife, and lit a cigarette. He was a big, heavy man and he looked uncomfortable.

"Tell me something about your marriage," I asked.

Before Max could respond, Lovelady burst out through her tears, "It was a wonderful marriage, it was unusual—perfect."

"I wonder how Max feels about it?"

Again Lovelady took over. "We were always very compatible, and we always had great sex." She started to cry as she spoke.

"What did you fight over?"

"Oh, we never fought. I know it's hard to believe, but we were completely harmonious. We were in love for nineteen years—until this happened."

Max ground his cigarette into the ashtray and looked as though he were ready to explode.

"Do you agree with this assessment, Max?"

"It's incredible how you select only what you want to believe," he said, almost whispering the words to his wife. "You liked it the way it was, so I must have liked it, too. Well, I didn't, you know. Our marriage is boring and has been for years."

"Her" marriage was certainly different from "his" marriage.[5] He was bored stiff and felt trapped. However, it seemed that marriage was only part of Max's discontent. He was plagued by a long-standing feud with his partner at the art gallery that he ran in Soho, his father had recently died, and his mother was making serious demands on him.

But Max blamed all his problems on the marriage. He expertly projected his problems onto Lovelady and called them hers. For instance, he skillfully avoided his problems with his own mother by describing Lovelady's problems with hers.

In the early session the goal was to separate Max's global dissatisfactions, defining some as marital and others as personal. Max wasn't interested. He was happy that Lovelady had a therapist because she had someone to help solve her problems. But he refused to participate any further in therapy. The problem, he said, was Lovelady's.

It's risky to work with only one partner when a marriage is in crisis, because it's almost impossible to rebalance the family. But in the face of Max's obstinacy, I agreed to work alone with Lovelady. The main thrust of therapy now was to help Lovelady initiate changes in the marriage.

Lovelady and I established a rapport almost from the beginning. But even though we liked each other, I was appalled by her goodness. She was not merely a good wife, she was very, very good. She kept the enormous loft they lived in immaculate and constantly looked for ways to make additions and improvements in it. She had recently installed a new kitchen—from sinks to stoves and worktables—doing most of the work herself. She grew an astonishing variety of fresh vegetables on the roof of their building and was known as a gourmet cook. She was involved with all her children's school and afterschool activities. She also contributed to the family income by selling her outstanding baked goods to Village gourmet shops. On top of all this, the Davises had a cabin in the mountains, which Lovelady also cared for as well as seeing to it that the family was packed and ready for their outdoor sojourn every weekend.

Lovelady anticipated everyone's needs and put her own aside. For instance, she never knew when *she* wanted sex because she habitually pursued her husband every night.

"You're joking," I said.

"Honestly—I did everything I knew how to take care of him . . ." and the flood of tears started again. Lovelady's reward for all this goodness was her husband's infidelity.

I marveled at her goodness. "Where's your natural meanness and selfishness?" I asked. "You remind me of all my imperfections." We joked about it, but I seriously suggested that she must be a deadbeat to live with. "Why don't you try to come up with something rotten to show your bad side?"

She came back the following week with a major event: when her mother asked her to drive to New Jersey one morning to bring a loaf of homemade bread to her card party, Lovelady said no. And her mother took it!

In light of this monstrous behavior, we made some progress. "Besides," Lovelady joked, "this depression is starting to get me down."

"I think there's more to your depression than being hurt," I said. "I think you're trying to get back at your husband and still preserve your good image. You don't have to be nasty or scream and yell—all you have to do is be depressed. It's an easy way to make him miserable. You look unhappy and mope around, and he feels guilty. The catch is, it's harder on you than it is on him."

Lovelady's habitual depression served two purposes: it constantly reminded Max that he had betrayed her, and it kept him in line. After all, if she was all right, he might walk out on her. Punishment and control—here were two powerful reasons for prolonging a depression that should have expired over a year before.

When she acknowledged that being a dutiful wife didn't guarantee personal security, Lovelady turned the present crisis to an advantage. Knowing that she might be left on her own prompted her to make changes in her life.

We set up some new standards for her. For the present she would have sex with Max only when he approached her, and only if she wanted to. Allowing Max to be the assertive one was an attempt to rebuild some of Lovelady's self-esteem and put her desirability to the test.

Actually Lovelady had a lot to be confident about. She found it easy to be free sexually and liked a variety of sexual experiences. Eliminating rigidly programmed nightly sex might allow a more genuine sexual relationship to develop between them.

After several nights of avoiding each other in bed, Max made the first move. After that their sexual relationship became established on a new, more spontaneous basis. Interestingly, they never spoke of this change, but it was the initial foundation of other refreshing changes in their marriage.

We applied the same technique to other parts of Lovelady's life to help her stop programming herself and her family. She began to expand her business and eventually opened her own shop; she wasn't home every day when her teenagers came in from school and didn't accompany them to all their activities. She stopped waiting up for her husband when he worked late and no longer organized weekend activities.

Changing Lovelady's life was not the ideal way to rebalance the marriage, but any change made by one person will affect others in the family. Max seemed relieved by her growing independence. He could now get close to her without experiencing the claustrophobia once generated by her slavelike devotion. With some of the marital pressure removed, he admitted he had other problems and tried to make some changes in his own life.

Lovelady and Max, after twenty years of marriage, had to confront mid-life switches and the knowledge that their children were becoming independent. To keep their marriage alive they had to face and refresh the staleness that Lovelady had called perfection.

DIVORCE THREATENS

Elizabeth Rowland's voice was shaking and her eyes were puffy from crying. Last week, she said, struggling for composure, her husband had packed a bag and left home. Four days later Betsy's hysteria and pleas for fair negotiation brought him back.

Vic Rowland poured out the rest of the story like a penitent in a confessional. He had started seeing a young woman from his office several months before, and a predictably brief affair had turned into an exciting romance. The woman, Rene, was bright, young, and glamorous. Manhattan was her playground, and almost every night, accompanied by Vic, she breezed through jazz clubs, restaurants, and the newest discos in town. Vic felt revitalized, and in a rash moment had packed his bag and left home. This flash of rebellion was quickly followed by remorse and guilt, which prompted him to return to his wife. But he wasn't prepared to give up the exciting life Rene held out to him.

Vic, chin down, hands in his pockets, looked like a defiant schoolboy being scolded by his distressed mother. Betsy, matronly and unforgiving, punctuated his commentary with exasperated sighs, eyes raised toward the ceiling.

Vic couldn't make up his mind about himself. He felt his nineteen-year-old marriage, although dependable, was heavily sedated. He was bored at work, acutely aware of growing older, and felt that he was running out of time.

Contrasted with this was the life he imagined with Rene. The sexual and intellectual excitement generated by this new relationship made him feel as though adventure was around the corner and opportunity still awaited him.

Betsy spoke of their beautiful home, the satisfactions of family life, the troubles they had shared over the years, and her deep commitment to him. She accused Vic of throwing their lives away for a brief flirtation with a woman half his age. She implored me to convince him to "come to his senses." She spoke as if Vic were a wayward youth who needed a good reprimand.

Vic vacillated between acting like a troubled adult and an unruly boy. At one moment the adult speaks: "This is not what I imagined my life would be like. I never wanted a house in the suburbs, I never wanted an ordinary desk job—it just kind of slipped up on me, and now I'm locked up in it. My life's over." Then he would turn sulky, shove his hands back in his pockets, and refuse to talk.

As far as Betsy was concerned, Vic didn't have any problems. Neither of them considered his adult concerns—career, life-style, money—as serious problems worthy of examination. "Nobody gets everything they want out of life," Betsy said. Vic's problems were not worth making a fuss over because, to her, they were irrational and would go away.

The Rowlands' two adolescent children were deeply troubled by what was happening to the family. Initially they had viewed their father through Betsy's eyes and declared him frivolous and irresponsible. But they were moved by Vic's explanation of his feelings.

Although Vic had returned home, his affair with Rene did not end. He continued to see her and to sleep with her whenever he could, although a "kind of pall" had settled over their previously carefree love affair. Affairs tend to lose some of their excitement when they are no longer secret and when they have to absorb open conflict from the marriage.

In this strained atmosphere Betsy and Vic tried to face up to some problems in their family. Vic hated the money-eating monster called a house, and he hated commuting. And marital sex, after nineteen years, was boring.

These fairly typical mid-life conflicts were resting on a deep flaw in the marriage. Vic had always been afraid to fight with Betsy, challenge her, or be honest with her about his feelings. He kept his troubles to himself and relied on her judgment.

For example, he said, when Betsy wanted to put in a swimming pool, he was reluctant to pour more money into a house that already stretched their budget, but he complacently had gone along. Betsy was shocked to hear Vic now voice strong opinions about issues she assumed they had agreed upon. She cried as he dismantled their life. And when she cried, he consoled her. This pattern took us back to the beginning: Vic choked down his own feelings to avoid upsetting Betsy, just as he had been doing for the last nineteen years.

With his son and daughter growing up, Vic felt their adolescent tension. He remembered his own youth, a stalled time in his life when he had failed successfully to liberate himself from his mother's rule. The struggle of his own son to become a man stimulated Vic's postponed rebellion.

All through the efforts to save their marriage, Betsy held the line. She refused to take their troubles seriously, insisting that the marriage would be fine if Vic would only give up Rene. To her, the affair was the central issue rather than a symptom of wider problems. (To Betsy, the affair was all that was wrong; to Vic, it was all that was right.)

In spite of three months of family therapy, the marital relationship remained rigid. Betsy could not extinguish the feeling that Vic was a recalcitrant, cranky boy who should stop being so selfish. Vic gave up and left home for good.

Defeated in one sense, he moved in with Rene in high anticipation. But their relationship, too, was doomed. Vic's previous unavailability as a married man had kept a tantalizing distance between him and Rene. Without the romantic cover, the affair was contaminated by the same issues of power and control that had plagued Vic's marriage. Rene tended to dominate Vic as Betsy had, and he was trapped in his role of trying to please. It became obvious that he had a weakness for demanding and critical women. Within a few months the affair was over.

But it had served a purpose. The affair got Vic out of an unhappy marriage and let him look at himself. He looked back at his past relationships and had to admit he had a problem with women, specifically his mother. He now tried to work out some of these problems with her directly.

Betsy, swamped by feelings of betrayal and abandonment, sued for divorce, accusing Vic of adultery. The divorce and its aftermath was bitter and filled with recriminations.

Predictably, the children had trouble leaving home after Vic and Betsy separated. The boy began to play the role once reserved for Vic, the mischievous child. He failed in school and started to use drugs, thus assuring Betsy that he needed her protection. Their daughter, ready to leave for college, decided to stay home and get a job for a year or so "to take the pressure off Mom for a while."

Vic continued in therapy as he launched himself into life as an independent male. The transition from married to single was rough. Vic felt disoriented. After twenty years as part of a couple, he was now paired at dinner parties with women billed as eligible. Was he obligated to make a pass? Would he offend if he wanted only friendship? Did he have to take her up on her offer of a weekend at her country place? These questions were raised over and over. He was perhaps overly sensitive to what women expected from him, but also the rules of the game had changed since he had been a bachelor, and Vic wasn't sure how to proceed.

I told him that I had heard it from the other side—women complain that men are sexually demanding and wonder whether paying for dinner entitles a man to spend the night in her bed. Eventually Vic met several women he liked; some became friends, others lovers. He is now seriously involved with a woman whom he sees several times a week.

Vic also had to find a new relationship with his children, who began to avoid him after the divorce. Vic's place had always been at the periphery of the family. Now that he was out of the house, he lost even his small connection with his children. He kept calling, however, and let them know that he wanted to establish a relationship with them. But he backed off quickly when they shunned him.

One of the most interesting studies of divorce among longer-lasting marriages involved the response of adolescents. A California research team found an understandable pattern when they interviewed teenagers whose parents had divorced:

> All adolescents experienced the divorce process as extremely painful and were extremely angry at their parents; similarly, there was sadness, a sense of betrayal, strong feelings of shame and embarrassment and anxiety about their future as marital partners and adequacy as sexual partners. There was often an unrealistic concern over finances. None felt responsible for the divorce. *All children tried to make use of distancing and withdrawal as a defense against experiencing the pain of family disruption.*[6] (ital ours)

The most fascinating statistic about the trauma of divorce is that "good adjustment" for children depends on a continuing relationship with the noncustodial parent.[7]

Although Vic didn't want to put the children in the middle or create more problems for them, he did want a personal relationship with them. One Sunday morning he invited his teenagers into the city for brunch at an expensive restaurant. Both showed up. Over French coffee and omelettes, Vic told his daughter and son that he loved them, that even though he and Betsy were getting a divorce, he still wanted to be part of their lives. "It was the hardest thing I ever did," he said. "Harder than anything with Betsy. I kept looking at the pink napkins on the table and wondering how to tell them so they wouldn't be embarrassed. They tried to be straight with me, but I think often kids don't know how they feel. It was hard for them to say they felt on the spot between me and Betsy, but that was the gist of it."

This meeting was a turning point in the relationship between Vic and his children. They started getting together regularly, sometimes just two of them, sometimes all three together. I think the divorce made it possible for the children to know their father for the first time.

Vic's postdivorce adjustment also involved rebuilding his own social network, finding ways to improve his relationship with his children, and trying to maintain co-parenting contact with Betsy. This last was difficult due to the legal battles and unresolved anger and guilt between Vic and Betsy.

Although the paperwork was done, the emotional divorce was incomplete. Sometimes emotional divorce—mourning the loss of an intact family, giving up fantasies of reunion, giving up anger and rebuilding relationships—takes two or three years. Some couples never succeed in putting their ghosts to rest. Children suffer most from divorce when this emotional wrenching apart drags on indefinitely.

Chapter 16

HAZARDOUS FAMILY PATTERNS IN STAGE 4

FAMILY CASUALTIES AND THE BIRTH OF FAMILY THERAPY

About thirty years ago studies of severely disturbed children and adolescents led to the development of family theory. Why did disturbed adolescents who improved in the environment of a hospital revert to mental illness as soon as they were released and returned home? If one child improved, why did another child in the same family become ill? Why did some patients show only minimal progress after years of conventional individual psychiatric treatment? These questions challenged some therapists, who looked for answers in family relationships, interactions, and patterns of communication. This new work created a theory about the way families operate, and a system to change destructive family patterns was evolved. Family therapy was born.

In the decade between 1950 and 1960, researchers in several different parts of the United States began to study family problems. History was made in the behavioral sciences when a California research team first observed and reported on the now-classic patterns of communication in families with a schizophrenic child. After studying the way family members communicated with each other, the researchers discovered that they routinely sent contradictory and confusing messages from the time the child was young.

As a simple example, a mother beckons her three-year-old son to her lap. As he climbs up, she sighs under her breath, "You're ruining my dress." The two requests or messages the child receives—"Climb on me, don't wrinkle my skirt"—are impossible to satisfy simultaneously. If the child responds to the message "don't ruin my dress" and retreats, the mother further confuses him by saying "Don't you love your mother anymore?" If the child stays on her lap, the mother fusses and blames him for ruining her outfit.

The researchers labeled the discovery the double-bind theory of communication.[8] The double bind means there's no way out of the dilemma for the child. He's damned if he does and damned if he doesn't. Although we all double bind our children at one time or another, families that produce schizophrenic children do it all the time. The confusing messages are frequent, subtly disguised, and insidious. Everyone in the family avoids straightforward communication, and no one discusses or acknowledges the contradictions.

Family members share a secret network of rules that govern everyone's behavior. The schizophrenic patient (often an adolescent) is chosen by the family to bear the burden of hidden tension in the family. The real disturbance was thought to be in the family members' relationships with one another, and the schizophrenic patient was a symptom of family problems. By being sick, the teenager helped stabilize the family.

The California group published prolifically in the 1950s and '60s, and today their articles are considered classics in the field of family therapy.[9]

On the East Coast several other pioneers independently developed their own frameworks for family therapy. The late Dr. Nathan Ackerman is considered by many to be the father of family therapy.[10] Nat Ackerman was a psychoanalyst who broke tradition in child psychiatry by approaching a child's neurosis as part of an interlocking system of family conflicts. He was famous among therapists for his controversial interviewing style, in which he would shock and provoke families into exposing their hidden problems. Ackerman was an active and sometimes startlingly provocative therapist. But his joking, poking, prodding, or interpreting was always directed toward discovering the family pathology, and his goal was to help the family change.

Another charismatic interviewer is Dr. Salvador Minuchin, who originally worked with delinquent boys in residential treatment. Minuchin also broke tradition when he focused on the families of these boys.[11] He was one of the few family therapists to work with working-class and poor families. Minuchin is currently creating new approaches for working with families where there is life-threatening psychosomatic illness.[12]

Dr. Murray Bowen, in Kansas and later in Washington, has created an approach to family therapy that places individual disturbance within the historical context of the three-generation family and shows how pathological relationships are transmitted from one generation to the next.[13] Bowen is one of the most widely recognized family theorizers and has trained several generations of family therapists.

In Baltimore and New Haven, Dr. Theodore Lidz focused on the disturbed marital relationships in families with schizophrenic offspring.[14]

Although not a theorizer, Dr. Carl Whitaker is perhaps the most intuitive and brilliant family therapist to watch in action. His teaching and demonstrations in Atlanta and Wisconsin have inspired family therapists to connect to the family's unconscious. He relies on his feelings as well as his intellect to help the families he works with and is not afraid of even the most disturbed families.

All these pioneers in family therapy broke away from traditional approaches to psychiatry and revolutionized the mental-health profession. At this point there are several different brands of family therapy. But most of the differences are in the style and technique of the therapist rather than in the theory itself. All family therapists agree on these basic concepts: behavior of family members is interlocking; family problems repeat from one generation to the next; and an individual's symptoms reflect wider problems in the way family members relate to one another.

When an adolescent's predictable problems are projected onto an already hazardous family pattern, crises explode staccato, one after another like a string of firecrackers on Chinese New Year.

In my experience most of the families who seek help from therapists are in Stage 4 of family life. They enter therapy because one of the children is creating a disaster in the family. This can be anything from disobedience to drug abuse, sexual promiscuity, or running away from home. The family is at a loss to explain the child's explosive behavior and usually believes he has "turned bad." In fact, a disturbed adolescent is revealing the stress in the family. His or her behavior acts as a pressure valve to release tension that is building up somewhere in the family. It is the same principle described in earlier stages of family life, but in Stage 4 the crisis is exacerbated by the normal stresses of adolescence, and the consequences can be extreme.

In earlier stages we described disengaged and enmeshed family patterns. Some families tend to be too detached, others tend to be sticky. But most families vacillate between the two styles. In Stage 4, as in other stages, extremes of either style create crises in family life.

As adolescents struggle with their natural inner turmoil, they are ready-made scapegoats for trouble in the family. Tensions which may have been subtle in earlier years are suddenly exaggerated in families that cannot tolerate the idea of adolescents growing up. Adolescents typically vacillate between independence and dependence, but the family *cannot bear* the idea of losing them, so the family creates a "solution" to this dilemma.

Family therapist Jay Haley writes,

> It is not accidental that people most frequently go crazy—become schizophrenic—in the late teens and early twenties—the age when children are expected to leave home and the family is in turmoil. Adolescent schizophrenia and other severe disturbances can be seen as an extreme method of attempting to solve what happens to a family when parents and children cannot tolerate being separated; the threatened separation can be aborted if

something goes wrong with the child. By developing a problem that incapacitates him socially, the child remains within the family system. The parents can continue to share the child as a source of concern and disagreement and they find it unnecessary to deal with each other without him. The child can continue to participate in triangular struggle with his parents, while offering himself and them his "mental illness" as an excuse for all difficulties.[15]

Some families in Stages 4 and 5 are so seriously flawed, so dysfunctionally organized, that they sacrifice their adolescent children to chronic mental illness.

PSEUDOMUTUALITY:[16] THE ENMESHED FAMILY IN STAGE 4

One of the major concepts that emerged from early research in family therapy was the term *pseudomutual family.* This is often the same family that in Stages 2 and 3 was called symbiotic or too close. In the earlier stages, in spite of the flawed pattern, the family stayed relatively balanced. But now, in Stage 4, when children have a powerful urge to be free, the enmeshed pattern is dangerous. The family that fails to release its children (or adults) is called pseudomutual, a family that through excessive harmony avoids *all* conflict. The prolonged dependence of children and parents no longer has value.

These families participate in rituals that deflect anger and embrace peace at any cost. Harmony and cooperation are considered family virtues. The most treacherous aspect of the pseudomutual family, from the therapist's point of view, is that it's almost impossible to get anyone in the family to admit there's anything wrong. In the American lexicon there is no such thing as a family that is too close. We believe that the happiest families are the closest families, and this is blatantly false. (In pseudomutual families nothing is "wrong" except that there is a seriously disturbed adolescent.)

Pseudomutual families are toxic environments for adolescents, who desperately need to be free and by natural inclination are difficult to live with. How can a teenager talk back when everyone is kind, loving, and understanding? In one family the youngest daughter was trying to assert her independence in a modest rebellious effort. She was a lonely girl and suffered long bouts of depression. Her father amazed me with his resourcefulness in neutralizing antagonism wherever it appeared. One day, as his daughter's small rebellion escalated in the safety of my office, he told her that he had been reading up on adolescence and calmly explained that rebellion was a necessary part of her development and he fully understood her turmoil. By practically prescribing her rebellion, he stole her protest.

"You just did it again," I said.

"Did what?"

"Made everything all nice . . ."

"What's wrong with trying to understand my child? What am I supposed to do?"

"You're not supposed to do anything—that's the whole point."

"I don't understand this. What's wrong with having a good relationship and understanding each other? Maybe I can help her over the rough parts."

"Don't help her—leave her alone. Cathy, you should be doing this, not me. Get on in there . . ."

"Gee, Daddy," Cathy said timidly, "I appreciate what you're trying to do for me . . ."

This is a good example of how pseudomutual families kill with kindness and make it impossible for children to grow up. These are "rubber fence" families[17]—the boundaries look soft and pliable, but there's no way out.

Pseudomutual families are versatile when it comes to squelching anger among members. Some enmeshed families that were loving in earlier stages of family life develop an authoritarian style when children become adolescents. Out of fear, parents exert excessive power to stay in control and keep children close to them.

Power is an important dynamic in all families when children become adolescents. In authoritarian families, parents gather all the power to themselves and are reluctant to give any up. They baby their adolescents and make them powerless. In a paradoxical way these families are leaderless. The leader in a family shows the way out; authoritarian parents shelter and protect, make the decisions, and shield their children from the world.

Pseudomutual families cannot bear conflict. Under this kind of restraint, pressure builds, and adolescent children frequently show signs of disturbance. But even the symptoms work against the child: the ill child brings the family even closer together with the illness. The disturbed adolescent becomes the family savior—a small sacrifice to preserve family harmony.

The original concept of the pseudomutual family was developed with reference to severely disturbed adolescents. The concept refers to a special family pattern that Dr. Lyman Wynne linked to schizophrenia. In such extreme cases the adolescent who cannot use rebellion to separate and differentiate himself or herself withdraws from the world and retreats into fantasy. Sometimes he or she becomes severely depressed or develops paranoia or such bizarre behavior as taking on a false identity. Nothing is wrong in the family—everyone is loving—but one member has gone crazy.

THE FAMILY TRAITOR

Eighteen-year-old Jacob Goldman was terrified that Nazis were about to rage through the Bronx, torturing and killing all the Jews. For seven days and nights he had refused to leave his house and sat on his mother's lap, weeping, terrorized by fantasies of merciless aggressors.

After first trying to get help within the local religious community, Jacob's parents reached my office for a consultation by a circuitous route. They were wary initially, because they thought of me as an outsider.

Benjamin and Ruth Goldman doted on both of their children, especially their son. Jacob had been an adorable infant and a model child, Ruth Goldman said. Even more so, they admitted, than their younger child, Deborah, who at fifteen was quiet but rather clinging.

Now, suddenly, Jacob was sick. And there was no conceivable reason. The Goldmans were surprised to hear that therapy would include the whole family, because they had assumed Jacob was the one who needed help. But they willingly complied with my request for family participation. They knew their child was in serious trouble and were willing to put themselves on the line to help him. As they left the consultation, Ruth Goldman said, "You'll see that we're just an ordinary family." Alice Through the Looking Glass, I later thought. For what I came to know was a family in which almost all normal behavior was turned upside down.

For the moment the immediate crisis was dangerous. Jacob spent most of the day in bed, and when he did finally drag himself out in the late afternoon, he couldn't dress himself. He lived in his pajamas, was afraid to get into the bath.

Although he clearly showed signs of serious mental illness, the pattern was not yet deeply entrenched. The best time for a therapist to intervene is at the beginning of a crisis, before the acute episode settles into a pathological pattern. The crisis upsets established family patterns, and this turmoil can be used to establish healthier patterns. I was anxious to get Jacob through the initial crisis, out of the house, and back to college. Only then could we begin to examine the events that led to the crisis. The first thing to do was quickly reverse the momentum of the pathological process with psychiatric consultation and antianxiety medication.

At this point Jacob still spent all his time when he was not in bed sitting with his mother in the living room, crying and fantasizing about the Nazis. Ruth Goldman was completely immobilized and couldn't leave him alone for five minutes. The immediate need was to create some distance between Jacob and his mother—literally to get him out of her lap—and open up the normal conflict between them.

Phase I. In the early sessions I looked for ways to bring out family disagreements. Before his illness Jacob had liked to explore New York by taking long walks into "foreign" neighborhoods. This had been a source of contention in the family, because his parents feared for his life in alien territory. (Jacob did occasionally venture into dangerous neighborhoods and in a real sense courted danger, but for the most part his journeys were merely romantic.) In a sense he was a pioneer.

I knew Jacob wasn't ready to resume his walking tours, but I felt these ventures indicated curiosity and a search for enlightenment and adventure. With a little encouragement, he and his mother started to quarrel about his walks.

Ruth put down his exploits as senseless and a sign of poor judgment. Jacob snapped back that he was old enough to take a walk by himself. Ruth looked shocked and coolly suggested that only a sick person would be rude to his mother.

At the end of the first session, I discussed my fee with the Goldmans. Both Ruth and Ben sat back in their chairs, and *Jacob* spoke up: "I think that's too much money," he said.

I was genuinely surprised. "Why are you negotiating the fee?" I thought. "You can't even get out of bed in the morning."

Jacob, a boy whose parents picked out his clothes, accompanied him to the barber, and supervised his bath, made all the important decisions in the family. When they decided to move into another apartment, it was Jacob who selected the place. When they went out to dinner, it was Jacob who chose the restaurant and carefully read the menu and checked the prices before they went in. It was Jacob who planned the family vacation and made all the reservations.

This was the first inkling I had of the topsy-turvy world of this family. Everything I thought was normal, they called sick. And what I called sick, they thought was normal.

We slogged ahead.

Within a month Jacob's condition stabilized; he stopped fantasizing, and his other more overt symptoms subsided. It was time for him to fight for some basic privileges, such as taking a walk alone or getting his hair cut by himself.

In all Jacob's small battles for self-respect, Ruth and Ben protested that he was rude, claimed that he must be sick, or said that he was making them sick by talking to them that way.

For instance, Jacob refused to join a religious group at college. When his mother pressured him, he stated his position calmly. Ruth Goldman nagged him, "Jacob, I don't know why you're acting this way!" Jacob became agitated and shouted to assert his opinion more forcefully. Then his mother had him. "See," Ruth said. "Look how upset you're getting."

By this time Jacob was very agitated, and his anger was used against him. He was in a double bind:[18] there was no way he could behave without being crazy by some definition. If he spoke up for himself, his mother said he must be crazy; if he let his parents control him, he was crazy, too. In the first instance he was *perceived* as crazy by his parents; in the second he actually was crazy.

My job was to take him out of this bind. I aligned myself with Jacob and supported his move for freedom. I put it to his parents that they would have to decide whether they wanted a well-behaved son who was mentally ill or a typical healthy adolescent who talked back.

When the situation was put in these terms, the Goldmans were forced to recognize the price they would have to pay for good behavior. They needed to increase their tolerance for conflict and consider the notions that people feel and act differently from one another and that niceness is not always a virtue.

Phase II. Within a few weeks Jacob returned to school; he tried to assert his rights over new territory. Owning his body and having the right to manage himself was a totally alien concept to Jacob and his family. He and his parents fought over both the important and the trivial: what classes to take in school, when to get a haircut, how to dress, when to bathe and shave, whether to have the holes in his shoes repaired.

Every issue was worthy of battle, and I encouraged Jacob to fight for his freedom. Now he was also a pioneer for his younger sister, who relied on him to declare independence for them both. At the same time, however, I sympathized with Ruth and Ben that normal adolescents were difficult people to live with.

Ruth Goldman was a vibrant, dark-eyed woman in her mid-forties. Even when she nagged her son, vitality and warmth spilled out of her. But as Jacob got better, Ruth fell apart. She grew depressed and was bothered by heart palpitations and sleeplessness. She would call me late at night to report incidents that in her opinion clearly indicated that Jacob was sick. This new independence was "not Jacob," she said. "He shouts at me, or doesn't pay any attention when I ask him to do something."

In about six months, just after his nineteenth birthday and at the beginning of the new semester, Jacob moved into a furnished apartment with another Jewish boy from school. Ruth and Ben were so ashamed you would have thought he had joined the Ku Klux Klan.

Jacob continued to meet his parents once a week in my office, and saw them at home every Friday and Saturday. Jacob was a strapping six-footer with grizzled coppery hair and deep brown eyes. He usually wore dungarees and a sweater or blue work shirt. He looked strong and handsome. Yet every time he came to a family session, his parents' opening remark was, "My God, you look awful." I thought he looked terrific and said so.

According to Ruth, Jacob was turning into a monster: he wore "hippie" clothes, he looked thin and pale, seemed nervous and agitated, questioned religious rituals, was secretive and insolent and selfish—and he was fresh.

I had to agree with her. Before the crisis Jacob always stayed at home and was obedient and well mannered, a religious son who listened to and obeyed his parents, was quiet but always confided in his mother. In fact, as Ruth said, "he was a lovely boy and a very happy child." Except he went crazy.

Phase III. Whenever Ruth grew alarmed over Jacob's behavior, her own depression lifted and her physical symptoms disappeared. I knew she didn't want her son to be sick, but she couldn't seem to tolerate his growing up. She needed him not to be well. Together we had to wonder why.

"If he's unable to manage, he'll need you. You'd do anything to keep him, even if it meant he has to be sick for the rest of his life. Why, Ruth?"

When I said it, Ruth put her face in her hands and cried. What she decided now would make the major difference in Jacob's recovery—and would at the same time cause suffering to herself. Ruth chose the hard road. She wanted Jacob to get better, even if it meant admitting that something was drastically wrong in her own life. To discover the problem meant she had to relive feelings and relationships of the past, open old wounds, and face things she would rather leave behind.

The answer to Ruth's dilemma was deeply buried in her relationship with her own parents. She had always been her parents' caretaker and still felt tyrannized and trapped by them, even though her father had died some years ago. Her responsibility had escalated recently as her mother grew older, and began to lean on Ruth more than ever. Ruth also admitted that she and her husband were not really happy together. Ben Goldman was like another son in the family, and there were the attendant sibling jealousies and conflicts between him and Jacob. The strongest alliance in the family was between Ruth and Jacob, with Ben and Deborah competing for Ruth's attention.

Ruth had two strong reasons to keep Jacob close to her: she was burdened by her mother, and her marriage offered little pleasure. If she released her son, she knew Deborah would not be far behind. She had to admit that she depended on her children for companionship and her need clashed with Jacob's need for freedom.

In this phase of therapy Ruth delved into her personal problems and frustrations. For several months she was depressed, grieved over her own lost opportunities as a child, and expressed her anger at her parents for holding her back to take care of them. And she heartily mourned the loss of her cherubic little boy.

Occasionally she would describe a possible clue that might prove that Jacob was still crazy or sick and needed "therapy." But Jacob continued at college, made friends, and developed a social life of his own.

Ruth and Ben revived some interest in each other and for the first time in twenty years went on a vacation alone together. And Ruth tried to free herself from her mother, although this was virtually impossible for her.

Jacob, because he actually went crazy, may be the first generation in this family to liberate himself from family tyranny. He had suffered such tremendous breakaway guilt that he was fully incapacitated by his destructive fantasies.[19] Here was another example of family pathology where the current problem mirrors an identical problem—in an identical stage—in the parent's family. The problem percolated through the generations until, in Jacob, it exploded.

DANGEROUS SPLITS: THE DISENGAGED FAMILY

At the other end of the familial pole are those families in which parents fail to present a coalition that offers discipline and leadership. This family has no center of gravity; members are alienated and lonely, drifting in separate worlds. Family life is chaotic. Children tend to lack inner discipline and are attracted to antisocial activity that may verge on delinquency. Street life offers the adventure teenagers crave, and much more—it offers a sense of belonging, and drugs that blot out loneliness. The drug world is a complex, tricky hustle of social relationships that entice the teenager who has no roots or structure at home. And the religious cults offer security.

I often hear parents protest that they have provided a good home for their children, given them everything, and suddenly their children have turned into monsters. These adolescent grief years can affect families in the suburbs, in the ghetto, in two-parent families, or in divorced homes. Disengaged is a style of living, not a prerogative of any particular class.

Parental Schism

Often the critical tie which is "disengaged" is the marital relationship. A rift between parents is usually established early in married life. By Stage 4 a schism between husband and wife creates an almost hopeless problem for the family. These rifts often result in power struggles in which one parent dominates and the other submits. In one family the father laid down the law in a booming, authoritative manner. The mother was so overwhelmingly indulgent that she couldn't set any limits on the children's behavior. Together these parents created a leadership vacuum where neither could help their children grow up as responsible adults. The mother encouraged self-indulgence, which the father punished. The father dwelled on the children's responsibilities, which the mother minimized. Predictably, all three of their adolescent children were aimless and drifting.

In the dominant/submissive marriage, the submissive parent may fight back through a teenage child, encouraging the adolescent to express all the anger and hostility the parent feels and also absorb the reaction from the other parent. The silent parent covertly supports the adolescent's rebellion and at the same time maintains loyalty to the spouse.

The bond between one parent and an adolescent strengthens over the years because of the inadequacy of the marital relationship. When a child is put in the middle in the marriage, or triangled, the natural separation process between parents and children is thwarted, often with devastating effect. When a child is the go-between for his parents, his normal development is perverted.[20] The teenager acts as a conduit for the parents, deflecting or absorbing their secret conflicts. He gains certain satisfaction from this role because he feels important and grown-up. Already nervous about leaving the family, the teenager senses his presence is needed to keep parents, however ill-matched, together, and he has an excuse to stay home. Teenagers vacillate about leaving home at this stage, and when they are offered legitimate reasons to stay, they usually oblige. The process of separation is stymied, and the child becomes trapped in the family.

The enmeshed family is overly protective. But the disengaged family has a leadership vacuum that can push the adolescent into delinquency.

TRIANGLES AND SCAPEGOATS

Triangles can develop in both enmeshed and disengaged families. Triangles established in early stages of family life can deepen into more severe patterns in Stage 4, and children may become a family's scapegoat. But most often a child is chosen to obscure the family's problems. It's not unlike school or work situations in which everyone agrees that one person in the class or office is a dud, that person's weirdness making all the others feel that they're all right and also creating a sense of belonging among them.

In the same way families elect one member to be sick and then filter all other problems through this one disturbed person. In every act, word, and deed, families punish their scapegoats. The scapegoat creates a commonality in the family, something they can all get together on. It is usual in these families for every member—except one—to appear normal, happy, and fulfilled.

THE SCAPEGOAT: THE POWER OF FAMILIES

Gabrielle Desseaux was a voluptuous beauty whose brittle voice betrayed her nervousness. "I really don't know why we're here," she said. "Lonnie had to miss his violin lesson and he resents it." Lon, the youngest child in the family, was a handsome, slightly nervous colt of a boy. Gabrielle selected a chair, and her son stood protectively next to her.

Across the room her husband Michael sat silently with their other child, Julia, a rather delicate seventeen-year-old whose long mane of blonde hair shadowed very pale skin. The cozy clustering of mother and son contrasted sharply with the frozen positions held by Michael and Julia.

Several weeks earlier the Desseauxs had sent Julia to me for individual therapy. As I began to know her, the severity of her problems impressed me. She told me she had quit high school several months before and was a heavy user of pot, angel dust, and cocaine. She had sex with men she picked up promiscuously in bars or on the street. She also said she had attempted suicide twice. As she spiraled down into a depression, another suicide attempt was on the horizon.

Over the next two weeks I felt increasingly uncomfortable about Julia's being "sent" to me. I began to worry about her over the weekend and gave her my home telephone number so she could reach me at any time of the day or night.

In the middle of our fifth session, my own anxiety heightened when Julia disclosed her suicidal fantasies. She didn't have a specific plan but saw suicide as a way out of her despair. I realized that I had to contact her family. If I didn't I would be denying the seriousness of Julia's problems. She might require medical intervention and possibly psychiatric hospitalization. By accepting her in individual therapy, I was, in effect, colluding with her family, which had expelled her and dumped her at my door. I told Julia my feelings, then called her parents and asked them to pick her up. Meanwhile I wasn't going to allow her to leave the office.

I made her a cup of hot tea, then settled down to do some paperwork until her parents came. Julia sat quietly in the waiting room, sipping the tea.

Several hours later I met Gabrielle and Michael Desseaux for the first time. They called me an alarmist. I described the suicidal risk and said that in my professional judgment, medical evaluation was clearly in order. I also said that Julia's difficulties in growing up might be compounded by current family problems, and that I had serious reservations about continuing to see her alone. Michael, a successful corporation lawyer, received this news coolly; he challenged me, "Can you be more specific?"

"*Sending* Julia for therapy reflects her isolation from the family—she's the bad child who needs shaping up. Julia is a ready-made scapegoat for any family tension. She's in serious trouble now, and it's getting worse. If you want me to work with her, I think you should all make yourselves available."

I included Julia's younger brother in this plan, although the boy was described by Julia and her parents as a high achiever and trouble free.

Both Gabrielle and Michael objected. "Lon has nothing to do with Julia's problems," Gabrielle said. "He's already too burdened by all this trouble and Julia's problems with drugs, her weird friends, and belligerent behavior."

The more the Desseauxs resisted involving the other child, the more I felt he was important. Theoretically everyone in the family contributes to making a scapegoat, and I suspected that Julia's brother actively participated in the scapegoat system.

Resistance to therapy is common in these situations. The whole point of creating a scapegoat is to avoid facing other problems. Families who create scapegoats will not willingly subject themselves to analysis and therapy.

The family had said the problem was Julia, and Julia played into the system. The problem was now redefined. Julia did have personal conflicts, but I was sure the family was using her to deflect their own problems.

They resisted family therapy vigorously, and we battled over the sessions. It was what family therapists Drs. Augustus Napier and Carl Whitaker call a battle for structure.[21] I was firmly committed to family therapy in this instance and threatened to withdraw if the Desseauxs didn't cooperate. Yet the family continued to choreograph a dance of avoidance.

We negotiated, and they agreed to try family therapy for several sessions as long as I also kept Julia in individual therapy. For family-therapy purists, the entire prescription would be family sessions. I knew that Julia had an important role in stabilizing a sick family, but she also had heavy individual conflicts. I compromised with the family.

Before the first family session the parents told me that Lon objected to the family session. Later that week Lon actually refused to participate. Gabrielle and Michael telephoned these messages and tried to convince me to give up the family sessions.

It was interesting that Lon, always extremely well behaved and cooperative, was the voice of family resistance—and that Gabrielle and Michael permitted a twelve-year-old boy to make decisions for them. Another clue to the family system: parents actually shaped the rules of the family but used children to convey their tensions and fears.

Lon acted on behalf of his parents and tried to get the family off the hook. At the last minute, however, they all appeared for the session. I made a mental note about this pattern (and would see it repeated for the next three weeks).

The session began chaotically. Everyone was annoyed that Julia's problems were interfering with their lives. Lon and Gabrielle verbally tripped all over each other in their eagerness to relate how terrible Julia was. Lon protected his mother by speaking for her. The conversation, no matter who spoke or what they talked about, always switched back to Julia. This was a striking pattern.

Family therapists tune in more to the pattern and direction of conversation than the actual content. I noted that Lon spoke for mother and mother spoke for Lon. I tracked the conversation, and each time someone wanted to avoid self-exploration or a problem with any other family member, the topic reverted to Julia. When I blocked the pattern, tension began to build.

Gabrielle broke down and started to cry; then she poured out her feelings. She was under great strain at home, worked full-time as a teacher, ran a large house, took care of the children, and also cared for her invalid mother. For years, she said, she had been thinking of running away.

In the face of her despair, Michael responded that he, too, felt hopeless, although he blamed his sadness on Julia. Then he turned on Gabrielle. "You and the children—especially Julia—use me to solve your problems, and then you ignore me. You're manipulators." Michael said that he felt impotent and used.

A demonstration occurred spontaneously a few minutes later when Lon and his mother began to argue about whether Lon should cut back on his violin lessons.

"I don't want to go three times a week—I want to play on the school tennis team," Lon said.

"But now is the important time, when discipline pays off—if you don't do it now, you won't make it."

When Michael tried to make a suggestion both mother and son whirled on him, eyes blazing.

"You don't know about this," Lon shouted.

"Keep out of it, Michael," Gabrielle said flatly and finally.

Michael was so alienated from the rest of the family that he needed some way in. Julia had been his favorite child; worrying about her gave Michael a purpose and kept him in the family. Should Julia ever manage to grow up, Lon was practicing to take over her role. The boy's conflicts with Gabrielle summoned Michael to mediate between them. As soon as he tried to help, his efforts were always neutralized and often cut completely.

Even though both husband and wife confessed to feeling despair, no sign of compassion or sympathy passed between them. Just below the irritated surface of this family, there was a sense of overwhelming sadness. When I said this in the session, they all nodded in agreement.

At the end of the first family interview, everyone was involved and interested. The family had begun to face their problems, and I felt encouraged about the future. Problems were coming to the surface, and the serious marital rift between Michael and Gabrielle, still not specifically acknowledged, looked as if it were about to show itself.

At the end of the hour, everyone agreed to come again the following week. Then Gabrielle turned to Lon and gave him a cue: "Are you sure you want to come?" she asked. The session had been so promising that I failed to pick up this expression of Gabrielle's resistance. Even if I had, I'm not sure it could have been overcome.

Predictably, over the following week the family lost ground. Several days before the next session, Michael called to say that Lon refused to attend. Gabrielle called later that same day to confirm that Lon absolutely refused to participate. "He just doesn't see the value of these sessions," she complained. "Julia needs help, not him."

That same week Julia came to her individual session and told me that her parents seemed sad and upset after therapy. She felt this was her fault and she wanted to spare them. I pointed out that her role in the family was to protect everyone—that as long as she agreed to be the problem, everyone else could safely avoid her or his own problems. "I think you are protecting your family by destroying yourself. Maybe you're scared of finding out the truth about them."

During the week the family united against Julia and returned for the next family session, once again presenting the picture of a reasonably happy family with a disturbed child.

I felt worn out. Families are powerful antagonists and can exhaust therapists, which is the reason family therapists sometimes work in pairs. This session was dominated by the family's resistance and was summed up when each person literally said, "I'm fine. Julia's sick."

There was a perverse quality to their resistance, which went something like this: "I will do anything—*anything*—to help Julia. Anything except explore myself and what goes on in my family."

Their insistence that everyone else was fine was belied by some interesting facts that surreptitiously bubbled to the surface. Lon, the accomplished twelve-year-old, was up to his eyebrows in violin and piano lessons, Boy Scouts and Little League. Sitting or standing, one foot twitched up and down involuntarily in a constant rhythmic tapping. Dark circles showed under his eyes because he had trouble sleeping at night.

Michael and Gabrielle, the devoted parents, hinted that some incident fifteen years earlier had caused a serious rift in their marriage. "If we're pushed about our marriage," Michael said, "it might lead to divorce." It was coincidental, they believed, that Julia's problems always flared up at the times when Michael and Gabrielle were dangerously close to divorce.

The message was strong and clear from the family: if we pursue this course, we will all be destroyed. Leave us alone, and everything will be fine.

I discussed the case in consultation with a colleague, who pointed out that I should watch for a sudden, false improvement in Julia's condition (technically, a phenomenon called a flight into health). Sure enough, as soon as I suggested to Julia that a broader family conflict might be involved in her problems, her outward symptoms diminished. This gave the family additional ammunition to resist therapy.

Julia was in the classic double bind of an adolescent embedded in her family: if she improved, her family had an excuse to withdraw from family therapy ("you don't need us"). Later on, they might sabotage her individual therapy to keep her just sick enough. Should she get worse, they might drive her out completely, to a hospital or into the drug world of the streets, or over the edge into suicide. Julia was caught. If she got better, the family would find a way to make her sick again. If she got worse, she would destroy herself.

One graphic example of the way they made her sick: Gabrielle and Lon were in the kitchen whispering about Julia. Julia came in, saw them with their heads together, and heard her name whispered. "What are you saying about me?" she complained. "I wish you wouldn't talk about me behind my back."

Her mother said, "We're not talking about you. You're so paranoid."

Julia's legitimate protest had been turned on her, making her believe that she was sick. (Confronted on this issue, mother and son protested against the idea that the exchange had been harmful: "We didn't want to hurt her feelings.")

My objective was to help Julia get better and gradually move her away from the thin edge of catastrophe and toward growing up. Until she was released from the family, her individual problems couldn't even be touched.

The Desseaux family was not ready to expose the family problems. They needed to keep Julia trapped so that they could hide behind her problems. Unfortunately they could rely on her to act up and demand their attention and keep them together. And as long as Julia played her part, she could avoid coming to terms with her own problems.

Unlike the situation with the Goldman family, I had no leverage with the Desseauxs because our goals were different. In the end the family was too powerful. They withdrew from therapy, taking Julia with them.

In therapy, clinicians don't always get what they want. Certainly in this situation family therapy was the best therapeutic strategy and would achieve the quickest results. Without it, I foresaw years of individual therapy for Julia, with only small prospect of improvement. Was it possible that Julia could have been helped by intensive individual therapy? Could she and I alone have compensated for the destructive force of the family that would continue to work against her? Could we have used what we had learned about her family to help her? I can only say maybe to each of these points.

Stage 4 is probably the most painful and exasperating stage of family life. As parents lose confidence in their sexual attractiveness and protest aging, they often seek outside affairs. At the same time their children are transformed into sexual beings, experiencing all the excitement of early sexual attraction.

There is a natural antagonism between generations as children reach adolescence. When a child is put in the middle of a marital relationship, this natural separation process is perverted, often with devastating and long-lasting effects.

Psychiatric problems for any member of the family at this stage signals a wider illness in the family as a whole. Sometimes one member of the family is elected to be "sick" and is scapegoated by the family. The unhappy relationships of all the members of the family are filtered through this one disturbed person.

Backing off, standing by, and watching children struggle with independence takes courage, patience, and companionship. Husband and wife need each other to confirm their capacity for love and sex and their importance to one another.

Stage 5
THE SHRINKING FAMILY

Turning Point: To force the family to stay the same or let the children go

Chapter 17

LOSSES

In the summer that my sister and I were married, my father died. Several people said later that he looked drawn, pale, and preoccupied at my wedding, but I never noticed. In some ways my marriage represented a great loss to him. He was closer to my sister Gail than to me, and her marriage, too, would have been a severe loss, but she was married in the shadow of his death, two weeks after we found his suicide note.

My father's suicide was a dramatic exaggeration of his place in our family: he was always on the outskirts of the emotional center. He never seemed to mind. He worked the hard and long hours of a pharmacist, building up a small, reliable business (which afforded us a comfortable middle-class life) and buried himself in detective stories and cigar smoke. As I grew up, his hours became more flexible and he got into the habit of sleeping later. He'd often be having eggs and toast in the kitchen when I came home from school. He seemed relaxed and happy.

My earliest recollection of our relationship haunts me even today. The memory may not be accurate, but no matter, for it is emotionally vivid and the sadness persists. I was about three years old, and my father was to take me to the zoo for an outing. Just the two of us. I was dressed in a freshly pressed party dress, blond hair in ribbons. I dreaded the outing. But I knew that I had to go and must not complain. I didn't want to hurt his feelings. I felt protective toward this vulnerable man who was my father. I felt somehow guilty for the rejection in my heart, but proud of myself for doing the dutiful thing. Arrogance and contempt colored our relationship from such an early point. I am sure my father felt I had little use for him.

In this small event the presence of my mother is more felt than observed. I sensed that she knew I did not want to go with my father, but the secret disdain was not to be acknowledged between us. I knew that. My mother and I had lots of pacts, and we were more than just close. I was born two years after an earlier pregnancy, which had resulted in a stillborn male child in the seventh month. I was to make up for my mother's hard early life, her late marriage, and the child that died in her uterus.

I was the third generation of eldest daughters to perpetuate the strong mother-daughter alliance that was the hallmark of my mother's family. That alliance didn't weaken when my mother married. Grandma always lived with us until she died when I was fifteen. My mother said she married father because he ate my grandmother's graham crackers and applesauce.

My father never objected to my grandmother's presence, perhaps because he missed his own mother. When he was only four years old, my father, Norman Roskeroff, was taken out of Russia by his father. His mother, left behind, died before she could follow her family to the New World, and Norman never saw her again. He was raised, along with an older brother and sister, by a stepmother who had six of her own children to worry about. The immigrant neighborhood in Buffalo in the early years of this century did not have streets paved with gold, and the big family was often cold and hungry. Norman grew up on the streets and became a tough fighter who often defended weaker kids from the street bullies. By the time he was a teenager, he was on his own, fending for himself. He had to be hard to survive, and it left its mark on him. There was a deep, hidden anger inside him that for the most part was only sensed by other people. But my mother touched his soft spot, and she brought him in from the cold.

She still loves to tell the story of how they met. My mother, Bernice Traub, who was at the time twenty-nine years old, met Sylvia Klein, who said that Bernice should meet her brother, Norman. Bernice agreed, and they arranged to have dinner together at the Town Casino, a popular restaurant of the time. There would be four of them: Bernice, Norman, Sylvia, and her husband, Ben Klein. Ben was an unusually handsome man, tall, lean, and with a gorgeous mane of thick hair. Norman was short, stocky, and balding. As Bernice approached the table at the restaurant, she assumed that Ben was her date.

"And he was so good-looking," my mother remembers wistfully as she tells this story over and over. When Sylvia turned to introduce her to my dad, she was stunned and disappointed. The story ends here, and when my sisters and I would push her for a resolution, she said she was not the least bit interested in him until he ate my grandmother's graham crackers. Then she knew he was a man she could count on.

Bernice had always worked hard to support her family. She had to walk several miles to her job as a stock girl because she couldn't spend the money to take a streetcar. Her father, a silver craftsman from Rumania, could barely make a living in this country. Throughout my mother's childhood she shared a bed with my grandmother. Her father died when Bernice was twenty-two. He had always been considered "beneath" my grandmother and was systematically excluded from the family.

My grandmother, Leah, learned to speak English without the trace of an accent and thought herself superior to the other East European immigrants. She wouldn't work in a factory because she was too proud to do unskilled labor. A combination of Leah's aspirations and Bernice's hard work and determination made my mother the first in her family to get a college education. She was a schoolteacher when she met Norman.

My parents were always compatible. My father was easy to live with, and my mother took charge casually and efficiently. Over the years, as my mother explained to us, she grew to love Daddy. My father looked like a man who was loved, and he adored my mother. Anything she said was all right with him. They discussed all his business problems, and my mother always helped him find a reasonable approach. But she also corrected his English when he used double negatives and often mentioned her efforts to "build him up."

My parents had a group of friends, mostly other pharmacists and their wives, who were regulars for bridge and Saturday-night kibbitzing. As the years went on and my father's business became more successful, we had comforts such as a lakeside cottage for summer vacations, and by the time I was a teenager, a trip to Florida every winter.

My mother adored me. When she checked me over after I was born, anxiously counting all my fingers and toes, she proclaimed me perfect. I love to see her face become animated as she tells this story. Just before I was born, my mother wanted to buy a house. My father hesitated; $5,000, the cost, was all they had. Mother insisted; Norman's objections dissolved. I didn't move from that house until I was married twenty-two years later.

Grandma lived in the house with us, and Mother and Grandma fought frequently. Their arguments are among the strongest memories of my childhood. My grandmother had no friends, having shunned all the women of her generation. She roamed through the house all day, a frail woman with aristocratic pretensions and a sharp tongue.

Mother fought back, explaining: "Grandma gets on my nerves." Grandma knew how everything should be done, from child rearing to housekeeping, and she was always advising, ordering, berating Mother. The battles for power raged ceaselessly. But mother usually won. When the argument came to its climax, she played her trump card: "It's my house," she would remind Grandma.

If the fighting became really intense, Mother would threaten to put Grandma in "a home." Then Grandma appealed to my father. With quiet tones and soothing words, he calmed my mother. He became the mediator between the two women. But as Grandma got older, she became more and more reclusive and was shunned by all of us. In the last years of her life, she stayed in her room almost all the time.

There were two strong relationships in our family: a powerful negative relationship between my mother and grandmother, and the strong positive tie between my mother and myself. When I reflect on it now, it seems that my appearance in the family displaced Grandma, that I came between the two women and usurped my grandmother's place.

Bernice was determined that her children and her home should be hers, and I remember the early battles which established my mother's territory. She fought her mother for supremacy over house and children until my grandmother relinquished her power and literally shrank in size and from view.

My mother took great pride in my development, and my performances and accomplishments were richly rewarded with love, approval, and acceptance. One family story (perhaps apocryphal) is that just before my first birthday I would crawl behind the living room couch and "practice" walking so that no one could see. On my birthday, for the small crowd assembled to celebrate the event, I walked for the first time in public—perfectly stable—"an accomplished walker."

In the family album, my mother is ecstatically extending her arms as I gingerly but steadily close in; Grandma smiles vaguely from the background. My father was the photographer.

A year after my first birthday, my sister Gail was born. She was my father's favorite and seemed to emulate his personality. Both were even-tempered and eager to please. In a household where the struggle for supremacy was a daily fact of life, they kept a low profile. There was little sibling rivalry between us, because my sister never competed.

My mother hints at the reason: whenever my needs conflicted with those of baby sister, my mother always took care of me first, since "the baby wouldn't know any different." My mother wanted to keep me from feeling jealous of my younger sister and to protect my favored position. When I was nine, a third daughter, Brenda, was born into the family, almost as an afterthought.

An only child herself, my mother perpetuated a variation of the only-child family within our family of three daughters. My sisters have never forgiven me or our mother. Today they maintain a close relationship with each other, from which I exclude myself and am actively excluded.

But in our childhood we had good times together. When we were very young, Sunday mornings were playful times. My father loved to romp with us in bed. I vividly remember his warm, early-morning smell and always thought it was especially his.

When we were of school age, my sister Gail and I explored the backyards, driveways, and streets of the middle-class neighborhood where we lived. Gangs of kids of every age and size played safely in our neighborhood, all virtually unsupervised. Street life was full of excitement, miniature camaraderie, a sense of belonging, and pure fun. We knew that we could always return home for help if our knees or feelings got bruised. Street life was an adventure.

My mother had aspirations for her eldest child that she never had for herself: the luxury of self-development. At five I began piano lessons, and I appeared on a children's amateur television program when I was seven. I was a very mediocre pianist and certainly no child prodigy. But "we" wanted to win so badly, we stuffed the mailboxes with postcards signed with false names. But I wasn't the tool of an ambitious mother—I loved winning for both of us. As overachievers go, I was reasonably successful over the years and accumulated my meaningless honors. In my heart, though, I felt it wasn't real. To this day I share the fear of the imposter—to be discovered a fake, to be found out.

Throughout my childhood, our family seemed to me safe, secure, and lively. There was always much talk, joking, and action. At dinner we were usually animated and excited. One of the rituals of the table was my mother's correction of our table manners. We objected loudly, saying that Daddy didn't adhere to the family rules against slurping and elbowing. Finally, after years of trying to reform Dad, Mom said that Daddy could eat any way he wanted. Dad, having at last triumphed on this issue, would jokingly respond, saying, "Do as I say, not as I do." Mom laughed. She knew when she was defeated. Rules could be applied differently, and we all knew it.

My father slowly overcame his painful self-consciousness, and as the years passed, he became more secure, serene, and confident. My mother, having won her major battles with Grandma, became calmer and less agitated. My youngest sister Brenda was born when my mother was forty-two, and she became the family plaything. She was adorable and cuddly, and the whole family loved her; we didn't seem to take her seriously. When I was older and the three of us went out for dinner, I pretended to be her mother. I loved the pretense because it made me feel so grown up.

My adolescence brought some changes to the family. I used the independence and toughness learned from my mother to break away from her a little. When I was fifteen, Grandma died of old age. The routine mourning rituals and burial rites were carried out with dignity. The only expression of the high degree of family tension that surrounded Grandma's death was a nervous giggle from me and my sister at several points in the ceremony. Several months later my parents took a cruise to the Mediterranean for three weeks—their first vacation by themselves. I took up skiing and boys. I hardly noticed Mom and Dad were gone. They returned tanned and happy, and we had a typical family gathering, complete with lively conversation and overcooked roast beef.

I went off to college, rejecting my mother's choice and choosing a small college for women that was farther from home and also exceeded even my mother's ambitions. Mother always wanted me to have more than she ever had, but she didn't want me to outgrow her.

My mother said, "If you get sick at college and have to return home, that's it for out-of-town college. You can go to the local university." Her announce-

ment sounded more and more like a prediction when Gail left for college two
years after my departure. Gail went to a large midwestern university. After
only one semester she returned home because she came down with mononu-
cleosis.

I was by this time launched. I loved college, resolved secretly never to
come home again to live, and had convinced my parents to send me to
Europe for the summer. I left for three months abroad as Gail was planning
her first venture out of the family. As siblings, we offered each other
minimal support as the family began to struggle with the disengagement
process. Gail was needed at home to balance the family, and she cooperated
by getting sick. Her cooperation was no accident. It was her turn to be the
favored child, and she wouldn't miss the opportunity. She tried to go out of
town to school again the next year but failed. I was concerned with my own
life and didn't interfere.

Then there was an ominous sign of change in the family, mirrored by my
father's behavior. To gain some recognition as a shrewd businessman, he
began to invest in speculative real estate deals. He was in over his head, but
kept pouring in his hard-earned money. That winter he had a mild heart
attack.

I was aware, when I came home the next summer, that my father was
worried about money. But then my mother and father suddenly decided to
build their dream house—smaller and cozier than the house I grew up in, a
creation to shelter the shrinking family. The new house was packed with
gadgets and the semblance of opulence. My mother was excited as she
showed me the plans and tried to engage me in the family's new venture,
but, although I feigned some interest, I looked down my nose at this
"builder's" house.

The summer passed; my father was reserved, my mother noisily enthusiastic. My mother, who had always been sensitive to status symbols but
resisted them herself, enjoyed her self-indulgence. I remained unimpressed.
I was preoccupied with thoughts of a man I had met over spring vacation
while skiing in Vermont. I wanted to see him but he wrote only once. I was
happy to return to school in the fall.

When I returned home at Thanksgiving, the situation had deteriorated
seriously. My father was obviously depressed. From their conversation I
found out that financial arrangements on the new house were going badly.
Construction had begun and my father had spent a great deal of money, but
the house was not as far along as he had hoped. He had no contract and
suspected that the real-estate sharpies might be taking him for a ride.

My mother also seemed worried, but she was busy with other plans. Her
two eldest daughters were seriously involved with men. My sister Gail was
engaged to a young man from a "fine family" in Buffalo who was a pre-med
student. I had planned to go skiing over Christmas with my friend. I told my
family that this was the man I hoped to marry.

Our family was undergoing extreme fragmentation. Two daughters were exiting. A third daughter had just entered adolescence. Two prospective sons-in-law and their families were introduced into the family, and their presence split the family even more by dividing loyalties. The schisms ran deep. Its members were departing too rapidly for the family to heal and integrate itself without feeling explosive fragmentation and amputation.

My father increasingly felt the family's malaise. He was isolated from those around him, and he alone faced the family's depletion of its resources. He focused on the concrete losses, the impending financial disaster, and the loss of self-esteem. At a time when he needed reassurance, he was too sad, too proud, and too deeply ashamed to get the legal help he needed on his own.

We all let him down. I was probably the most selfish, avidly gathering my trousseau and planning a lavish wedding. My self-centeredness was encouraged by my mother's wish that her eldest have the best. My sister Gail, ordinarily my father's ally, was involved with her own man. Brenda, the youngest sister and another of Daddy's girls, withdrew from the family into the narcissistic world of adolescence.

For years I secretly blamed my mother for my father's suicide. Where was she when he was so depressed, so withdrawn, that he barely spoke for days? I know now how much easier it was to blame her than to question myself. I had seen my father during spring vacation the summer before I married. I saw how troubled he was, how worried, how desperate. I had talked briefly to my mother, who immediately became agitated and helpless. But I never spoke to my father. For a long time I could not ask myself why. I knew the answer. I was planning my wedding. I was in love with life, ready to leave my family in exchange for the exciting prospects of living in New York near my husband's family. I would transfer my loyalties for as little as a Gucci handbag.

My father, cut off from his family, felt he was losing everything: his dignity, self-respect, and pride went with the money he had invested badly. He planned his death so as not to embarrass the family. Just two weeks before my sister's marriage, and while I was still on my honeymoon, my father drove across the state line and in a lonely hotel room took an overdose of sleeping pills.

It has taken years to recover from the shock of my father's suicide and to overcome the accusations and guilt that such a desperate act leaves the survivors. In twos and threes and in our private thoughts, we have talked and examined and explained the facts, and our feelings, and our regrets. It is part of our family history. At worst we secretly blame each other, isolate one another, and make his death a family secret, a taboo. At best we face our culpability, try to heal each other's hurts, and keep my father's memory alive.

* * *

My exposure to family therapy in graduate school coincided with leaving my family, getting married, and mourning my father's death. I was drawn to family therapy for reasons I could not then explain.

During the next eight years as a professional social worker, I received intensive training in family therapy with some of the best-known family therapists of the era. Examining family relationships, exploring conflicting sets of loyalties, wrenching separations, and unspoken secrets in my own family made the concepts of family therapy come alive for me. I was committed to a career as a family therapist and went back to Columbia University as a doctoral candidate.

My husband and I had our first child. The emotional link to my original family nourished my attachment to my husband and infant son. But the memories of my childhood were at odds with the circumstances of my father's death. That a basically happy family could be fractured by violent losses persisted to influence my work without my knowing it.

I began to write about the stress families experience from life-cycle events—birth, marriage, death—and began to chart, out of my personal and professional experience, the sequences of interpersonal changes that family members have to make.

I began to think about the circumstances which cause "normal" families to become stuck and to identify the conditions which combine at points in the life cycle and create that extra pressure which turns normal families from their course. Life's marker events, unexpected stress, and trouble spots in the previous generation were factors that seemed to contribute to the difficulty that families have in making the quantum leap from one stage of family life to another.

It is the "normal" as opposed to the obviously pathological family that has interested me. My ideas about the family life cycle are based on the assumption that families are naturally programmed for change and that they are both resistant to and capable of such change. But I also remember that families can be threatened by dangers they are not aware of and changes they do not know how to make.

Chapter 18

LETTING GO NATURALLY

Stage 5 means there are empty bedrooms in the house. They are used infrequently by children who are fully grown and almost mature, children who return from college, work, or travel for brief visits. Husbands and wives eat alone and no longer need to retreat to their bedroom for privacy.

Letting go is a natural progression from Stage 4, when children and parents struggled to free themselves from dependency on each other. Now children actually leave to make lives of their own. The family must confront its shrinking size, recoup from the shock of profound losses, and acknowledge that the family is undergoing the most radical transformation of its history.

Until now the membership of the family was a constant. Shifts in each stage were based on the changing needs of family members. But the family as a unit, unless parents divorced, stayed the same. Intact. The whole point of Stage 5 is launching children into the world.

Families let go in ways consistent with their personal styles. Disengaged families tend to release members suddenly. Overly close families wean their departing children slowly. Disturbed families trap their children and bind them to the family indefinitely.

For every family, impending and current departures add stress to all its relationships and jeopardize family survival. Under the stress of a series of exits, family cohesiveness can disappear and the family may remain ruptured.

WOMEN IN CRISIS

This period is especially stressful to women who are traditional homemakers. The vanishing focus of their lives can be traumatic. Sociologist Pauline B. Bart[1] describes the state of acute self-depreciation recognized among women in their forties and fifties. According to Bart, the steep decline in self-esteem results from loss of the central role of the caring mother and often leads to a severe depression that requires hospitalization. The displaced homemaker is more than out of a job. She may lose her identity.

At one time the hormonal changes connected with menopause were believed to cause this depression in women over fifty. Now contemporary behavioral science theory relates mid-life depression to changes in women's social role. The woman without commitments outside the family has to reorient her life at this stage. She must find a major focus for herself outside the family.

Many women welcome the shift and make the transition gracefully. They take courses, begin hobbies or volunteer work, or even start late careers. They enjoy and relish their free time. Some, for the first time in years, can pursue their own interests.

THE TWO-SEATER MERCEDES

In healthy families the marriage is vital enough to generate closeness between partners when children leave. The parenting function is virtually extinguished, and couples face each other without a child as go-between. For some couples Stage 5 brings an opportunity to revitalize their marriage. Time together is cherished, and a new life evolves. Companionship and romance are revived.

Couples who rediscovered each other in Stage 4 in the midst of adolescent chaos are in the best position to enjoy their relationship alone, as two adults, without children. As the children vacate the house one by one over a period of several years, husband and wife are comfortable with each other and relieved that disco music is no longer blaring in the background. Empty rooms bring peace, not bareness.

I recently talked with a couple who had two preteen children. The father was talking about romancing his wife in courtship. He loved his kids and was a family man, but he said that he and his wife had substituted family activities for socializing together. Being alone with his wife for a drive in the country, without lively conversation from the backseat, had become a secret obsession with him. He has a plan that when their last child goes off to college, he will buy a two-seater Mercedes sportscar. It's exactly this quality of looking forward to being alone that makes the transition to Stage 5 easier.

In fact one of the hallmarks of Stage 5 is that generations tend to group together: adults turn to adults; brothers and sisters turn to each other. Just as adults replace their loss by deepening their relationship, brothers and sisters can help each other move out of the family by creating a support system of their own.

SIBLING SUPPORT: BROTHERHOOD AND SISTERHOOD ARE POWERFUL[2]

Part of the regrouping along generational lines that helps families accomplish the momentous shifts required in Stage 5 involves the sibling system.

The way brothers and sisters help each other has been overlooked for a long time, partly because of the emphasis on sibling rivalry. Favoritism, competition, and jealousy commonly interfere with sibling cooperation, but they are the dark side of a brighter picture. In Stages 4 and 5 sisters and brothers at war since childhood discover ways to count on each other.

Rivalry keeps sisters and brothers from being allies. But comparisons tell siblings how they differ from one another in temperament, interests, talents, and outlook. All through life siblings bounce off each other as a way of finding out who they are as well as who they are not; what they are and what they want to be. Just as parents and other adults are models to emulate and criticize, brothers and sisters are foils for measuring growth and finding uniqueness.

Siblings who tattle on one another in younger years turn to each other as confidants in adolescence. If they are close in age, they are likely to confide their secrets and guard each other's privacy. They are natural allies, struggling for the same rights, sharing common insecurities and similar antagonisms to adults.

In Stages 4 and 5 brothers and sisters also need each other to counter parental authority. Siblings can form purposeful alliances to fight for later curfews, bigger allowances, and the privilege to travel alone. The argument may be persuasive if brother and sister can tag Dad alone. Up against Mom and Dad together, they are outnumbered, easily picked off, put down, or simply overruled.

A few years later the oldest "pioneers" for younger sisters and brothers.[3] He or she is the first to try marijuana, drive the family car, travel to Europe. The oldest gets the family used to the weird things adolescents do and makes it easier for younger brothers and sisters. Family rules change because one sibling initiates and wins permission for the others to follow.

In Stage 5 the first sibling to leave the nest paves the way for the others. For brothers and sisters left behind, it may be a sad loss. The balance of power in the family is destabilized, and children left behind feel vulnerable and overwhelmed by parental control. Sometimes a docile teenager becomes an overnight antagonist soon after an older sibling has left for college. This is fairly common in families and reflects a temporary loss of power in the sibling system.

Only in the last few years have family therapists become sensitive to the power of the sibling subgroup within the family. It is natural and healthy for siblings to have different roles, responsibilities, and privileges, based on differences in age. Family therapists encourage these differences but at the same time try to get siblings to depend on each other.

When brothers and sisters are too competitive or distant and unable to group together, it's because parents have made them divided for their own purposes. "Good" and "bad" siblings are created by the family. "Bad" siblings are almost always family scapegoats, and "good" siblings suffer privately from the problems buried in the family. None of these divisions makes whole people.

One pattern of sibling exploitation is so common that family therapists have given it a name: the family with a parental child.[4]

The parental child is not just an older child who shows leadership to younger siblings. The parental child is delegated by the parents to take over for them. This situation is common in large families, single-parent families, and working families, who may lean too hard and rely too much on the eldest female (and sometimes male) child to supervise younger children or run a household without realizing that the child is being trapped.

Perhaps more than in any other stage, the needs of the adolescent clash with the role of the parental child. The child tends to become withdrawn and depressed. To normalize the situation, parents have to move into leadership and return the parental child to the sibling subgroup.

PASSING THE TORCH[5]

As young-adult children help each other leave the nest, parents reexamine their relationships to their parents. Husband and wife are well into the mid-life crisis. Their own parents are elderly. Have they "won" adult status from their parents? Do their parents respect their adult achievements? Or are they still waiting to be appreciated by a stern father or taken seriously by a doting mother?

Have their parents made room by turning over the power, authority, and status held by the eldest living generation? Every healthy family must confront this problem at this stage.

In disturbed families, patriarchs are loath to retire, and adult children are controlled by aging parents till their parents die. In healthy families, elderly parents retreat gracefully from the central position and grant their adult sons and daughters the role of family leader.

One clue to how well the family will survive in Stage 5 has to do with how willing the older generations are to grant adult status to the younger generation. If a mother is still under Grandma's thumb, it's a sign that adult status is hard to come by in this family. A father who still takes orders from his father will have trouble letting his children go. The family problems continue and worsen with each successive generation.

Every family therapist assesses the way adults treat other adults in the three-generation family. The last family portrait in this stage, Family Legacies, examines how a close family discovered this problem in the aftermath of death and had to face the lie that had cemented family ties and distorted family relationships.

Chapter 19

HOLDING ON UNNATURALLY

Once children take on important roles in stabilizing their parents' marriage, they find it hard to give up these positions. The whole family is secretly determined to keep the family the same. Families dedicated to maintaining the status quo are in serious trouble in Stage 5. These families go to extremes to keep their children stuck in the family.

Because these families equate separation with abandonment, they cultivate a heavy-duty fear called breakaway guilt[6] in their adolescents. Parents cleverly avoid being abandoned by teaching their children to be helpless, fearful, and dependent. Independent, autonomous behavior automatically triggers guilt and overwhelming anxiety. Children learn to protect their parents from feeling abandoned by never being capable enough to leave home.

The following story shows how a family had to detour back to Stage 4 to pick up the threads that would make separation possible.

THE BENEVOLENT DICTATOR

Will Olson seated himself comfortably in my chair and stretched out his legs. "That's my chair, Mr. Olson. Do you want to take another seat?"

"Whoops, sorry, Doc." He got up quickly and selected a chair between his two daughters. Will grinned at me, but he had let me know that he was the power in the family.

In a dazzling display of verbosity, Will outlined his younger daughter's problem. Felicia, twenty-one years old, was desperately unhappy. After one and a half years at Midwestern University, she had returned home to live and planned to attend NYU. She had no friends. When she was at Midwestern she would call home long distance every night, sometimes two and three times, crying and complaining that she was lonely and miserable. She begged her parents for advice and guidance, then systematically proved that their suggestions couldn't work.

"We try to help her in every way we can," Will said earnestly. "We listen to her troubles, take her with us when we go out, make sure we have all her favorite foods in the house. But she seems more unhappy than ever." He described the many advantages Felicia had been given—the family trips to Europe, visits with Mom and Dad to museums and theaters, the best schools.

When Will paused to take a breath, I leaped into the monologue and asked if anyone else had anything to say. Before the words were out of my mouth, Will raised his voice and rolled on. It was a filibuster. This time he didn't stop for breath as he rolled out more and more details of Felicia's life.

I finally interrupted in my most officious manner to ask if anyone else in the family got a chance to talk except Will. Bonnie, the older daughter, who was a teacher, said that she had learned a lot about her family when she studied psychology, and that if she could see me alone, she would share her insights.

I half-heartedly said I might take her up on her offer but that now I was concerned that the whole family let Dad do the talking. Felicia's inability to leave home, her loneliness, the clinging to her parents were all signals that the family was having trouble letting the children go.

"I know how Will views the family problem," I said, "But how do the rest of you see the situation?"

I looked at Will's wife, Jean Olson, inviting her to join in. She sat with her back stiff, hands folded in her lap. Jean calmly described Felicia's room: "Her clothes and belongings are spread out into two upstairs bedrooms. Her own room is so crowded that she's moved into Bonnie's old room." Now that her twenty-five-year-old sister had married and moved into a house with her husband, Felicia was literally filling two spaces.

It seemed that Jean was not as sympathetic about Felicia's problems as her husband was. Will immediately spoke up to soften the tension that was building up in Jean's voice, and in his rational, friendly way gave Felicia a few tips on cleaning her room.

"Wait a minute, Will. Felicia's shit is covering the top floor of the house and Jean doesn't like it. She has a right to say so."

"Doc, that's not a nice way to talk," he countered. "The kid is just a little disorganized and needs some pointers on how to keep her things in order. There's nothing wrong with that."

It was clear that Will was determined to keep the peace. He was the rule keeper, and the most important rule was that all the family relationships were harmonious, everyone cooperated, and there was never any conflict among them. This arrangement had successfully stifled all anger, rebellion, and defiance, and made it almost impossible for Felicia and Bonnie to separate from the family.

By making herself needy and dependent Felicia was continuing a tradition of parental involvement in her life, enticing her parents into helping her, and then defeating them by continuing to be unhappy no matter how much they did for her.

This behavior is typical in early adolescence as parents and children struggle to free themselves of overly close ties with each other. Usually, parents and adolescents get fed up and back away from one another. This backing away frees young people and lets them strike out on their own.

The overprotective style of the Olson family should have died a natural death when Felicia was in her mid-teens. For some reason, this stage of family life had continued beyond its natural life, and Felicia was stuck in adolescence. She was having trouble growing up, making friends, and creating a world of her own. Instead of using college as a springboard into a broader existence, she was narrowing her life, literally retreating into the center of the family.

From her earlier comments about Felicia's room, I sensed that with a little encouragement Jean might break the family rule of total harmony. I pressed her to explain her view of the situation.

"I don't think this has anything to do with her problem," she said, "but she really is very messy." Jean spoke of Felicia in ways that were typical of any mother describing an adolescent daughter: Felicia was sloppy; she left the dishes in the sink, failed to clean her bathroom, played her stereo too loud. Felicia smiled provocatively as her mother spoke.

Will was noticeably uncomfortable. Even in this very ordinary family recital, the tension was too much for him, and he tried to reduce the heat building up between Jean and Felicia. He tried to smooth things over.

"I'm sure that doesn't have anything to do with her feeling so bad," he said. "She just needs a little help in the housekeeping department." He began to reiterate all of Felicia's nice qualities and summed up: "We just want to find a way to make her feel happier." Jean withdrew and said no more.

As a couple, they seemed united, with Jean supporting everything Will said, whether she believed it or not. If she didn't agree with him, she retreated. "I don't like to fight with him," she said.

Felicia mentioned that her parents always looked like one person, joined and undifferentiated. She never thought of them as two people. Yet as I looked at the family, I noticed that Felicia was sitting between Mom and Dad, and Bonnie sat on the other side of Mom. The parents were separated and surrounded by children. I shifted the seating arrangement and asked the girls to sit on the other side of the room.

Jean and Will had a pseudomutual relationship that set the tone for all the relationships in the family.[7] Their closeness was a façade, paid for at the expense of Jean's having a voice in the family. Why was Jean so overpowered by Will? What was she afraid of? Jean was not a passive woman by nature. She was a volunteer administrator of a large fund-raising organization and was active in community affairs. Why was she reduced to nothingness in her own family?

For one thing, Jean said, she was afraid that if she disagreed with Will, he would get excited. "Will has a heart condition," she said. "I really fear for him." Will's physical ailment had been incorporated into the family system to reinforce its basic pattern and to resist change.

Jean told a story about her original family. She and her brother used to fight over who would have the last piece of candy, but the fight was the opposite of what they really wanted. Protestations of "you have it"—"no, you take it," competitive generosity, false altruism were the hallmarks of her early life.

In her adult life, Jean was falsely generous to her husband by giving him all the power. Their marriage was a partnership from which one partner had resigned. With two daughters approaching womanhood, Jean's surrender to Will was a poor model of self-esteem.

Will and Jean were bathed in a compatibility that prevented their conflicts from erupting. To learn what they were so carefully protecting, I needed to understand more about their relationship. But the Olsons had not come for marital counseling. They were in family therapy because they were concerned for their daughter Felicia, who, although she was a young adult in years, was stalemated in early adolescence. This is a common dilemma for many families: the basic problem is marital but no one wants to know it.

Although they did not believe their marriage was part of their daughter's problem, Will and Jean agreed to come alone to a session the following week. The first basic thing we uncovered was that they both had a methodical approach to life. In their respective professions orderliness was an asset and systematization paid off. Time was carefully structured and chaos was unbearable.

As any parent of teenagers will tell you, chaos is a part of family life. Not only must parents have a reasonably high thermostat for tension, but an almost unlimited tolerance for the unpredictable. Neither of the Olson's had these qualities.

Yet they had managed quite well when the girls were young. From the beginning Will had been the more willing nurturer in the family. "He was so protective and loving towards the children," Jean said. "He was interested in every stage of their development from the time they were little babies."

Jean, easily rattled and exhausted by the children, found it easy to turn over more and more child-care responsibilities to such a willing father. As the girls grew older, Will spent his evenings and all his spare time helping them with their homework, acting as art director for their shoe-box projects, and supervising every aspect of their lives. "Will and I never had any time together, no private life together."

Will assumed that Jean was satisfied with their "close-knit" family style. But, in fact, a profound distance grew up between husband and wife.

We looked back to the older generation for patterns that repeat themselves. We already knew that Jean had been trained to assume this giving up attitude. What was the pattern in Will's family?

Will, the youngest child in his family, visited his elderly parents several times a week. Often he would skip dinner and drive for two hours to their house in the country just to look in on them, then turn around and drive back. Every weekend, every day off, every vacation, Will visited his parents. He was kind and generous and, as everyone in the family knew, a "soft touch." Will exhausted himself doing things for his family.

Will's family had always been close, but now that his parents were growing old, he quarreled with his brother and sister because "they don't do enough for the folks."

"It's not so much that they don't do enough," Jean pointed out. "But they don't do what Will thinks should be done."

Will, normally good natured and smiling, was angry that his brother and sister didn't spend more time with their parents. But he ignored the fact that his brother cared for the property around their parents' old home, and all three siblings shared the extra expenses for their parents.

Will was running—and ruining—everyone's life with his goodness. Despite the distance between them, the Olsons' marriage was stable and durable, and there was no threat of divorce. But the parent-child bonds were stronger than the marital bonds. If parenthood was extinguished by children leaving home, the marriage would be threatened.

After Bonnie got married, Felicia's continued dependence kept Will in business, and sustained the familiar distance between husband and wife. Bonnie had failed to pioneer for her sister. In fact, her departure seemed to increase Felicia's dependency. Bonnie admitted that the more her parents fussed over Felicia the less attention they paid to her and her new husband. And she liked it that way. So she never had tried to help her sister win her wings into the wider world.

What would happen in the family now if Jean began to take a stronger position? After so many years could the marriage adjust to a new set of rules?

I knew that if Jean took a more active role with her daughters there would be some extra pressure on the marriage, and the familiar balance between closeness/distance would shift. I suggested that Will and Jean prepare themselves by beginning to spend some time alone.

We focused on the changes needed in the family relationship to help the children move on. Will and Jean did not want to radically alter their lives, so we concentrated on just those aspects of marriage that directly affected the release of the children.

Giving Jean a voice in the family was critical. She had to exercise her right to have an opinion and could no longer submerge her views. Jean was less tolerant than Will of Felicia's sloppiness and dependency. It was important for her to directly confront her daughter on these issues. There were many examples of Felicia's demands, and the Olsons endlessly trying to please her. For example, Felicia expected to be driven to her dance class every day during the summer. Jean complied because it was a family rule never to say no. But she really felt Felicia should walk or make her own arrangements.

I pushed Jean to set limits, say no, bring the battle between parents and children out in the open. Will, of course, objected. Given his own nature, it would be almost impossible for him to tolerate conflict. But it wasn't impossible for Jean. If she could change, she would help the girls.

Over the next few months we worked with all family combinations, sometimes all four members together, often in pairs because the family tended to create triangular relationships and they needed to sustain one-to-one relationships.

In those sessions when Will and Jean came alone, Jean could freely complain about the kids (which Will found unbearable if the girls were present). They planned a two-week vacation together, which was a long time in materializing because Will worried that Felicia would languish without them.

In the midst of our work together, a family secret was exploded. At this point, Will and Jean were enjoying each other as a couple, and Jean was taking a stronger role in the family. Felicia was now viewed by both her parents as an insufferable adolescent. For a while at least, they had to let their twenty-one-year-old daughter be a sixteen-year-old adolescent, a privilege they had denied her when she was really sixteen.

The family myth was that Will was like a strong fortress that protected the rest of them. Everyone agreed that he was overprotective, but always added, "He's just trying to take care of us for our own good." But Felicia began to put her finger on the noxious elements of her father's benevolence. Will's loving protection undermined her confidence.

For example, on Felicia's first day at college, Will insisted on taking her to school. NYU is located almost in the heart of Manhattan, practically Felicia's backyard. Yet Will said he was worried about her traveling alone on the subway and didn't seem to think she could hail a cab by herself. His protectiveness made her feel weak and incompetent. He assumed she was both helpless and irresponsible. Furthermore, he created a picture of a world populated by dangers. The only safe place was in the family, with Daddy at the helm.

When the girls were small, they couldn't roller skate in front of the house unless he was with them; couldn't play in the schoolyard after school because they might get hurt; couldn't go to other kids' houses because something might happen and there wouldn't be a grownup around (Will was the only grownup); could not go to see a play or a movie without their parents—even if other adults were present. Will had completely convinced the girls—and Jean—that this was the way a close, loving family behaved. They didn't need anyone else because they had each other.

Whenever she had any desire to hang out with the kids on the block, or go to a party, Felicia was overcome with guilt feelings. She worried about hurting anyone and spent days trying to make a decision. If she went, would Daddy feel hurt? If she didn't would the kids be hurt? In desperation, she would put the problem at Will's feet, and Will would assure her that she didn't want to go anyway.

Both Felicia and Bonnie felt isolated from the outside world. Felicia especially kept herself from joining in, was easily rattled, and worried excessively about hurting people's feelings.

By not joining the outside world, the girls protected Will and made sure he felt needed. Will—big, brash, confident—really felt quite uncomfortable in the world. He used his family as a shield. Although he was extremely likable, Will had few personal friends. He was an ultimate giver, and he treated adults the same way he treated his children. He would give them anything, if in return they let him rule.

After her parents began to renew their personal relationship Felicia worked on career problems and developed relationships outside the family. She graduated from college and continued to move in and out of the family as she struggled with her fears of the wider world.

Chapter 20

FAMILY SECRETS

Every family has secrets that family members loyally guard. Some secrets are common—hostility disguised as affection, tyranny in the guise of benevolence, sexual infidelity, marital rifts. Others are more unusual—illegitimacy, mental illness in the family, alcoholism, incest, suicide. The nature of the secret is not important. What matters is how family members *perceive* the secret, and how much they invest in protecting the secret. Some families protect secrets and destroy their children in the process.

To keep a secret, many lies—or myths—have to be made up. These myths build like an inverse pyramid: a secret no bigger than a pea is on the bottom, and the myths build up on top of it until the whole structure begins to tremble of its own weight. The bigger the investment, the more myths and lies the family tells. The pressure increases, family relationships become distorted, and often the family shatters.

Children are especially burdened because they sense the secret but they can't tattle. They live in a shadow of partial truths, taboos, vague answers, and contradictions that don't make sense.

Most secrets are buried in the history of the family, and sometimes family members don't even know exactly what the secret is. These secrets are kept from the world and also from the family itself. The myths surrounding the secret are passed on from generation to generation and are hard to shake.[8]

Family secrets can be protected for several generations, but with each successive generation the recycled secret and its growing volume of myths and lies distort the family more. Family secrets and myths, like all family problems, are not passed on if they are exposed, confronted, and dealt with.

PRISONERS

Dolores DiBono was frightened when her twenty-year-old daughter rang the doorbell at four o'clock one morning. "She said she had a new job as a go-go dancer in a nightclub and had just gotten off work and thought she'd drop in. And we live way up in Bronxville. She seemed high and spaced out. She said, 'Why don't we have a nightcap?' and got a bottle of Scotch from the liquor cabinet and started drinking it straight, out of a water glass. Finally she just passed out on the sofa. She's been doing this sort of thing for months—coming and going at all hours of the day and night. Sometimes she stays an hour, sometimes a week. Once she came home with a black eye and a swollen lip and said she was mugged coming out of the subway. We don't know what to do for her anymore, and we're scared something awful's going to happen to her."

Although Sharon was no longer a child in the strict sense of the word, a consultation with the whole family was needed, since it was her mother who called and the family seemed caught up in her behavior. But on the day of the family appointment, Sharon showed up alone.

"My folks couldn't make it," she said. "It's Friday and they had plans to go away for the weekend."

"I guess that means I'm supposed to fix you up and send you back a reformed daughter?"

"I guess so," Sharon said.

I didn't like the assignment. Lots of kids are sent to therapists the way Sharon had been sent to me. The family says, "You're the crazy one—leave us out of this." From that moment on, if the therapist accepts the assignment, he or she is working for the parents, and the therapy is dead-ended for the adolescent, who, by refusing to cooperate with the therapist, finds an ideal way to defeat his or her parents.

Sharon and I considered each other. She was restless and fidgeted in her chair, looking out the window, at the ceiling, at each piece of furniture in the office; then she looked directly at me, her eyes full of disdain and challenge. She was a beautiful girl, with dark hair and luminous gray eyes. But her jeans and blue silk shirt looked soiled and her makeup was turning orange, as if it had been on for days. Mascara collected in smudges like thumbprints beneath her eyes.

By mutual consent we decided to spend at least one hour together. Sharon painted a vivid description of her secret life. Her family knew she had dropped out of college and was living with a black man named Hal, who they believed supported her. The family disapproved of Hal because they suspected he used dope, although Sharon said, "They really hate him because he's black. They say they don't, but they're lying." Actually, according to Sharon, Hal was both a sometime user and a full-time dealer. "He deals everything," she said proudly, "typewriters, calculators, hot computers. Even guns. I mean, we walk down the street in the neighborhood and *everybody* shakes his hand. Hal is everybody's man."

Sharon was clearly excited by Hal and the power he generated. "Just nothing fazes him, you know—everything's possible with Hal. You want it—you got it."

There was a snag in the relationship. Sharon had depended on Hal for everything, from fur coats to cigarette money. Ninety percent of the time they lived high, but they hit a financial crisis every time the rent was due. "We have money for all the fabulous stuff, but when it comes to the nitty-gritty like the electric bill or the telephone bill, we're always short." Sharon and Hal luxuriated in sniffing coke, drove a white Cadillac, and took flash trips to San Juan and Las Vegas, but frequently had no money for food.

Sharon loved the ups, but the big downs were hard to cope with. She felt she was a victim of Hal's mercurial approach to money and that the only way she could influence their roller-coaster financial affairs was to acquire money of her own. She tried a string of jobs, but they never lasted more than a couple of weeks. For a while she worked as an office temporary and would often take an assignment only to walk out in the middle of the day, not even collecting the pay she had earned. Sometimes she never even arrived. As we talked, she yawned. It was 11 A.M. and she had been up all night. Sharon and Hal partied all night and slept in the day.

It hadn't taken long for Sharon, wanting big money and part-time evening work, to find a solution to her problem. Young and pretty, she became a high-priced prostitute. "I'm a working girl," she said, "if you know what that is. Sometimes I make as much as a thousand dollars a day—more than you'll ever see. All women are prostitutes anyway," she continued, "giving sex to men. I'm just more honest about it, and this way I'm in control of my body." She privately sneered at the men who thought they turned her on.

"Does your family know about any of this?"

"They don't know a thing. They'd never dream their baby could do what I do. My father, especially. He's such a goddamned perfect goody-goody. God, he'd fall over dead if he knew."

"How about your mother?"

"I don't know—she's kind of vague. She doesn't know what's happening half the time anyway. I mean, she'd feel miserable and cry and think she'd done something awful."

For the moment I sidestepped the issue of prostitution, but agreed with Sharon that her desire for independence and control over her life was important. She told me she was one of the few prostitutes who didn't turn her money over to a pimp. She was an independent operator. Yet even this was not giving her what she wanted.

"Every time I get ahead, I have to bail Hal out, loan him money to make his dope buys, which he never catches up on." She had come home one morning to find their expensive East Side apartment stripped of its custom-made furniture and her fur coats missing. Hal had needed money fast and had sold their belongings to a junk dealer.

"It sounds like the only thing that keeps Hal from being your pimp is a trick of language."

Sharon was furious when I said this. "He's not my pimp. It's my money—I do what I like with it. And I do what I like with my life."

"Then what's your problem? Why don't you leave him if he's causing you so much trouble?"

"He'd come after me—or he'd send someone after me. I left him once, and these three guys caught me on the street and beat the shit out of me."

"Was that when you went home and told your mother you'd been mugged?"

"Yeah."

Whenever Sharon needed money or when she was sick, she returned to her family. These crises occurred at least once a month, sometimes more, and kept the action going between Sharon and her parents. Her mother called her every day, lent her money, and brought her groceries and homemade lasagna. Her father had high expectations for his daughter and couldn't stand the idea that she was wasting her life. Whenever Sharon came home, he lectured her and demanded that she get her life straightened out. After a week or ten days, Sharon would leave again and go back to Hal. She had been repeating this cycle for more than a year.

"Sharon, what appeals to you about your life?"

"Mostly the money—I like living high. I like driving a big car and wearing a mink coat. I like going to any club or restaurant I want to. The other night we went out and spent three hundred dollars on dinner. I like it."

"What don't you like?"

"There's only one thing I don't like. I don't like the financial insecurity. If Hal was just a little more reliable about money, I wouldn't have any complaints."

"Even about your job?"

"I like my job."

"Sounds like you're in a bind. I mean, you don't like Hal's number with money, but you can't change him and you can't get rid of him. I think you need to find a way to get on with your life and stop bouncing back and forth between Hal and your folks. Don't you?"

"I guess so."

"Why don't we get your parents in here to work with us for a while?"

The following week Dolores and Joe DiBono came in with Sharon. Joe was a big man who carried himself like a prizefighter. Dolores, a tall blonde in her early forties, was a perfect match for him. They were a gorgeous couple, brimming with style and affluence. Sharon, too, was dressed to kill, even though it was nine o'clock in the morning. She wore a scarlet silk chemise top that left her shoulders and much of her breasts bare, skintight jeans, and heels at least four inches high. Her hair exploded in a cloudy frizz around her face and halfway down her back. She sat directly across the room from her parents but didn't look at them.

Joe plunged in. "Sharon's floundering around, and we think she needs some help getting back on the track. Her mother's alarmed at her behavior and so am I. And we don't like her living with this guy Hal."

Sharon flared up immediately. "You don't even know him—you won't even have him over. He might contaminate you with his blackness."

"I don't care if he's green—he's a lowlife."

The DiBonos didn't seem to know what Hal did for a living but they suspected that he was a user and were panicked at the sight of his custom Cadillac, the flashy clothes, and no visible means of support.

Dolores and Joe, although they were wise to the ways of the world, had no idea that their daughter was a hooker. They had come up the hard way, both children of poor families. Joe was determined to make a better life for himself and his family. He devised an early form of fast-food family restaurants, a diner-cum-cafeteria that eventually grew into a chain.

After their first restaurant became successful, Dolores stopped working and stayed home with their two young daughters. Joe became enormously successful and influential in community affairs. His restaurants sponsored a multitude of educational and outdoor programs for young people, particularly deprived and handicapped children.

In the session Joe took charge and laid it out for me. Both Dolores and Sharon remained silent, seemingly in awe of his power.

"Sharon," Joe boomed, "we don't like the way you're living your life. You have no sense of responsibility and you're running around with the wrong people. I can get you a nice job in an office, a good nine-to-five job, and you can reapply to college. You'll come home to live and leave that no-good Hal up to me."

Sharon gazed at the ceiling.

Dolores said, "Sheri, sweetie, you don't look like you're eating right. Do you and Hal keep enough food in the house? Do you need to go to a doctor? I think you're too thin."

"Oh, Mom, come on. You're always fussing over us."

"I just want what's best for you, honey. I worry about you all the time."

"Mom, I'm a big girl. Don't worry about me. I can take care of myself."

"If you could take care of yourself," Joe boomed again, "we wouldn't be here!"

There was a pause, then, "Did you eat that lasagna I brought over the other night?"

"Yes, Mom . . . it was yummy."

I saw over and over again that Dolores and Sharon were allied, and that Joe had a reserved seat outside the family.

Sharon at twenty was too old to be still expressing abolescent rebellion. There had to be more to her behavior than adolescent acting-out. Sharon's problems started when her older sister finally managed to leave home for college after several years of stalemate. For some reason Dolores and Joe were holding their kids back. But it was hard to figure. They seemed geuninely affectionate toward one another. They were young and lively. Why were they afraid to be alone?

I moved Sharon's chair nearer to my desk and asked her to merely observe or consult with me if she had anything to say. Then I asked Dolores and Joe to talk about some personal problem between them, anything, no matter how silly or trivial it seemed. I asked Dolores to go first.

Shyly she began to describe a minor domestic problem (which I later learned was a long-standing, deeply festering gripe). "I never know when Joe will be home for dinner, and sometimes I spend a whole evening waiting for him, trying to keep the food warm. Sometimes he calls at eight or nine and says that he's stuck at a meeting and won't be home at all."

"Dolores, Joe's sitting right here. You can work it out directly with him. Talk to him."

Joe interrupted. "Listen, I sit on eight different boards. It's impossible for me to control my hours. And I can't break up a meeting just to run out and telephone you when I'm not even sure how long we're going to be. It's ridiculous. What am I going to say, 'Listen, I'm still in a meeting, I don't know what time it'll be over?' What good would that do you?"

Dolores shrugged her shoulders and gave up. She looked back to me.

"It must be a frustrating situation for you," I said. "It's important to you. Don't give up."

Again Joe verbally overpowered her. "It's just a fact of life that you have to live with. I don't see why it's such a big deal. We're wasting our time."

Sharon, seeing her mother defeated, couldn't stay out of their exchange. "You think you're such a big shot," she yelled at her father. "Such an important person with your meetings and your boards and all your crap. Big fucking deal."

"This is between your parents, Sharon. Why are you butting in?"

"Because she won't do it herself. She never stands up for herself."

"What would happen if you didn't speak for your mother?"

"He'd just walk right over her. She's soft."

"What do you mean, soft? How soft?"

Sharon screamed at her mother, "You get abused and exploited and taken advantage of by men."

In this brief exchange the complete family pattern was suddenly illuminated as though a flare had exploded above a dark landscape.

Sharon was the frustrated, angry voice of her powerless mother. Sharon accused Joe of being "high and mighty. It's easy for you to talk about me—you're perfect. Everything's easy for you. You never make mistakes, and you never fail. And you expect everybody else to be as good as you."

In one sense Dolores put Joe on a pedestal and supported his tremendous need to feel important. Then from her weakened position, she set Sharon on him to tear him down.

Buy why? Why was this elaborate system necessary—this building up and tearing down of Joe's ego? Why did he seem to need and demand glory, yet so docilely accept ridicule? What did Sharon's secret life as a prostitute have to do with all this?

The DiBonos had described their problem in terms of Sharon's behavior so many times that it seemed hopeless to get anything fresh out of them. They had drawn the picture of successful father, happy home, and delinquent daughter so often that they were now doing it with their eyes shut. But I kept asking questions, because invariably the corner the light doesn't reach is the one the dime rolled into.

We began to piece together the details of the DiBonos' youth and their early relationship. Joe tried to explain how hard it was for him and Dolores to make something of their lives. Joe grew up in the slums of Baltimore. "Then after we got married," he said, "I realized that I had to make something of my life."

"How old were you when you got married?"

"Twenty-two."

"What did you do before that?"

There was a long silence before Joe said, "Nothing much, this and that."

"Did you go to college?"

"No."

"Daddy!"

"I never went to college—everybody thinks I did. I didn't even finish high school."

"Oh, Joe, you don't have to tell them everything."

I ignored Dolores's interruption. "You dropped out of high school. Then what did you do between that time and the time you got married? I'm just trying to understand about your early life and your own family."

There was a long silence. I could hear the clock ticking in the room.

"I was in prison."

I had suspected there was another secret in the DiBono family, but I did not suspect for a moment that it was a secret as crucial as Joe's.

"I was in prison," he repeated, and he might as well have dropped a bomb in the office. Sharon was absolutely rigid in her chair. I was not so much shocked as caught off guard. Dolores sat quietly, tears streaming down her face.

Joe began to tell the story as if he had been rehearsing all his life for this moment.

When he was fifteen years old, he, along with other boys in his neighborhood, was a member of a gang. One night, armed with knives and Saturday night specials, the boys broke into a warehouse. The night guard heard them and sounded the alarm. In their flight, the boys fired haphazardly. Bullets slammed into the warehouse walls, and ricocheted off the steel loading platform; the guard was wounded by a flying stray bullet. The gang was captured by the police and convicted of armed robbery and assault with a deadly weapon. Joe spent the next five years in prison.

At twenty, Joe was an ex-con, back on the street with a lifetime of misery and guilt already behind him. He had to take the sleaziest jobs where references weren't required and no one asked where he went to school. He washed dishes, swept floors, and bussed tables.

At one big restaurant where he got a job washing dishes, the boss liked him and Joe worked his way up into kitchen jobs and eventually got to be a cook's assistant. Here he learned the ins and outs of restaurant work. From there, he was able to get other jobs in other restaurants, using his old employer as a reference. No one checked further.

From that grim, unhappy time of his life, Joe built a life and a position in the world that is the envy of many people, including his own family. The peculiar aspect of the situation is that he has never been recognized or appreciated for his most remarkable achievement, creating this valuable life out of complete defeat. People assume he had advantages common to most men of his position. But it's well known that ex-offenders have a tough time staying straight on the outside, and it's rare for a person who's served time in prison, with no money or family to help him, to create the life and position that Joe DiBono had.

But Joe lived a masquerade. His associates assumed he was well educated and had a college degree. He had only a high-school-equivalency diploma, earned while he was in reform school. He had never been inside a college, except on scholarship committees. Joe mixed and mingled with university presidents and politicians, but he always felt like an outsider.

All families have secrets. They usually involve sore points the family has tried to ignore because recognition would somehow make things worse. For example, a husband and wife grow bored with each other sexually and no longer sleep together, but never talk about it. They sense that to discuss it might expose something seriously wrong in the marriage; that words alone would create upheaval or possibly even separation and divorce. It seems easier to ignore the problem and continue the family pattern that is only partially rewarding.

In this situation, however, the family secret was not only kept from the world but from the family itself. Only Dolores knew about Joe's past. The children hadn't the slightest idea that their father was not everything he appeared to be. Their dad was the great man—accomplished, polished, successful, humanitarian, self-made.

This deeply hidden secret had twisted the family system, beginning with Joe himself. He was so afraid that his past would emerge, that it wasn't enough to be good or successful, he had to be invincible. He was so afraid that the criminal still resided in his soul that he tried to extinguish every flaw in his character, every minor infraction of social law. He was not simply husband and father, he was the perfect person. This was the myth that protected the secret.

Dolores, his partner in life, was forced to help him preserve the masquerade to the extent that she was afraid to challenge him or criticize him for anything. Over the years, the myth of Joe's infallibility had grown into an enormous burden.

Husbands and wives cannot live like this, no matter how much they love each other. Since Dolores could not speak against Joe, Sharon did it for her. Sharon didn't even know what she was doing—she didn't know about the family secret, yet she effectively and consistently kicked away at Joe's pedestal, sneering at him and ridiculing him, scoffing at the great man whose perfection made her feel so inadequate. Sharon harbored her own secret life as well. She was destroying herself to prove to Joe that he was not—could not be—Mr. Wonderful, not because he had been in prison but because his own daughter was a prostitute. "If I make a mess of my life," Sharon seemed to be saying, "you're not perfect." At the same time she created a relationship with Hal that almost exactly mirrored the darker side of her parents.

Sharon thought she was tougher and more able to take care of herself than she really was. She played at being an adult by living the high life with Hal. When she crashed, her parents gave her a home and another role to play. Swinging between Hal and her parents, she had the best of both worlds—the comforts of middle-class care (clean house, stable environment) and the high, instant gratification of the street, where everything was the pleasure of the moment.

At this point Joe and Dolores decided to use family therapy for themselves. This was the right time in their lives for them to take a look at their marriage: their children were grown and, except for Sharon, out of the nest. There was no reason for Dolores to be sitting around the house all day waiting for Joe to come home. They both admitted this. There was almost no resistance from either of them to getting Dolores's life back on the track.

Over the next few months Dolores made some radical changes in her life. When people are ready to change, it doesn't take long for them to do it. Dolores went to night school, got involved in local community projects, joined some of the committees and clubs that Joe was active in, and began to have a social life of her own. She no longer made dinner and waited for Joe to come home.

It was interesting that mother and daughter were in exactly the same stage of growth, even though in the conventional world Dolores passed for well adjusted and Sharon looked dangerously neurotic. Education, work, and personal identity eluded them. Who and what were they as women? Could they manage for themselves? Were they important? Did they count? Could they live with men without being exploited?

But Sharon was unable to follow the adjustments made by her mother. Although Joe and Dolores no longer needed her to keep their secret, Sharon herself was not ready to shift gears in her life. She was too deeply embedded to readily abandon her position now, even though she was no longer needed to cut her Dad down to size or remind her parents of their past.

When a family distorts itself to protect someone, even the person who looks like the victim gets something out of it. I asked myself what Sharon got out of this situation. Coming home whenever she was in trouble—which was often—assured her that she was loved, that she mattered, that she had power. It kept her from feeling completely worthless, a feeling that cropped up in her life with Hal. It also let her express anger toward her father. She enjoyed flaunting her life-style in Joe's face.

Sharon could not give it up. But I knew part of her wanted to. She started to lose weight and went down to a dangerous level. Week after week I saw her growing thinner until I brought a scale into the office and made her stand on it. She was down to ninety pounds. She hadn't eaten in days, she said, and when she did, she threw up. I insisted that she see a doctor. Her health became so critical that she had to quit "working" and move back home. "I'm too skinny," she said. "The customers don't like me anymore."

Was Sharon protecting herself from prostitution by risking her life? Was she simply trading one form of self-destruction for another?

Sharon recovered her health, but she resisted any basic changes in herself. Within weeks she was back at work and back in the apartment she shared with Hal. And a few weeks after that, she knocked on her parents' door begging them for money.

She was determined to continue her life as it was. "It's Hal that's screwing everything up," she insisted. "If he'd only leave me alone, I'd be all right." She counterpunched every suggestion.

"What if you stopped turning tricks and took a straight job?"

"Where am I going to make a thousand dollars a day? Forget it."

"At least Hal would leave you alone if you didn't have any money."

"Sure; but that's the whole point. I wouldn't have any money. I like money."

"If you like money so much and if you like your work as much as you say, why don't you go to another town and start all over again. You could go to any big city and do what you're doing here. Hal's not going to follow you to Chicago or Los Angeles."

Sharon thought this over for a moment. I could almost see the wheels turning. What would happen if she went somewhere else, where she had no family to run to, no boyfriend to pressure her?

"That's impossible," she said finally, "and you know it."

"I don't know it. I only know what you tell me. Why is it impossible?"

"I'd probably get killed, for one thing. I mean, you don't just drop into town and get a job in a high-class place like I've got here. You've got to know people, have connections."

Sharon and I were going around in circles and we both knew it. She was determined to block all access to change. It was still vital to her to stay trapped in the situation with Hal.

"Sounds like you're stuck, then."

Joe and Dolores felt absolutely helpless. I felt the best way to help Sharon was to stop letting her drag herself back home every time she was in trouble.

Dolores said, "I don't think I can do that. She's our daughter, and our home is her home. We can't turn her away when she's in trouble."

"Besides," Joe said, "she'd just go to someone else—street people. We'd rather she'd come home to us when she's in trouble."

"Well, she would try to go to other people. But her friends aren't likely to accept her problems for very long, especially when it comes to lending her money. They'll help her once or twice, then tell her to get herself straightened out. They don't feel guilty about her like you do. Eventually she would have to realize that she has to take care of herself."

"You hope," Dolores said.

"Yes—I hope. I can't guarantee it and I don't know what will happen. But I know this way isn't helping anyone, certainly not Sharon. It only fuels her up so she can go back and hurt herself all over again. One of these days Hal's going to hit her too hard, or she'll overdose."

Joe and Dolores couldn't reject her, and I didn't blame them. It's easy for a therapist to tell parents that they have to bottom-line it with their kids, but how do parents turn away the children they love when they come home for help?

We had already discussed how Dolores and Sharon were in a similar stage of life, even though one was some twenty years older than the other. Our remaining hope was that the changes Dolores made for herself would eventually affect Sharon. Originally Sharon had inherited her fears and insecurities from Dolores. Now, perhaps, as her mother strides forward and personally solves some of the problems that plague them both, these changes also will filter down to her daughter.

Now that the secret is out, Sharon is no longer required to voice Dolores's protests or remind her parents of the past with her dangerous life-style. Her job was to blow the family cover, and it's over now. Sharon should have a chance to face her own problems more directly than ever before. But it is impossible to predict whether she will be able to benefit from the changes that have taken place in the larger fabric of her family. Family habits are strong, and members are deeply affected by family history.

Only time tells how much of a toll family secrets take. Some secrets die hard. One family uncovered a family secret at the grave.

FAMILY LEGACIES

In the early summer of 1979, the remaining members of Philip Dobson's family convened in New York.

Philip's wife and children had scattered like a flock of dispersed homing pigeons when he died almost a year earlier, and now his son and daughters flew into various airports around the city and made their way to the small apartment rented by their mother on Manhattan's upper West Side. Irene Dobson, Philip's widow, waited for them with a kind of heart-thumping anticipation.

For several weeks each member of the family had looked forward to the reunion with a mixture of pleasure and anguish, for their meeting was neither a day of mourning nor a day of celebration. The children had come to help their mother dismantle their big West Side co-op and sort out all their personal belongings. The apartment had already been stripped of most of its furniture and was a hollow, echoing reminder of the happy family they had been.

Not that they weren't happy to see each other, but in some ways the family members so close to Philip Dobson were strangers to each other.

The four people who came together now were radically different from the grieving family members who had taken their departure a year before. Irene, the wife and mother, was now a husbandless, childless woman. Susan, the baby of the family, was now a married woman expecting a child of her own. Leslie, the oldest, was garnering an advanced degree and dreaming of entering the political arena. And Robert, the middle child, was a wandering evangelist.

"I was so eager to see them," Irene said. "But as soon as the kissing and hugging and crying was over, we started to have problems. Part of the problem was that the apartment is so small. It's only a studio, so we had to rent a roll-away bed and Robert slept on the floor, and it was such a mess on a day-to-day living arrangement."

From the first day of the reunion, the Dobsons started to irritate each other. "Even Leslie, who's been such a help to me this last year, seemed to turn against me. I felt my children were aligned against me and I against them, but I didn't know why. We had always been so close when Philip was alive."

"When Philip was alive" a phrase repeated almost endlessly by Irene. "Mom never needed anyone but Daddy," the girls said. "He was everything to her."

"Mother seems to think that she's the only one who should mourn for Daddy," Susan complained. "She talks about him all the time, how much in love they were, how much she misses him. It's true, but she doesn't leave room for us. It's like we're all supposed to gather around her and protect her in her grief like she's a great bee."

Leslie, the child closest to Irene, was worn out. "I can't bear to be with her, she clings so. No matter what I do, I can't seem to give her enough. If any of us talks about how we remember Daddy, she interrupts and tells us we've got it all wrong. Then she goes on for hours about what he was really like, as if he died yesterday instead of a year ago."

Robert, a peripheral figure in the family, was annoyed that his mother was around all the time. "Everytime we want to do something, we feel we have to take her with us. We can't even go to a movie or for a walk around the block without Mother looking as if we've abandoned her. I'm fed up with the whole scene."

Leslie continued, "I think Mother's mourning is out of whack. She doesn't seem to be getting over Daddy's death at all. She can't seem to stand on her own. It's strange because she's an unusually accomplished person. It's not that she wants someone to take care of her or pay the rent or anything like that. She wants something I can't give her—she wants Daddy."

Irene reacted to their complaint. "I resent the fact that because a year has passed, I'm supposed to be over it. You all expect me to forget about Philip. How can a year's grieving compensate for twenty-five years of marriage?"

In a way the children were right. Most people who have lost a loved one feel their sharp grief begin to subside after a year has passed. Irene did seem to be hanging on to her mourning. But an essential point had been missed. Philip died almost at the moment his children were leaving home. Susan had married only a few days before her father's death and had gone to Central America with her husband to join the Peace Corps immediately following the funeral. Leslie had moved out of the family apartment into her own apartment near the university where she was starting to study for her Ph.D. in political science. And Robert had dropped out of college and bought a one-way bus ticket to Los Angeles.

They had had no time to mourn together. As the Dobsons came together again this summer following Philip's death, they were forced into a belated mourning, made all the more bitter for having been thwarted for a year. In fact, all of the Dobson's were still in mourning. Now to their grief they added personal resentments. Susan, especially, from thousands of miles away, had felt left out of the family. Leslie, the only child left to cope with Irene's severe grief, was overburdened and resented it. And Irene, although happy to see her children, felt pushed out of her small apartment and out of her children's lives.

In the midst of this Irene tried to preserve the family unity by demanding that her children stay close. But she denied them the right to mourn by claiming all grief for herself. "Losing a husband is worse than losing a father," she told them. The children objected to her yardstick for death; the great love affair between their parents had grown tiresome.

In an attempt to spread the grief through the family, the children got together and reminisced about their father. Irene felt excluded; now the children usurped her grief as she had theirs. The truth is that parents mean something different to children than spouses do to each other. Brothers and sisters do share a special mourning when they lose a parent. They grieve as individual sons and daughters, and also need to grieve together.

There was someone else who begged to be recognized in this family crisis: the ghost of Philip, the warm and supportive husband and parent who somehow instinctively knew when anyone needed help. He was tremendously in love with his wife and devoted to his children. They all relied on him for nurturing. Each person in the family felt that Philip was the center of his or her life. Philip was the most cherished, most loved, most important member of the family. He also had been a powerful shock absorber, protecting his family from emotional run-ins with each other.

Now, cooped up together like wounded survivors, they bumped into each other's emotional injuries. They burned up energy trying to avoid each other, both physically and emotionally. Tension was high and mounting higher.

The children tried repeatedly to duplicate their father's selfless giving and keep his place alive in a futile attempt to give Irene what she needed. Leslie, sobbing, says, "I just can't do it—I can't be Daddy for everyone. Daddy was special." At this stage everyone had to find a way to give Daddy up.

The family failed to realize that with one person missing, they had to reorganize themselves. Irene expected the family to behave as they always had when Philip was alive. But his death created a gap in their emotional circuits. What was needed was a new format for the family, a different way of getting along together.

An additional problem was that Philip had died just as his children were on the brink of maturity, yet before any of them had fully completed the separation process from "old" adolescence into full-fledged adults.

Is this the reason that everyone in the family identified with Leslie's recurring nightmare that at Philip's funeral she crawls into the grave, the earth covering and suffocating her? Leslie has the same dream night after night. Why did the children feel as if they were buried with their father?

As the summer dragged on, Irene and the children began to fight openly in anger. They all felt guilty about this, because they weren't accustomed to expressing anger. But their anger was only a sign that the mourning process was in motion and moving toward culmination.

Irene was suddenly fed up with the children complaining about her. "I've had enough of being the bad guy," she said. "Here they all come, invading my apartment, taking over my life, demanding that I 'get over Daddy's dying,' whatever that means, and expecting me to do everything their way. The hell with them."

This shook everyone up enough to make the children take another look at their mother. Irene in her late forties was a fragile-looking woman, still very beautiful. Almost black eyes, dark hair without a trace of gray. She was trying to make a new life for herself. But her children gave her no credit for it. Because she demanded too much, they refused to give her anything—no compassion for being vulnerable and alone in that mid-life period when children leave the nest, no sympathy for having to give up the family home chock full of memories of a lifetime, and no understanding that after twenty-five years of loving one man, she goes to bed every night alone.

Irene faced her loneliness. She felt its terror, but also her strength. It was when she packed up the last of their belongings in the old apartment that she uncovered a family secret that had never been faced before.

Exposing this secret rocked the family and inextricably altered their view of their past and the entire perception of themselves as a family. Everything the Dobsons were as a family was suddenly and irrevocably destroyed by this one realization. But facing the secret helped Irene and the children complete the mourning process and seal the grave.

The family had always been short of money. Irene was a harpist whose income, although it was small, often exceeded her husband's. During Philip's lifetime he had worked in his father's business and drew a modest weekly salary. His father kept the books and doled out the paychecks. Philip assumed he was a partner in the business and that an annuity was building up that he would come into one day. In effect, he received a clerk's salary while, second only to his father, he assumed major responsibility for the company.

The three-generation family was extremely close; weekends and holidays were always spent with grandparents. Irene and the children assumed, along with Philip, that he was his father's partner.

But Philip's father never passed the torch, never relinquished his power, never allowed his adult son to take over. By staying in the business in some undefined, illusive status, Philip passively waited for his father to recognize him. He had quietly mentioned to his wife shortly before he died that he wished his father would show some appreciation of his work.

When Philip died, Irene expected his father to acknowledge her husband's status. But it turned out that Philip had no pension and no share of the business. In fact, the insurance policy on his life was just enough to pay for his funeral.

Still, while this hurt Irene terribly, she did not come to terms with it until after she was forced to sell the family apartment. She wanted desperately to keep the big apartment for her children, a home full of memories where they could all come together. But although the co-op was paid for the monthly maintenance was climbing higher every year. Besides her salary Irene had not a dollar to call her own and no inheritance for her children. Her main worry was seeing her children through college.

The only way for Irene to ease the financial burden was to ask Philip's father to settle a sum of money on his son's heirs. This was not merely money. To Irene, a settlement would be a symbol that the years Philip had worked were valuable and that his father did in fact respect him.

She carefully estimated the money needed for Leslie to complete her education, for Robert (if he would) to get through school, and for a gift for Susan's baby. The sum total she arrived at was appallingly small considering the number of years Philip had given to the business and the fact that his father was an extremely wealthy man. With these figures written down, Irene decided to confront her father-in-law. Leslie accompanied her mother on her quest for Philip's rightful share.

Irene broke down completely when Grandfather said that she could see a lawyer, but as far as he was concerned, he had no legal responsibility to her or the children. "But what about your moral responsibility?" Irene cried.

Grandpa walked out of the room, leaving his daughter-in-law in tears and his granddaughter in shock. As if nothing had changed, Grandpa still expected to have Sunday dinner with the family.

This was more than a new twist in the family system; it was a major rupture. Irene and the children had been trying to work out their grief around their feelings about losing the ideal, perfect father. Their adoration for Philip had interfered with putting his memory to rest.

Now they were confronted with an unexpected picture of their father, and he wasn't there to help them. Who was Philip Dobson? A loving husband and parent? A confident man content with his life, happy in his work, devoted to his children and his own parents? Or was he a man lacking the courage to demand his rights, a man humiliated by his own father?

As the impact of this news resounded, Philip's children were quickly disillusioned. Their happy family image was destroyed in a flash of awareness. The picture of loving grandparents, parents, and children was shattered like glass. The Dobsons were frauds.

It emerged now that Grandpa had had contempt for Philip; that year after year he had humiliated his son by refusing to recognize him. While Philip devoted his life to making Grandpa rich, Grandpa treated him with even less consideration than his file clerk, who at least got a Christmas bonus. Grandpa now treated his son's family with the same contempt, as charity wards instead of rightful heirs, and offered them a loan with interest.

The focus of the family was obscured. Who was Philip? Who was Grandpa?

The issue was whether parents can recognize their children as adults. It was interesting that the issue between Philip and his parents apparently could not be resolved because Philip, dead at age fifty-five, had never achieved separation from his father and, therefore, never achieved full adulthood. We could only guess why Philip believed that any challenge to his father would have created irreparable separation; that if he did not play along, his father would forever exclude him. He was probably wrong in this assumption. But even if he was correct, it would have been better to win independence although it meant losing his father.

But Philip wasn't here to work this out with his father. Now his battle was fought by his children. Each child had to solve Philip's problem by deciding what to do about Grandpa.

Irene, predictably, wanted them to reach a family-policy decision, officially ending their relationship with both grandparents. "I won't live a lie," she told them. "How can we go on being friendly with them when we know they had no respect for Philip?"

The children bucked her; each one wanted to make her or his own decision. They were not nearly so clear about their feelings. "You must have known all along," they accused Irene. "You must have known that Grandpa used Daddy. You lived a lie for years, and so did Daddy."

Susan, beginning a family of her own, favored sustaining the three-generational family tie because she wanted her children to enjoy the extended family. She also felt that it wasn't all Grandpa's fault. "Daddy was to blame, too. We all knew in some way what was going on. If Daddy had faced up to Grandpa a long time ago, he would have been okay. Grandpa didn't force him to stay in the business. And besides, Grandpa is getting old. I don't want to punish him now."

Leslie, the only witness to her mother's humiliation before her grandfather, was not so quick to forgive. She was an independent, compassionate woman who felt less compulsion to continue the family line for its own sake, although she was close to Irene (if, at the moment, somewhat overwhelmed by her mother's needs). "It's one thing to maintain family ties, but it's something else to maintain those ties just because they're family. Why should I continue to go through the motions with by grandparents when I know they had contempt for my father. I loved my father and he loved me. That's the relationship that counts, even though he's dead."

Leslie perfunctorily maintained the relationship with her grandparents, but concentrated on getting on with her life. She said, "I don't think I'll ever feel the same about them. How can I? Everything we had built our family relationship on was a lie."

And Robert—well, Robert was drifting. He was out of it, vague and uninterested. Robert was almost a ghost in the family system.

In this desperate family problem I was reminded again that therapy doesn't come with a set of rules. Family therapy is discovery for everyone, including the therapist. There are no easy answers, no rights and wrongs, just ways for people to work together.

For the children it meant learning who their father really was—a good man, yet trod upon by his own father and unable to stand up for himself. This knowledge freed his children and made it possible for them to loosen their overly close family ties. They no longer held the mythical image of a perfect father. They were learning to be individuals rather than a cohesive family with no individual identities.

I asked myself what would have happened if Philip Dobson were still alive? How—and where—would the unspoken problem between Philip and his father have shown up? Theoretically at least, when a person fails to win his adulthood from his parents, the problem is passed along to his children.

I thought about the Dobsons, and my thoughts gathered around the elusive Robert. And there it was—Philip's son, Robert, who couldn't finish college, who couldn't find a job, who had no friends, who, because he could not grow from adolescence to adulthood, wandered aimlessly across the country trying to lose himself in religious ecstasy and seeking salvation.

Over and over the theme I have seen is that adult status is hard to win when families are too close. Philip lived in his father's pocket, and with his wife created another family that was too close—"sickeningly close," as Leslie once described her mother and father.

The Dobsons worked hard to extinguish family ghosts. It's possible that the family can now help Robert to freedom, to make a life for himself.

Stage 5 radically alters the face of family life. From two generations sharing a household, the family is fragmented into smaller units. Letting go is both sad and liberating. It's an opportunity for parents to rediscover themselves as individuals and also as partners. There is often a certain desperation in Stage 5, but it leads toward a rewarding continuance of the family life cycle, an affirmation of all the strengths inherent in the family. In this stage the family has to allow the departure of the children as a natural outgrowth of their maturity.

Stage 6

THE EMPTY NEST

Turning Point: To continue alone or find companionship in each other

Chapter 21

REVITALIZING MARRIAGE IN MID-LIFE

The natural culmination of Stages 4 and 5 occurs in Stage 6. In the previous stages the family readied itself for the full independence of its children. The family is in the throes of Stage 6 when the youngest child leaves home for good. Couples stripped of their primary parental functions face each other directly, without children as intervening buffers, and they look toward the future with some trepidation. But the turning point of Stage 6 is an opportunity for couples to renew a personal and intimate life together.

How well this recoupling process works depends largely on the depth and quality of the original marital bond formed in the earliest stages of family life. The way husband and wife solved conflicts and balanced closeness and distance in Stage 1 will affect the transition into Stage 6 some twenty years later. If they created an intimate and compatible relationship early in the marriage, the turning point will be much easier.

Some wives and husbands find themselves miles apart, bored with each other, irritable, and indifferent. Their major shared interest has been their children. It's becoming increasingly common for such couples (especially those with chronic marital problems) to become acutely and openly dissatisfied after twenty years or more of married life.[1] Sometimes this is a prelude to separation and divorce. In other situations family therapy can help revitalize a stale relationship.

Charles Potter, approaching his fiftieth birthday, practically dragged his wife Marion into therapy. "For twenty-three years we've been bickering," he said. "We have three beautiful daughters, a lovely house, and no financial worries. And I think we love each other. I don't know what's the matter with us, but I hate this constant arguing. I think we could both enjoy life more without it."

A brief period of marital therapy helped them realize that finding fault with one another was their distorted way of showing affection and need. People sometimes get in the habit of showing their affection by picking on a loved one. The bickering keeps them from getting too close. Charles and Marion had to learn to express affection without also creating distance by continuous carping.

Couples who have diverted their personal problems into parental satisfaction are faced with empty marriages when children leave home. Marital problems they have ignored or buried during the years of active parenting are likely to resurface in Stage 6 and complicate the transition.

Husbands and wives in Stage 6 need to look for ways to renovate their marriage, recover some lost parts of their early relationship, discard others, and rearrange the marriage's design. Sometimes renovation can be almost physical. After twenty-five years of marriage one woman's major dilemma centered on what to do with an old sofa, the largest, shabbiest piece of furniture in her house. Should she have it recovered, replaced, or throw it out? Similarly, as she and her husband struggled to make over their marriage, each toyed with the idea of giving it up altogether and finding new loves.

Mid-Life Crisis

Re-creating the original balance between two people is sometimes aggravated by mid-life crisis.[2] Husbands and wives in Stage 6 may have to renew their companionship in the light of individual change. Frequently one partner makes a crucial shift and expands his or her life, while the other partner stays the same. At a time when men are usually riding the crest of their careers, contemporary women in mid-life often are beginning a new spurt of self-development. The ambitions of husbands and wives sometimes clash in mid-life, and the impact heightens the divorce potential.

Smaller Families

Many couples are still young (often only in their mid- to late forties) when the last child leaves home, a pattern that forces the empty-nest period to coincide with mid-life crisis for both parents. The collision of mid-life crisis with the departure of children is partially a result of smaller families. The birth of the last child in the average family today is approximately eight and a half years after marriage,[3] which makes the years devoted to family building shorter than among previous generations.

Because all of the children are gone sooner, couples share many more years together alone. Mothers have more time for themselves and less need to devote the major part of their lives to childbearing and rearing. Husbands, relieved of some of their financial obligations while they are still young, often ease up on job pressures and sometimes make major shifts to more rewarding, though less lucrative, jobs.

Smaller families emphasize marriage as the central force of family unity. The quality of the marital bond is crucial, because by the time families face the transition into Stage 6, they are just two-thirds of the way through the family life cycle.

The combination of smaller families, mid-life crisis, and revitalizing marriage makes this a critical time for many families.

Chapter 22

DYNASTY

Alexander Lyons remembered every detail of the night forty years before when the world he had known was changed forever. He was a slim, dark boy of almost eleven then.

He stood at the window three stories above the street and looked out between two tall buildings across the way and over a wide, ragged sea of roofs split into crooked sections by the streets. A heavy wind swept across the sky, dragging dingy clouds through the night. A burst of rain suddenly rattled the windows.

Alexander had never before been awake at three o'clock in the morning. In the lamplight his mother hurried him and two of his brothers into their clothes. Each son wore two pairs of woolen knickers, two undershirts, two cotton shirts, two sweaters, a jacket, and over all this a bulky canvas raincoat. Each stuffed an extra pair of socks and underwear in a coat pocket.

Alex's mother helped him struggle into the heavy coat and then bent to securely retie the shoelaces of his heavy walking shoes. This done, Clara Lyons added a second shirtwaist and gray cardigan over her own serge dress, wrapped herself in a greatcoat, and pulled down the brim of her hat.

There was a quiet tap at the door. The three boys whispered farewell to their grown up brothers and sisters and dutifully kissed their father on the cheek. Their mother embraced her other children and husband. There were no tears. On the landing a tall man, dark in the shadows, waited. The father handed the man a small felt pouch and shook his hand. "That's all of it," he said.

The man guided the small party to a gray sedan parked at the curb. He drove the big car swiftly, without lights, through the wet streets. Even darkened and wary, the city seemed to throb. The car sped past the massive Century Hotel, looming like a castle in the dark, past long blocks of battered factories, to the waterfront and the coal barges with lace curtains draped across the cabin windows. They rode without speaking for fifteen or twenty minutes, then the car turned onto a wide-planked pier, stopped, released its passengers, and disappeared into the night.

Alex looked up at the hulking body of a merchant freighter chained to the pier. An hour later, with the boys and their mother aboard, the ship slipped into the oil-slicked Scheldt and churned down the river more than fifty miles until it reached the freedom of the North Sea.

The month was February; across the north Atlantic the sea was cold and treacherous. Alex, like his brothers and mother, was empty-handed, with only the clothes on his back. But tightly wrapped in white tissue paper, packed into the heel of the shoe his mother had so carefully tied, was a handful of small, flawlessly cut diamonds.

Alexander celebrated his eleventh birthday on his way to America. Three months later, the German army broke the Belgian line on either side of Courtrai, and in the early hours of May 28, 1940, Leopold, king of the Belgians, surrendered his armies to the German Command. It would be more than ten years before the Lyons family was reunited.

When Sigman Lyons brought his four oldest children and their families to the United States in 1951, his younger sons were well on their way to fabulous success. Alex, now twenty-two, was the genius behind their fortunes. Using his family's import-export connections, he had traded diamonds through Africa and Belgium. But the fact that Alex was the brains of the family was an unacknowledged truth. He was the youngest, and traditionally age conferred status in the family. While Alex supported and expanded the family business, he kept a low profile.

In the old European tradition, the younger brothers who had "saved" the family made room for their older brothers and sisters and deferred to them as the oldest, giving them respect and status as their rightful due. Both sisters had married before the war, and their husbands, along with the two oldest brothers, assumed roles in the family business. Although Sigman was titular head of the family, he left the business end to his sons.

The family credo was: We are one; everything I have belongs to you. No one had a set income or salary. There was one family pot and each person took as much as he needed.

For all their apparent unity, the division between the two groups of siblings, initially perpetrated by the war, carried over into their new life, and two distinct factions formed in the family. The three youngest brothers were inseparable. All had married and moved to a secluded compound of respectable estates on Long Island. Children were born, but wives and new families were kept outside the strong alliance of brothers.

Many years later, Alex's wife, Celia, would say, "They were the real family—Alex and Henri and Oscar. Wives were not included. I was always an outsider."

After the years of war and deprivation, the four oldest siblings and their families luxuriated in their newfound wealth. They bought mansions and hired large household staffs. Although the older brothers and brothers-in-law held prestigious positions in the family business, none of them seemed to take responsibility seriously. They kept short office hours and took long vacations. If they went abroad on business they gambled and ran up extravagant expense accounts.

For twenty-five years tension brewed among the brothers and sisters, and the two family camps hardened against each other. But no open rift ensued until their father died in 1976.

Sigman Lyons had always been the man who wasn't there; Alex was the leader in the family. But something happened when Sigman died. Even though Alex had had little contact with his father, Sigman was the link between Alex and his older siblings.

Alex remembered Sigman as an unassuming man, a weak character compared to his striking, assertive wife. Clara Lyons berated Sigman, complained to her sons behind his back, and made him seem a ridiculous figure. In fact, Alex said, "I never really knew my father. I stood at his grave, and it was like burying a stranger."

When Sigman died, Alex felt the time had come to finally make the break. "I've paid my dues," he said. "I don't owe them anything anymore."

Alex and his brothers Henri and Oscar kept the diamond end of the business, and the older group took the import-export end. The two factions permanently broke off relations.

The year the family split, Alex's son, Peter, finished college and entered the family business. Peter made a brilliant start, showing the same flair and enthusiasm for empire building as his father. Then four years later, when he was twenty-five, Peter suddenly went to pieces. He stopped going to the office, slept long into the afternoon, snorted cocaine daily, and became disoriented. Weeks went by and Peter's depression deepened.

Alex worried that his son might harm himself; he called the family together and they considered hospitalizing Peter. Henri's wife suggested they consult a family therapist. It was under the desperate threat of committing Peter to a hospital that the whole family came for the first session.

They were a handsome group. Alex particularly stood out, a man in his prime. He was tall and powerfully built, with hair graying at the temples and dark eyes. Peter was as tall and dark as his father, but his long hair almost brushed his shoulders and his well-tailored jeans and cashmere sweater contrasted sharply with his father's three-piece suit.

Everyone expressed concern for Peter. "We're very worried," Alex said. "He has a lot of responsibility at work, and he's falling apart."

"Can you talk to us, Peter?" Celia asked. "We're so worried. Please tell us what's bothering you."

Peter slouched in his chair, his long legs stretched out in front of him. He glared at his uncles and his parents as if he could barely choke down his rage. He didn't answer his mother.

"I feel I can't trust you anymore," Alex continued. "How can I trust you with my business? You didn't even show up for the transfer at Cartier's. We all depend on you."

Peter's bitterness and pent-up resentment poured out of him. "If you depend on me so much, why does Henri go through the papers on my desk? If I'm so important to you, why do you criticize me all the time. You brought that other guy in and put him over me. I can't take orders from him. Why should I? He's not in the family. And Oscar is always on my back. Why can't you leave me alone?"

"I remind you that you haven't been yourself," Alex said, exchanging glances with his brothers. "All you do is party. You're not meeting your responsibilities."

They went around and around. Peter defended himself petulantly. "Why do you always pick on me? Just because I'm the youngest in the business, you're always on me."

Ultimately, Peter gave up. Alex "won." Henry and Oscar seemed satisfied. But Celia was obviously distraught. "Alex overpowers everyone," she said.

The similarity between father and son was striking. They were both wheeler-dealers, and they both loved money and power. Despite Alex's criticism of Peter, he respected his son's intelligence and marveled at his ability to juggle several deals at once.

As the family prepared to leave the session, Celia spoke confidentially to me: "As long as I can remember, Alex has complained about being the youngest. Even though he took care of everyone, he always had to defer to the others, and could never challenge or disagree with them. He always stifled himself. I feel like I'm hearing it all over again."

At the end of the first session, the family was aggrieved and upset, presenting the best profile for future change. They decided to continue therapy sessions. Because of the power of the brother triumvirate, Henri and Oscar were not asked to join the next family session, and only the immediate family—Alex, Celia, and Peter—continued. At different times in the ensuing weeks other members of the family occasionally joined them.

In the weeks that followed, Alex emerged as the central figure, and he and Peter began openly to do battle. Like a late-blooming adolescent, Peter fought for his rights. He wanted to be his own man and run his part of the business without supervision. Oddly, one important issue was whether he could dress casually at the office—jeans and open-necked shirts instead of three-piece suits like his father and uncles wore. It's interesting that such small things as clothes often represent complex problems. What someone wears and the way he cuts his hair symbolize the right to be an individual and project one's own image. Whether Peter had a right to wear what he chose mirrored the larger issue of whether he was free to be his own man.

Alex, a reluctant granter of independence, began to examine his overprotectiveness and control. After one heated exchange Alex mumbled, "This is very hard for me. I have to wean my son away. But I still want to take care of him." It was an understandable conflict in light of his own experience during the war.

"We all depended on each other," Alex told us. "But I ended up being the one who took care of everyone. I still do. I'm tired of it. The family brings you into the world and protects you until you can protect them. Then it buries you." This same conflict—wanting to protect and wanting to escape—ran through the whole pattern of Alex's family life.

He said, "I have never had a month off in my life. I don't even know if I enjoy work or not. I do it because I have to, because the family can't survive without me. I am sick to death of it."

In the last few years the vise had tightened around him. His brothers were growing older and leaning on him even more. Alex felt himself sinking further and further into the role of the family supporter.

"I guess I was hoping you would bail me out," he told Peter. "If you could take over, I'd be off the hook. Maybe I was asking too much from you."

All his adult life Alex had been the strongest in the family. Yet he had never been recognized as the head of the family. He had become tired, "tired of picking up the pieces and fixing everyone up." He wanted out but couldn't admit it. He felt extremely guilty that he wanted to break free of his responsibilities to the family. Peter's depression and subsequent failure at work solved Alex's problem for him.

Alex reasoned that if Peter could assume responsibility in business, then he could cut loose. But if Peter failed, Alex would be forced to resume his burdens. He had set Peter up. He gave him too much responsibility too fast. He wanted Peter to do everything. Alex gave power, hoping that Peter would be responsible enough to set him free. At the same time he resented his son for having it so easy. "No one ever gave me anything," he said. He shadowed Peter, tried to control him, and ultimately took away the power he had bestowed.

This mixture of giving and taking reflected Alex's own crisis. He wanted to bail out, but he also wanted to take care of and control the family.

As soon as Alex took notice of his own problems, Peter's burden lightened. His depression lifted, and he resumed his work at the office. For all his brilliance and success, Peter had the normal insecurities of any young adult, but he no longer felt so used by his father.

Once Peter began to feel better, the family hesitated to go further and began to resist therapy. With the immediate problem solved, they began missing appointments and talked about terminating therapy.

Peter was relieved that his parents were in therapy with him and that his father was opening up his life. "I don't think I ever knew him before," Peter said. In a private telephone call Peter told me that he was worried that his parents were splitting up. "They've had separate rooms for a long time now."

Celia and Alex treated this separation casually, but Peter thought his parents might be divorcing. Was this another case of a son keeping his parents together by going crazy?

After about two months of family therapy, Celia and Alex turned up at a session alone. Peter had a reason for not attending and had called in beforehand. I suspected an attempt, conscious or unconscious, to get Celia and Alex alone together. I silently agreed that it was about time.

Alex and Celia were uncomfortable in the office. For a long time they talked exclusively about Peter, pouring over his past misdeeds, his childhood tantrums, and his visits to many child therapists. The triangle was obvious. Peter complained to his mother about his father. Celia told Alex. Together they worried about their son.

Throughout the session Alex and Celia talked about their son, their brothers and sisters, and then their parents. Their concern for the members of their family was genuine. But they never talked about themselves.

"Where do things stand between the two of you?" I asked. They were evasive. Everything, they said, was fine.

"Peter thinks your marriage is a shell. He's worried that it's all over between you."

They were shocked that Peter knew their secret. Celia started to cry. Alex talked. "About three years ago I met a young woman; Celia found a letter from her in my desk."

"And?"

"He denied everything," Celia said. "But that's when he moved to another room."

"You've never discussed it?"

"No. He never told me anything. I never knew what was wrong."

It was, in fact, a mere flirtation that had never materialized into an affair. But it gave Alex an excuse to pull away. Alex had continued to pay all Celia's bills and gave her a monthly stipend. She felt as if she were on a string.

"I hardly ever saw him, but I was completely dependent on him. If I wanted to go anywhere, I had to call him and ask him for the money. He always knew exactly where I was, and I never knew what he was doing. I wanted money of my own."

Alex couldn't understand her point of view and assured her that he would always take care of her. After months of pleading, he had finally agreed on a cash settlement for Celia, granting her independence. Now they led separate lives.

* * *

That afternoon Alex and Celia couldn't speak to each other directly. Celia said, "I'm willing to look the other way. I don't want to know what he's doing when he's not with me. But I'd like to be with him sometimes."

"I'd like us to move to New York and start all over again."

"He really wants his own apartment. He likes to be with young people. I crowd him."

"We could get another place for both of us. She could pick any apartment she wants."

"I don't think I can."

"I think you're afraid to relinquish your independence again," I said. "If you make your life over for Alex, you take a chance that afterward he won't want you. You're very vulnerable right now."

"Look at him! He could have a twenty-five-year-old if he wants. He loves young people. He's good-looking and rich. I'm fifty-one and I'm old."

"You know," Alex said, "I have no real friends. There's no one to talk to. Young women are beautiful, but you have to explain everything to them. They don't know anything that happened before 1955."

Celia is proud and beautiful, and vulnerable. Alex is reticent. They couldn't look at each other.

"You know, since the children have grown up, there's a void between you. You need to find each other again."

"Don't you call this the empty-nest syndrome?" Alex said. "Aren't I a perfect case of mid-life crisis?"

We nodded, laughed, sighed.

The marital problem between Celia and Alex was only secondary to the central issue: Alex was going through a delayed mid-life crisis. The imagined extramarital affair—a red herring that took place just when he split the two factions of his original family apart—was part of trying to free himself. Breaking away from the oldest faction was like getting rid of *some* of the burden.

Peter's difficulties serve two purposes in the family: failing to live up to Alex's expectations, he keeps his father tied to the family and the business. And he keeps his parents together by giving them something in common.

Therapy went rapidly for the Lyons family. Peter bounced back quickly and returned to work with energy and enthusiasm. Celia and Alex continued to go to therapy together for several more months, and Celia eventually moved into New York with Alex.

In the business the brothers made some important changes. Before, Peter's duties had expanded and contracted at Alex's whim. But now his work role and responsibilities were clearly defined. Alex and his brothers began to leave him alone.

The next few years will be critical for the family. There is little possibility that the whole family will reunite. Alex still wants to give up some of his business responsibilities, but both of his brothers are in poor health. He might sell the business, but he wants Peter to inherit. His brother Oscar has two young sons whom he wants someday to have a part of the business. It's possible that Peter and his cousins will perpetuate the family dynasty in generations to come. The work the family does together now may give them more room to enjoy the benefits of a close-knit dynastic family.

Chapter 23

ILLNESS AS CRISIS IN STAGE 6

The marriage in Stage 6 is often subjected to a severe stress—a major illness of one of the partners. Illness, though not predictable, occurs so frequently at this time of life that it is practically a necessity to consider it a part of Stage 6.

Illness is an emotional as well as a medical crisis. Prolonged vulnerability and dependence can twist the marital relationship and force major adjustments. Serious illness puts some marriages in jeopardy.

Breast cancer is the foremost disease among women in their forties and fifties. About one out of eleven American women will develop breast cancer some time during their lives, and for many, mastectomies or surgical removal of the breast will be performed.

Obviously breast cancer and the accompanying medical procedures are a major life crisis. It is a cruel irony that breast cancer most often strikes at a time when a woman needs her strength and confidence to face typical mid-life changes. Just at the age that men begin to feel they're growing older and often need to test their virility, women lose confidence in their desirability. Women who have breast surgery face an actual loss—an amputation—of part of their bodies. For the fortunate ones a breast is the cost of restraining a ravenous disease, and favorable prognosis can offset the loss. But more than one marriage has failed to survive the trauma even though the prognosis for physical recovery was good.

The crisis is complicated if marital bonds are tenuous. In those marriages where men and women equate the dimensions of a woman's body with the dimensions of her person, breast surgery can be traumatic beyond repair.

"My husband never got over it," one woman told me. "I couldn't believe it. I felt so lousy myself, but he was like a petulant child. He never came near me. We finally split up because I was feeling so terrible about myself all the time. It's hard enough to face death, but to feel unloved makes it that much worse. All my friends wanted to kill him. But I'm not sure we had such a great marriage if we couldn't get past this."

Strong marriages can sustain the shock; partners sometimes briefly recoil from each other and then adjust to the loss. "We had a terrific sex life before my surgery," another woman said. "I was terrified afterward that my husband would be repulsed by my body. I know *I* was—at least initially. Then it dawned on me that I was lucky to be alive. And I was still a complete person even though I have only one breast. We started making love in the dark at first, and it was different, more loving I think. It took a few months to bring our sex life back to normal, where we felt completely relaxed about it, but it eventually worked out."

When one partner becomes ill, new life-styles often have to be created to sustain marriage. "After my husband had a major heart attack," a fifty-five-year-old woman said, "our life changed overnight. One day we were young and energetic—we went everywhere and did everything. The next, he was an invalid, and I was a nurse. It was almost two years before we adjusted to the change in our life-style that his illness demanded. But ultimately it brought us closer together; it made us enjoy what we have more. It was a reminder that we wouldn't live forever."

Men who become ill in their fifties and sixties often suffer an almost irreversible depression. One couple who came for general marital counseling in mid-life quite suddenly had to face an unexpected medical crisis.

Rose Laslow could look back on a lifetime of service to those who needed her. Now fifty, she had always been a good daughter to her parents, a good wife to her husband, a good mother to her children. The rewards she felt from a close family life made up for personal sacrifices. "I've always felt that women by nature are better caretakers. It always made me happy to take care of my family and help my husband."

Rose and her husband Teddy had raised three well-adjusted children, although all three daughters had been slow to leave home and had lived with their parents even after they finished college. Meg now was married; Colleen recently got an important new job and moved to another state; and Victoria, the youngest, also in the process of establishing a career, had moved to New York.

For the first time in their married life, Rose and Teddy were alone. Faced with this new arrangement, a certain undercurrent of tension that had existed in the marriage for years turned into open hostility. The Laslows began to fight over everything. Rose complained that Teddy was too self-centered and demanding; he expected her to cater to him constantly. ("Where are my socks? Why can't you put my things where they belong?") Teddy said Rose was bitchy and miserable to live with. ("Find your own socks. Am I your servant?")

Over thirty years of married life, the Laslows had created a moderately healthy version of the child-centered family. Their system allowed all members of the family to grow except Rose, who, as the primary caretaker, was the center of gravity in the home. Now, forced retirement from nurturing a whole family and a new role as Teddy's personal valet made her furious.

Around and around they went, looking for old battles to wage. Rose said Teddy's demands made her bitchy: "He wants me to do everything for him—he'll never change." Teddy said her bitchiness made him worse: "It really gets my back up."

Their constant bickering kept them safely apart, and also safely away from the real issue. But what was the real issue?

After all these years Rose wanted something for herself, but she didn't know how to get it. With the family focus removed, she was unsure of herself. To make matters worse, as her self-assurance ebbed, Teddy stopped making love to her.

The sexual problem was a simple metaphor for their inability to find pleasure with one another, but Rose equated sexual rejection with the other deprivations she had sustained in her life. Just as she had stayed home and missed out on pleasure and excitement in the outside world, she was now also being denied pleasure in bed. She grew increasingly bitter; her frustration exacerbated the nighttime silence between them as they lay side by side but miles apart.

When Rose first came for counseling, she and Teddy were fighting all the time, and there was a desperate, nasty quality to their bickering. Teddy, who shared Rose's profound sense of family responsibility, agreed to join Rose for therapy.

It's not unusual for couples to seek counseling in this stage of family life. When a home is suddenly vacated by one or several of its important occupants, a marriage is easily thrown off balance. Husbands and wives look at each other without the shadows of children blurring the distance between them. Flaws come into startlingly clear focus, and old wounds hurt again as they take a long look at each other; then, rejecting the vision, they try to look away to avoid an unpleasant picture. Frequently couples delay their inevitable personal confrontation by refocusing attention on their children.

Rose and Teddy could achieve a small measure of compatibility when they talked about their children. Both parents talked to Colleen on the telephone several times a week and offered her practical and emotional support; after the call they would talk together long into the night about their child's struggle to achieve professional recognition. Together mother and father also indulged Victoria. Although Victoria was more confident and self-assured than her sisters, she often asked her parents for expensive presents. Whenever she asked for something, Teddy and Rose would shop together until they found just the right thing. "It's all right," Teddy said. "She works hard and she deserves nice things." "She gets what she wants," Rose said.

The most important part of Teddy's life had always been outside the family, and now at the peak of his career, he hid in his office and buried himself in work, finding personal satisfaction without being forced to confront the emptiness of his marriage. Rose didn't have this option. Without the caretaker role to sustain her, she faced emptiness on all sides of her life.

There were two tasks for the family: Rose and Teddy had to build a new relationship without parenting as its focal point, and Rose needed to develop herself as an individual.

Rose had an ambition to be a nutritionist in a hospital, but to achieve this goal she needed a graduate degree. She was a natural advocate for the sick, old, and incapacitated. She had an enormous capacity to help others, and her choice of profession was well aligned with her natural instincts and abilities. I encouraged her to pursue this goal, and both Rose and Teddy agreed that she should try to go back to school. As she considered the task, her widowed aunt became seriously ill, and Rose put aside her plans. An old resentment rose in her breast as her personal plans were spoiled, but she was accustomed to self-sacrifice. Rose's extraordinary efforts on her aunt's behalf renewed her familiar role as caretaker.

After the crisis passed and her aunt's health stabilized, Rose hesitated. The momentum of her original desire had been sapped. She felt now that she was too old to go to graduate school and would be out of place. Even if she managed to finish her master's degree, she said, she would be in her mid-fifties by the time she started to look for a job.

For several weeks Rose was preoccupied with the idea of time running out on her. Finally, intense self-examination coupled with this same sense of urgency pressured her into making a decision to try again. She went back to school.

Once back in school, she thrived on the intellectual stimulation and began to expand her personal life. As she made these motions in the outside world, she and Teddy also tried to revive their marriage. They began to travel together on weekend jaunts and even took some time off together, which they had never done before. Now that both of them were busy and under pressure outside their own relationship, they stopped fighting and began to look to each other for friendship and support. Their sexual problem continued, but it did not seem to be a pressing issue.

In only a few months they began to rebalance their marriage and make the essential shift into Stage 6. At this point we agreed that they had made the best of the therapy and our sessions ended. Then, suddenly, an unanticipated crisis threatened to destroy all the successful work they had done. Three days after Rose began her final semester of graduate work, Teddy suffered a massive coronary, and subsequently a double coronary bypass was performed.

A medical crisis is a major emotional upheaval for both husband and wife.

For Rose and Teddy, two people still unaccustomed to being alone together, an emergency that demands closeness for survival was bound to create serious problems.

Once again Rose's own needs were superseded by someone else's needs. Just as she approached a hard-won goal, she was cut down. Rose had to take a leave of absence from school. On the threshold of a professional debut, her degree and in fact her future were in jeopardy. She was worried and concerned for Teddy, but she also resented him for "taking it away from me." Sitting at his bedside day after day, Rose couldn't help hating him. But she was steadfast.

In a much more dreadful way, Teddy's future was also in jeopardy. For three long weeks he staved off death. At last he was removed from intensive care, and six weeks later he was released from the hospital. But back at home he still required around-the-clock nursing.

Teddy had always been aggressive and strong, a man in full control of his life. Now his helplessness nearly destroyed him. He was completely off balance. Severe bouts of depression would overcome him. The depression itself was new to him and even more terrifying than his illness. Unsure and frightened, he looked for ways to prove his power and strength. From his bed he criticized Rose mercilessly and overwhelmed her with demands. He was bitter over this stroke of fate and took out his bitterness and frustration on Rose.

She did everything he asked, and resented him profoundly.

The aftermath of the medical crisis was an extremely rough period for both of them. There was a burgeoning danger that the illness would become their emotional center and dominate their lives. Teddy's tendency to bully and Rose's tendency toward self-sacrifice could create a situation in which Rose would stay home forever to nurse Teddy, and Teddy would retreat into invalidism, ruining both their lives.

It took a great deal of courage for Rose to go back to school and finish while Teddy still needed constant attention. But she decided that she had to in order to save herself. For the first time in her life, she was able to fulfill her commitment to herself without abandoning those who needed her. By making this effort she made herself freer to give to her husband, both emotionally and practically.

Six months later, about the same time that Teddy got back on his feet and went back to work, Rose graduated with her class.

This is one of those stories that in the telling sounds deceptively simple. It can seduce you into believing that family problems are readily solved if everyone either gets a job or goes to graduate school. The ability to examine one's life and to change it at mid-life is no simple matter. Add a medical emergency with a long recuperative period, and that is a major family crisis.

That the Laslows were able to overcome these odds—for Rose to develop a career, for Teddy to regain his health and continue his work, and also for them to renew and improve their relationship—was a testimony to their personal courage.

Although many additional stresses—individual change, smaller families, mid-life crisis, illness—can severely unbalance marriage, the central issue in Stage 6 is how a couple, individually and together, copes with the void that is created when children leave home.

Chapter 24

RAPPROCHEMENT

PARENTS AND CHILDREN: LIKING EACH OTHER

Children complete the separation process by creating new friendships and new loves. This tearing away is made easier when parents realize that the distance is usually not permanent. Once children establish their independence and discover their own identities, they naturally drift back toward their parents and become part of a loosely structured extended family. Stage 6 is a period of rapprochement.

From the point of view of the younger generation, the distance once needed to separate is no longer necessary. "Who are my parents as people?" asked a single woman in her late twenties. She was ready to renew their acquaintance on an adult-to-adult basis. From the parents' point of view, they can enjoy their children for the first time as equals.

Sometimes young adults are not completely independent financially and still need parents for some support. This leads to trouble when parents use money to control their children or children use it as an excuse to prolong their dependence and remain entrapped within their families, not forming full lives of their own.

There are other ways that parents and children continue to cling to each other. One thirty-year-old woman cannot seem to make the break with her parents even though she is fully independent financially. In a well-modulated voice she answers the page over the PA system in the hospital where she is on staff; her tone immediately changes: "Oh, hi, Ma. No, I'm not too busy to talk to you."

This scene repeats itself several times a day. In Diana's traditional Catholic family the rule is that a woman's primary role is to marry and raise a family. Those who lead their own lives are disloyal to the family.

Diana's parents heavily criticize her career. Her mother bombards her: "Some girls get too involved with work. Men don't like women who are too independent." Or, "Guess who just got engaged?"

For Diana's parents the world is changing too fast, and they feel obsolete. How did their little girl become so accomplished? She travels all around the world, while they've never left the Bronx. They feel closest to their eldest daughter, whose life mirrors theirs though she lives in a suburban split-level house. Diana's intelligence and determination scare them. When their efforts to seduce and control fail ("Your sister has a lovely boy she'd like to introduce you to"), they lay on a brutal attack that could be funny if it weren't meant to be vicious ("Diana, I wonder if you're a lesbian?").

In order for rapprochement between parents and their adult children to occur, parents have to face the fact that their children aren't children. The standards, expectations, and control which were exerted in shaping a *child's* development are no longer appropriate. Unfortunately, some parents never get it right and deprive themselves of a warm, mutually supportive relationship with their offspring.

In healthy families, parents and children achieve a level of mutual respect and acceptance. Even though they are relieved of major responsibility for their children, parents can still play important roles as friends, sounding boards, and career consultants. It takes a certain amount of practice to work out the new balance. There's an old story my husband likes to tell, which illustrates the balance and lack of it:

A widowed mother calls her married son at work:

MOTHER: I never see you. Why don't you call me?

SON (mumbling): Sorry, Mom. I've been awfully busy.

MOTHER: I'd like to see you once in a while.

SON: How about Wednesday? Can you come to dinner Wednesday night?

MOTHER: Oh, I wish I could. But Wednesday night I'm busy.

SON: Well, how about Thursday?

MOTHER: I'd like to, but I'm invited out.

SON: Well, Friday we're leaving for Vermont for the weekend. Would you like to come?

MOTHER: I'd love to, but I have a luncheon date Saturday and I plan to visit your father's grave on Sunday. When was the last time you visited the cemetery where your father is buried?

SON (long silence): Well, how about next week? When are you free?

MOTHER: Next week? So long? Oh (sigh) I guess that will have to do.

Later that same day.

MOTHER (calling son): Well, I broke my plans for Wednesday, Thursday,

Friday, Saturday, and Sunday. I can come for dinner Wednesday and Thursday, and go to Vermont with you for the weekend.

SON (Stunned): Well . . . um . . . okay.

The mother and son are trying to find a new balance between closeness and distance, and trying to get used to the idea that they lead separate lives. She was busy and so was he. Whose commitments were more important? Who would give in? And under what conditions? In an effort to reconnect on a new basis, they overshot the mark and the balance was upset. In this instance the mother won the mild power struggle because she defined—and he accepted—the terms of their meeting.

BECOMING IN-LAWS

As children marry and bring new husbands and wives into the household, the family almost simultaneously contracts and expands. Does the family accept and approve of the children's choice of lovers or mates? Do they make room for the newcomers, or keep them outside the family? Do they co-opt them, taking them over and blurring the boundary between new young couples and the family? Or do they allow them lives of their own?

Some parents want their new sons- and daughters-in-law to call them Mom and Dad. This may be an attempt to create an illusion of a bigger family, with the emphasis on adding rather than losing members. "I'm not losing a daughter, I'm gaining a son." Some parents like it because it's familiar and it's a role they are comfortable with. Others need this title to feel reassured that they won't be displaced.

Enmeshed families tend to absorb their children's mates. One couple lavished expensive gifts on their son and daughter-in-law and built them a small country house. It was no coincidence that the house was just down the road from the parents' weekend retreat. The young couple, initially lured by the luxury of a second home they couldn't possibly afford on their own, later felt that the emotional mortgage came at too high a price.

In another family, each time a twenty-six-year-old son brought a girl friend to a family gathering, the conversation automatically shifted to engagements and weddings. The young man and his date were put on the spot. "And what are *your* plans?" The son's plans were to visit his family alone.

In disengaged families, parents show little interest in the romances of their adult children and give a new daughter- or son-in-law a restrained welcome. In one family a mid-life divorce had solved chronic marital tension. When the youngest daughter, Kathy, announced her engagement to the man she had been living with, her father was displeased. He told a friend, "I think she's making a big mistake." But he couldn't—or wouldn't—tell Kathy herself.

He worried, but remained silent. Then one morning he came across a newspaper article which reported that many fathers were no longer footing the bill for their daughters' weddings. He clipped it and sent it to Kathy with a short note: "This might be of interest."

Kathy was furious. "I got the message," she said, "but it wasn't about finances."

Father and daughter finally talked openly together. The air between them cleared. Shortly afterward Kathy set the date for her wedding. Her father did pay for the event, and walked down the aisle with his daughter on his arm.

BECOMING GRANDPARENTS

When adult children marry and have children of their own, a new generation comes into being. As new grandparents, a couple experiences the birth of their own children all over again. Mothers and daughters often share a unique experience at this time. Many women say that they feel closer to their mothers after the birth of their first child. And the birth of a grandchild re-creates a sense of maternal pride in the new grandmother.

Many men, for various reasons, denied an emotional role in the family and unable to develop close relationships with their own children, find a new opportunity with their grandsons and granddaughters. My husband and I both regret that our fathers and children missed the pleasure of knowing each other.

Most couples today become grandparents while they are still relatively young, often in their mid-forties and early fifties.[4] They become great-grandparents in their early and mid-seventies.[5]

Grandparents fill a unique place in the lives of their grandchildren. My daughter Jennifer came home from school one day mulling over the good fortune of her best friend. "Emily is so lucky," she said.

I sensed this was the-grass-is-always-greener syndrome, but couldn't help asking, "Why is Emily so much more fortunate than you?"

"Because her grandmother lives right next door, in the same building, and Emily gets to see her every single day."

The birth of grandchildren creates a bridge which spans three and sometimes four generations, and connects many elements of the family. For new parents and grandparents the event is a celebration of family unity and continuity. Grandchildren link generations together and give grandparents a vital new role in the lives of their children. Partially excluded by their children's marriage (having held back from intruding on the young couple's private relationship), middle-aged parents usually welcome grandparenthood.

Grandparents can play a supportive and loving role in the lives of their grandchildren. They can help and reinforce parents and become major figures in a child's life. Or they may be disruptive and sabotage parents. They may be vague, shadowy figures that grandchildren see only once or twice a year. Whether grandparents play a positive or negative role depends largely on the history of the family.

When grandchildren are born, old family themes and conflicts that have faded are often urgently revived. At the same time, the three- and four-generation family is an opportunity to continue relationships and compensate for personal losses. Grandchildren provide that sense of continuity and heritage.

. 'There is a myth in our culture that interfering grandmothers one-up the mother, criticize her parenting style, and try to reduce the status of parents. Perhaps this myth persists because of the singular maternal role available to women in our society. Some grandmothers, having lost their own maternal role and much of their purpose in life, do try to displace their daughters in an effort to sustain meaning in their lives. But research shows that grandmothers are most often perceived as interfering by their daughters-in-law, *not* their daughters. Sociologist Lucy Rose Fischer at the University of Minnesota discovered that "having children generally improves the relationship between a mother and daughter, but causes the relationship between the young woman and her mother-in-law to deteriorate." According to Fischer's research, daughters-in-law resent advice about child care offered by their mothers-in-law, but the same advice from their mothers is acceptable.[6]

These days some grandmothers are so busy with their own lives that they aren't around enough to interfere. Often young mothers complain because their mothers are not available to render child-care services. The fact is that most young couples expect and want their parents to offer occasional child-care service as part of the grandparent role. They tend to resent it when their parents are so busy they can't accommodate them. Most grandparents, even those who are active and busy with their own lives, get enough pleasure from their grandchildren to make some time available. It's another example of how the three generations are mutually dependent and offer support to each other for everyone's benefit.

Grandfathers seem to have a more consistently positive image. Being a grandfather affords some men a chance to be caretakers for the first time. The patriarchal, powerful father who was demanding and critical of his son indulges his grandson. His gruffness softens when his granddaughter smiles.

The grandfather-grandson relationship is often closer and more affectionate than the relationship between grandfather and son. Sometimes a new father resents the closeness between his father and his son, a closeness that he never enjoyed with his father. But more often it gives everyone pleasure and effectively heals old wounds.

Grandparents frequently have the pleasure and joy of children without the responsibility. Some consider this the ideal family. There are few pressures or obligations for either grandparent or child, no need to be perfect or measure up to impossible standards. Grandparents build the confidence and self-esteem of grandchildren because they love without judgment.

Chapter 25

AGING PARENTS

An important aspect of Stage 6 is a couple's relationship with their own aging parents. In our forties and fifties we often provide support for our parents that they once provided for us. "Aging parents," writes gerontologist Margaret Blenkner, "can no longer be looked to as a rock of support in times of emotional trouble or economic stress but may themselves need their offsprings' comfort and support."[7]

Some people see this as a role reversal: children become parents to their dependent parents. But role reversal is a misleading description of the altered parent-child relationship. An adult's capacity to support his or her aging parents—in all the various meanings of the word—is a measure of "filial maturity."[8] Although the person is still a child and the parents are still parents, a new dimension is added to show that the parent-child relationship can encompass change throughout life.

Gerontologists Geraldine Spark and Elaine Brody write: "The behavior of a brain-damaged old person may appear child-like, but he is not a child. Half a century or more of adulthood cannot be wiped out."[9]

We often think that parents help children achieve complete independence. In fact, in healthy families there is always a flexible interdependence between generations that continues throughout the life cycle. There is neither total separation nor total dependence.[10]

The main theme of surviving family life is that families can meet the changing needs of all their members. Most shifts in family life are made to accommodate independence as children and parents all strain for individuality within the family system. But the diminishing physical capacities of older people frequently are a prelude to progressive dependence.

When this new shift takes place, a different relationship is bound to evolve between adult children and their parents. Adult "children" now share and relive the past with their aging parents. And aging parents gain a new appreciation of their children as responsible, caring adults.

HAZARDOUS PATTERNS IN STAGE 6: BURDEN BEARERS [11]

The natural concern and support for aging parents is distorted in some families. It's unnatural for one adult child to assume major, unrelenting responsibility for an aged parent when there are brothers and sisters to help.

Will Olson, who drove 120 miles round trip to visit his parents almost every day, fulfilled this role. As his father grew older he became frail and was often bedridden. Every night Will would sit by his bedside for hours, even though his father was usually asleep. Will's brother, who visited only occasionally, had always been his father's favorite.

Ruth Goldman visited her widowed mother at her home every day and assumed full responsibility for her physical and emotional care. Ruth cleaned house, did the grocery shopping and cooking for her mother, assisted in her personal care, and mediated in her mother's disagreements with other members of the family (just as she had mediated between her mother and father when her father was still alive). When her mother had a series of minor medical emergencies, Ruth practically carried her back and forth to the doctor. Ruth was nurse, housekeeper, and domestic counselor.

As her mother grew older (she is now in her late seventies), she relied on Ruth even more. Yet she constantly criticized her, accused her of not doing enough or doing the wrong thing, or blamed her for the friction between herself and her brother and sister. If Ruth left early one afternoon, her mother accused her of abandoning her.

Needless to say, Ruth looked haggard and was exhausted. She had chronic medical problems of her own and was often in pain. Her two younger brothers, who lived nearby, were too busy to help.

Ruth rationalized that her mother couldn't manage without her. This is probably true.

Why did Ruth continue to martyr herself? What did she get out of it?

She was needed, and being needed made her feel worthwhile. She counteracted low self-esteem by extraordinary self-sacrifice. Her lifelong struggle had been to make both her parents love her. But the harder she tried, the more she felt their chronic dissatisfaction and her own inability to please them.

Inside, Ruth was angry that her mother didn't recognize or appreciate her efforts. But then her rage would backfire, and she was instantly contrite. She said she felt "like a bad person" for having these "terrible feelings" about her old, frail mother. In response, she redoubled her sacrificial giving.

Burden bearers like Ruth and Will reflect several dysfunctional family patterns. Both the Olson and Goldman families have had overclose relationships between parents and children. Will Olson and Ruth Goldman had difficulty letting go of their own children in Stages 4 and 5 of family life.

Their problems were a continuation of the basic difficulty in past generations. Ruth's eighteen-year-old son Jacob couldn't break away from his mother because Ruth had never successfully separated from *her* mother. And Will's daughters could not leave home because Will still confused loyalty with servitude. These families have never known how to let go of their children.

Frequently burden bearers are the least favored children who are still trying to win the affection of their aged parents. They are overwhelmed by feelings of profound inadequacy, of always being second best. Through childhood and into adult life, the family system pitted brothers and sisters against one another in a subtle contest for parental affection. Because the family rule is usually pseudomutual, siblings learn to bear the brutal class structure of favored/unfavored child in bitter silence.

At this time of her life, Ruth began to make tiny steps toward independence (mostly to protect her health), but then she redoubled her efforts to care for her mother. Being burdened is a dangerous trap. It always leads to resentment, and feeling resentful made Ruth feel guilty. She had to set some limits on her time and energy so she could feel satisfaction, not defeat, for her efforts. The best she could hope for at this late time in her mother's life was that she would not sacrifice her own health to her mother.

These problems that have festered for decades can seldom be solved in the present generation. Ruth and her mother (and father) had missed their opportunity for a healthy separation. But Ruth can solve the problem for herself and her son by breaking the pattern and letting her own son go. It's possible that Ruth and Jacob will be able to end this destructive pattern in the family.

Burden bearers carry their responsibilities so far that they pervert their relationship with their parents. Genuine maturity involves responsibility, obligation, and love—without guilt. It is a natural shift in mid-life that comes from having successfully separated from parents.

Filial maturity also implies that adult children can face their parents' old age and inevitable death. Burden bearers, on the other hand, have grandiose, omnipotent fantasies that if they try hard enough they can keep their parents alive forever.

Ruth adamantly refused to believe that her mother was slowly dying. She thought that with extraordinary effort she could prolong her mother's life indefinitely. She took the total responsibility for her mother's survival. And when her mother dies, as she must, Ruth may believe it is her fault.

Burden bearers often care for their parents at the expense of their spouses. They use aged parents to keep distance in the marital relationship, just as they placed children between themselves and their spouses in the early stages of family life. In some cases aged parents fill the void left by children who have left home.

Filial maturity, on the other hand, does not interfere with the renewing of marriage in this stage of family life. In mid-life couples can actually strengthen their personal relationship as they share responsibility for their aged parents.

THE MYTH OF DUMPING THE AGED

It is true that our society as a whole has been slow to respond to the changing needs and contributions of older people. But it is a myth that the aged are abandoned and dumped by their families. In most families close ties are continued, and in healthy families life is enriched for all generations by continued contact and sharing.

Stereotypes still exist: old people are sick, senile, rigid, incapable of being a flexible part of the family. Families have to grit their collective teeth and put up with the idiosyncrasies and demands of older members. While these stereotypes are real for some families, they are, surprisingly, in the minority.

Our feeling of repugnance toward old age in this culture distorts reality. It's a kind of stereotyping based on social values that equate youth with beauty and old age with defects. This cultural void is responsible, at least in part, for the myth that the oldest generation in a family is pushed aside, ignored, or barely tolerated out of obligation. The myth has outstripped the reality. In fact, 84 percent of men and women over age sixty-five live within an hour's drive from one of their children. Four out of five see an adult child as often as once a week, and many visit every day or two. Many of these visits include grandchildren and other family members.[12] In one study conducted in an urban area, more than half of the older generation saw children and grandchildren every day or nearly every day.[13]

These are hardly the statistics of disengaged families or segregated older people. Of all elderly people, only about 5 percent live in institutions of any kind. And when families do place their older members it's usually because they are elderly or ill themselves, and have exhausted all other alternatives.

There are of course many problems when illness finally strikes and dying is painful and prolonged. These are hard times for families, during which the younger generations have opportunities, perhaps for the first time, to pay their debts. "My father," said a seventy-year-old woman, "was a wonderful man. After my mother died, he came to live with us, the last five years of his life. When he got sick, we took care of him. It was in many ways a sad, miserable time—yet it was a privilege for us. Two of the children were still at home, and it was hard on them. I always said I wouldn't live with any of my children—but this illness and dying is a part of life."

Family therapist Jay Haley suggests that every family needs to confront the difficult problem of caring for older family members. " . . . how the young take care of the old," Haley writes, "becomes the model for how they will be taken care of as they grow old, as the family cycle continues without end."[14]

How family relationships are managed during this stage strongly affects the youngest generation. Grandparents and great-grandparents are models, teachers, and helpers in the family; they foster a sense of family history and pride. How the family copes with the aging and inevitable death of its oldest generation is a model of commitment and responsibility. The death of a grandparent or great-grandparent often is a young person's first experience with human mortality. These painful experiences help shape the lives of the youngest generation and prepare them for the losses they will confront in their own lifetimes.

When their elderly parents die, adult children in mid-life are left at the frontier of death. A generation passes on, and the next generation fills the vacuum. By caring for the older generation in Stage 6, a couple prepares to step into the position of family leadership. The birth of children at the other end of the life cycle insures the continuation of the family.

Stage 7
THREE GENERATIONS TOGETHER

Turning Point: To coerce family closeness through guilt or to encourage and perpetuate family life

Chapter 26

RADICAL CHANGES

The family forms a full circle. As the two-generation family becomes one that spans three, and sometimes four, generations, the couple, first just parents, become also grandparents and often great-grandparents. As family relationships continue through the generations, the life of the family is extended almost infinitely. At this stage parents and children reconnect in new ways, and the extended family becomes whole. Although aging parents inevitably face death and their children confront loss, the extended family can be exceptionally rewarding for all three generations. If the family has faced and resolved problems through its life, Stage 7 of family life is naturally secure and loving.

Finding and making a new life in one's seventies and eighties is a situation unique in our time. "At the turn of the century," write Geraldine Spark and Elaine Brody, "only one in twenty-five Americans was 65 or over. Now the aged represent one of every ten in the total population—20 million strong—and are increasing both numerically and proportionally. Most families include more older people all the time."[1]

Older people confront many kinds of losses in Stage 7: decline of physical ability, loss of work, change in social status, and frequently loss of family home as large houses are exchanged for smaller ones. Retirement; moving; death of a spouse, friends, other close relations—all these changes create profound stress at this time of life. How well people cope with these important life changes depends largely on their individual strengths and also on the stability of the extended family.

For the older generation the major task in Stage 7 is to come to terms with the choices they have made in their lives and face the inevitability of death.[2] Married couples draw closer as they cope with their increased dependency; all members of the family try to heal the wounds of the past, document the family's history, and reminisce about good times that were shared.

Aging is a complex process colored by many factors. *How* a person ages is affected by the quality of marriage and family relationships. For instance, married people live longer than single people. Psychoanalyst Dr. Stanley Cath stresses that rewarding marital and family relationships can offset the physical depletion that older people experience. "Every crisis in marriage," he writes, "has a potentiality for increased closeness or distance." In crisis, husband and wife each have the potential to destroy self-respect and self-esteem, or to renew their love. The need for love and respect from other people, especially one's spouse and children, never ceases. This support is even more valuable in later years, when severe stress events tend to accumulate.[3]

THE DISENGAGED COUPLE IN STAGE 7

In Stage 1 marital problems reflect the wish that our partner will make up for our own personal inadequacies. In the last stage of life personal shortcomings are experienced more directly. Because aging involves a kind of personal assessment based on a lifetime of experience, we have a keener sense of our own limitations. The earlier "solution" of denying our problems by demanding that spouses be perfect is not practical in later years: self-doubt and self-hate as we grow older can produce serious marital tensions, especially when the couple has a disengaged style of relating.[4] Either too distant or hostile for many years, they are now especially vulnerable in Stage 7 because their relationship does nothing to help them come to terms with life.

In fact, as Cath points out, older people who have a heavy dose of self-hate tend to convert those feelings into mistrust and suspiciousness. In early marriage, "I am disappointed in myself" is translated into "I wish my spouse would be perfect." For an older couple the same idea becomes "She/he hates and attacks me."

Cath explains this psychological maneuver succinctly: "Anxiety is lessened by feeling hated by someone else other than the self."[5] His analysis accounts for the paranoid, sometimes bizarre suspiciousness some older partners have toward each other. The last years of their relationship are lived in a hostile atmosphere charged with constant bickering, provocative arguing, and resentment. Adult children often are called upon to intervene and mediate; the triangular pattern that existed earlier in family life when children were young is continued.

Some couples remain alienated or continue bickering for the rest of their lives. Their patterns of hostility are so firmly entrenched that they don't seem to know any other way of getting along together.

THE ENMESHED COUPLE IN STAGE 7

The enmeshed or symbiotic couple faces a different problem in Stage 7. As they grow older, their fusion deepens into even greater dependency. For enmeshed couples death of a spouse is an ultimate, devastating crisis. The identity and self-esteem of the surviving partner is completely destroyed.

But occasionally the widowed partner rises like a phoenix and grows into a new, different personality.

Cath writes: ". . . On rare occasions we are surprised to find, instead of a helplessly depressed and self-castigating patient, an individual emancipated for the first time who is able to live independently, even if still in a seriously disturbed and neurotic way."[6] But more often mourning is prolonged and devastating. Some widows and widowers die within days or weeks of their spouses. Others shut themselves away from society, even refusing to leave their homes, until the years they have left dwindle away.

RETIREMENT

No matter how eagerly it is anticipated, retirement is a major transition. Some people make the adjustment smoothly and begin a new phase of personal development and pleasure. For many, however, retirement is a shock that produces repercussions of emptiness and demoralization.

Work in our society has many meanings. Along with economic independence, work awards status and dignity. Gainful employment is tangible proof that one is a productive member of the community. For most people work structures the day. Time is organized around the balance between work and leisure. Work also frames one's social life, creating a natural network of colleagues and personal attachments. Retirement means giving up more than a job. People need new ways to anchor themselves; flexibility and resourcefulness are essential for making a positive transition.

Today it is still, in the main, husbands who retire from a lifetime of work outside the home, only to find themselves without resources. But the experience of husbands with retirement is strikingly similar to the loss that wives sustain when the years of active parenting end. One difference is that wives who have been homemakers still have a certain amount of work to do in maintaining the house, preparing meals, and caring for husbands.

For most couples the most difficult part of retirement is that husbands and wives are thrown together around the clock. In closer contact than ever before, they are irritated at the loss of privacy and independence.

"I still had plenty to do," said sixty-seven-year-old Daisy Graham, "but my husband was at a loss. I couldn't even go to the store alone; Jim was always right behind me. It drove me crazy.

"Up and down the aisles we'd go. I'd select items from the shelves and put them in the shopping cart. Then Jim would take them all out again and put them back on the shelf. 'We already have that,' he'd say."

Jim Graham, an active, resourceful man, said he grew old overnight when he retired from his own business and moved to a retirement community. "In three weeks, I was sick to death of playing golf. When we weren't actually playing golf, we talked about playing golf. I was completely, totally bored."

Jim didn't wait for his boredom to become a way of life. "I went out and looked for a job and took the first thing I found. Later I tried several different jobs until I found one I liked. Working for somebody else, I don't have the headaches of running a business. I really enjoy this."

Loss of employment isn't the only change that retirement brings. Often the connection between the couple and the outside world is cut, and before a new way of life can be formed, the marriage is thrown off balance. Marital problems often crop up at this time, and sometimes the problem is serious. As in other stages of family life, stress may be expressed by one member who develops a symptom.

Wives frequently develop an incapacitating symptom when their husbands retire. In one family Marge Lopes, the sixty-four-year-old wife of a retired factory foreman, suddenly became afraid to go out alone. Her husband Leon had to accompany her everywhere and was even needed to drive her to her poker or canasta game and the hairdresser.

Jay Haley's analysis regarding the shifts in marriage at the point of retirement adds some insight into this couple's dilemma:

> When a wife developed a symptom her disability could be seen as a way of supporting her husband through a crisis. The problem arose at the time of her husband's retirement, when he was deposed from an active, helpful life to what in his view was being put on the shelf with no useful function. When his wife developed her problem, he had something important to do—help his wife recover.[7]

In this instance Marge was showing her devotion. She curtailed her own independence to ease the retirement transition and make sure her husband continued to have status in the relationship. Marge and Leon adjusted the balance between them when Leon became president of the local senior citizens' club. Marge's mysterious fears began to subside, and she soon made other arrangements to get around without her husband.

Retirement is sometimes more stressful when a couple sells their family home and moves to another community. Activities change, places change, and friends change—suddenly. But with patience and effort to make new lives as individuals as well as a couple, most people find they can weather the shift within a year or two. They find new interests and make new friends. Life often becomes easier in its daily responsibilities. A simpler way of life develops. And as they look back and evaluate their lives, couples approach marriage with a new mellowness and pleasure in the opportunity for closeness.

Mary and Tom O'Reilly play tennis every day for about an hour. They play from the back court, rhythmically hitting out with carefully placed strokes. There are no overhead smashes or volleys down the line. Loud thunks sound as balls hit sweet spots on gut. Graceful and lean, Mary and

Tom have just celebrated their fifty-fifth wedding anniversary. They are closer now than at any time in their married life. They reflect on the stability of their relationship and view marriage as the sustaining force in their lives.

During the transition, wrinkles occur in even the best marriages. The biggest potential problem is that the couple will fail to find new interests to replace their several losses and as a result begin to lean too heavily on each other. But most couples make the transition and take advantage of the best part of retirement: the opportunity to find new interests and indulge in travel and hobbies for which they never had time before. Retired couples need to look for ways to expand and add dimension to their lives.

WIDOWHOOD

It is a hard fact that one partner will generally die before the other; of all life crises, the death of a spouse is the most severe.

In our culture, men die at a younger age than women. Women outlive men by an average of almost nine years, and there are nearly three times as many widows as widowers in the United States; most of these are women over sixty-five years of age.[8,9] For many families the oldest generation is not an elderly couple, but a single, elderly woman.

One difficult aspect of widowhood is the swift change in social life. Several men and women shared their thoughts in a group session. "I'm not a couple anymore," said Lynn Firth, a sixty-five-year-old widow, "and couples shun me. They don't want a single woman in their social circle. It was quite a shock at first, but I've learned to make friends with other single women and it's all right now. But in the retirement community where I live, the couples and the singles don't mix."

Sophie Burke agreed that it was a tough adjustment. "Yet in some ways this is the happiest time of my life. I don't have any responsibilities to anyone. I am totally committed to myself. I have privacy and freedom. I guess you could say I'm an independent woman for the first time in my life."

Becoming a widow forces a woman to put herself first. Sometimes this is a radical switch. Lynn added, "I used to feel that if I couldn't help my children solve their problems, I had failed as a parent. I couldn't bear to see my kids unhappy. But I've let go of that. I had to for my own sanity. After my husband died, they seemed to lean on me for everything. I was running out of stamina and money, too. I made a conscious effort to take care of myself first. It turned out better for all of us. We don't 'lay guilt trips on each other,' as they say. They try to solve their own problems, and I try to solve mine. If we can help each other, we do. We enjoy each other more now."

Men are viewed from different perspectives. Sophie said: "So many of the men you meet when you're a widow think they're really a prize just because they wear pants and they're alive and kicking. But my husband really *was* a prize. I'm not interested in marrying someone just to have a man in the house, even though I get lonely sometimes. Who doesn't?"

And some men resent being packaged as eligible. Harold Rachmil told us: "Somebody's always trying to marry me off. Every time I'm asked to dinner, I know I'll have a new lady for a dinner partner and everyone watches to see if we hit it off. I feel like a prize specimen—and Lord knows I'm not—but I can never relax."

Similar to the newly divorced woman, widowed women want to hold onto their independence, a positive dividend of their painful experience. "I could have gotten married again," Lynn said. "There are still a few old boys around. But most of them just want someone to take care of them, and I've done all that. It's one thing to take care of a husband you've lived with for thirty or forty years. But why take in a stranger and cook and clean house for him? Do I need that?"

And yet some widows and widowers in their sixties, seventies, and even eighties do manage to find each other and make new lives together.

REMARRIAGE IN STAGE 7

After an extended grieving due to the circumstances of my father's death, my mother remarried when she was sixty-seven. "I need companionship," she said simply. Her reasons for remarrying were uncomplicated, she chose well, and her second marriage is a good one.

Second marriages can help provide companionship and stretch finances. But a second marriage in Stage 7 is often a romantic as well as a practical affair. Sexual desire and attraction continue to stimulate relationships throughout the life cycle. The sexual revolution has affected all generations. For some older people, especially widowed women, sexual experimentation is thrilling. Often for the first time in their lives, women in their sixties and seventies "permit" themselves sexual pleasure and seek erotic sensation. Sometimes, having missed the opportunity in their youth, widows engage in a brief series of passionate love affairs before settling on a sedate new husband.

Second marriages benefit from less stringent standards than first marriages, but they are plagued by tensions over children and money. These late-life marriages seem to work best when only one or neither spouse has children. The marital relationship becomes the primary attachment, and if adult children and grandchildren intrude, they do so from only one direction.

Money can be a serious and chronic problem, especially if the bride has more money (usually inherited from her dead spouse) than her new husband. The traditional male-female power hierarchy is upset by this inequality, because older men in our society are still used to bringing in the money and calling the shots.

Tension over money is often an expression of a conflict of loyalty. Older adults feel obligated to pass down the family inheritance to children and grandchildren (rather than to share it with a new spouse, buy a new car, or upgrade their life style). Loyalty to the original family is expressed by preserving dollars.

Many widows brinking on a new marriage try to preserve their money and their independence by drawing a prenuptial agreement to protect their assets. These arrangements are usually made in a straightforward way and can help avoid future misunderstandings.

In spite of these problems, most older people who remarry find a happy relationship. They seldom expect to mold or change their mates into the perfect partner. They are realistic about love and appreciate and accept their new spouses as they are. These marriages, perhaps not always made in heaven, have a good chance of surviving.

Chapter 27

TWO-GENERATION CLOSENESS/OVERCLOSENESS

PATHOLOGICAL DEPENDENCY VS. HEALTHY ATTACHMENT[10]

As parents grow older, their influence declines, and the balance of power shifts to the middle generation. Although the generations continue to be interdependent, by Stage 7 the aged couple are off center in the extended family. There's a distinct difference between healthy attachment between generations and pathological dependency. Mrs. Sullivan and her daughter Patricia live within walking distance of each other. In spite of the fact that they visit almost daily, they also talk for hours on the phone. Patricia consults her mother about even the smallest decision, and in effect the seventy-year-old matriarch supervises her daughter's life.

In another family Sam Edwards calls his daughter for the third time in one day. He feels he has no reason for living since his wife passed away three months ago. He is sad and despairing. His daughter tries to convince him that life is worth living, that with time he will adjust to making a new life for himself. Every day she drives the thirty-five miles to his house in the suburbs, cleans for him, shops, tries to get him to eat. Her usually meticulous father is so listless he doesn't shave or even bother to change his clothes. He refuses to see a doctor. Sam says, "I can't go on. I want to die. I'm going to kill myself." His daughter invites him to spend a month with her and her family.

These are pictures of pathological dependency. The first suggests that the psychological separation between Mrs. Sullivan and her daughter is long overdue. In the second instance Sam is having trouble completing the mourning process for his wife. His daughter is in direct line to inherit the role of burden bearer for her father.

All families at this stage are concerned with the decline of their oldest generation. In healthy families older people are not so afraid of being alone that they need to exert guilt to keep their children and grandchildren close.

And adult children are concerned and voluntarily take responsibility when necessary, without the burden of guilt.

Throughout family life, guilt is a primary mechanism among troubled families where emotional separation equals abandonment. In Stage 7, guilt reverberates in the phrase, "When am I going to see you?" Guilt underlies the accusation, "You don't care about me." This routine is constantly replayed. Its foundations are the unspoken rules between parents and children: "Whatever you do, it's not enough and will never be enough (because I'm afraid that without guilt you will leave me)." It works because sons and daughters believe that by living their own lives, they will make their parents suffer.

Money and Power

Money is another way aging parents provoke guilt and maintain control. In some dynastic families with money, the oldest of the clan remain in the position of family leadership not only because they are independent but because they hold the keys to the family safe.

Elderly parents control the family business and the family money. In some overly close families, the oldest generation is reluctant to relinquish power to the middle generation. These family clans celebrate frequent reunions that bring aging parents, aunts and uncles, all the children and grandchildren together. Family affairs and family business affect everyone in the family. Adult children usually are in the family business, sometimes three and even four generations old, and led by a matriarch or patriarch or both.

Brothers and sisters compete for favoritism, and the future leader is appointed and made ready to step in when there is a vacuum. Rifts, splits, and rivalries that exist just below the surface burgeon when the clan leader dies. The dead leader's brothers and sisters may then gang up on his heirs, or the heirs divide against each other. In these dynastic families, one never graduates into adulthood through maturity; only one *inherits* adult status when the leader dies. Only through death is room made at the top.

The dynastic family is the affluent version of excessive dependency that exists in enmeshed families at all stages of the life cycle. The point is the same: as power diminishes, money is used by the oldest generation to hang on.

Esther Kamen wanted to and could help her daughter, but couldn't stop herself from extracting a price.

"How much did you say you needed for that down payment on your house?" Esther asked Susan.

"I didn't say," Susan replied. "I'm not sure. We're scraping together all our savings. It's my dream house. We're so cramped in this apartment with the two kids."

"Well, we're not rich people," Esther said. "We don't have much. But we'll give you whatever you need. I hope Dad doesn't get sick again. Those medical bills."

"Hasn't Dad been feeling well?"

"He looks so tired and worn out. You'd see if you visited more often."

"I was just there on Sunday!" Susan said defensively. "He looked fine."

"That was one of his good days!"

"I have to go now, Mom. The baby's crying."

"We'll try to give you what we can. Maybe you can get a bank loan."

"Don't worry about it, Mother. We'll manage."

Money is sometimes used to barter for affection. Both Esther and Susan understood that emotional debts would never be paid off with money, but they couldn't help themselves from getting tangled up in this futile game.

Esther played because she felt money was the only resource she had left, and the only thing she had that would interest her children. She tried to counteract her feelings of depletion. As long as she had money, she proved she wasn't dependent. Yet she believed she was losing her position with her children. Money gave her leverage and power with them. At the same time she resented them for her loss of esteem and felt that they owed her something.

Susan played the game up to a point because she wanted the house, and deep down she also felt she was owed something.

Such families are not comfortable with separation and cannot manage to be close without the tie of guilt, which is used to maintain power and control. Aging parents may also use money as a promise or a threat to control their children.

Financial support to aging parents when necessary is an expression of responsibility by adult children. Social Security, pensions, and Medicare help ensure economic independence for older people, and today few adult children fully support their parents. Nevertheless, these benefits are weak hedges against economic deprivation and inflation. As a group, the elderly frequently fall below poverty level, second only to female heads of households. But older people do not like to take money from their children. Dignity, self-respect, and pride—important in all stages of family life—continue to be essential themes in Stage 7. Even so, when necessary, older people should acknowledge that they need help, and adult children should try to assist without making parents lose face.

If children feel they were deprived when they were young, they may resent this drain on their emotions and finances. If family members over the years only gave to each other grudgingly, they will have a hard time giving and taking now. Old people may deny they need help or, conversely, demand to be taken care of. Children may withdraw or give with resentment.

When parents have to move in with an adult child, they often feel they must humble themselves, that they no longer have a right to make demands or take up space in the world, that they have to live by the rules laid down in their son's or daughter's house—that, in fact, they will cease to be their own men or women.

Here, too, past is prologue. How well the family manages these crises when the oldest generation loses power depends on the quality of the parent/child relationship and the *history* of the family.

Responsibility Without Guilt

Jane Dyson, recently widowed, considered moving to Florida. She planned to sell the family home and, using the income from the sale, buy a condominium in a retirement community. Her daughter was living in Europe, and her son had a family of his own and was very involved with his career. Jane felt the move to a warmer climate, plus the opportunity to meet people who shared her own interests, would be the best plan for her. Yet the change was a radical one.

Her son, Stewart, offered to make a trip south with her to look at condos. In fact they made two trips together, and Jane decided to go ahead with her plans. Four months later she moved. But the adjustment was harsher than she had expected. She experienced a kind of culture shock, suffered more than ever from her several losses, and, in this unfamiliar territory, grieved for her dead husband.

When Stewart telephoned her on his usual Sunday night, Jane broke down and cried. Early the next morning Stewart flew to Florida and spent half the week with his mother, taking her to dinner, accompanying her to an art lecture, playing bridge as her partner, allowing himself to be lovingly introduced as her only son. On Thursday he went back to New York.

Several weeks later, her spirits revived, Jane chattered amicably on the phone with her son, told him about her new friends, and asked him to bring the family the next time he visited.

She was not entirely through the transition, but she felt she could now handle the loss and loneliness by herself. "I always told my kids not to come crying to me or their dad anytime they had a little problem. But they could count on me for a big cry. Well, it's a two-way street."

How does pathological dependency differ from healthy attachment between generations?[11] In the first instance parents and children desperately cling together and cease to grow as individuals. The relationship is based on one generation being overresponsible and the other generation being underresponsible. The imbalance created by the failure to be responsible for one's own life locks the generations into distorted roles and excessive dependency on each other.

In healthy attachments, boundaries between generations are clear and support is offered on a temporary rather than a permanent basis. The motto of these families is: Whatever you need to improve your own life, I will try to provide. Assistance, as Jane Dyson said, is a two-way street, offered by both the aging parent and the mature child, each trying to help the other to be more self-sufficient. Support is given as the encouragement of one friend to another, although the bond is more profound.

If the adult child/aging parent relationship at this stage of family life reflects pathological attachment, the family is stuck in dependency. It is as if they never progressed emotionally beyond Stage 2. Parents and children continue to be overly dependent, overly protective, and completely enmeshed. In Stage 7, only death can force a separation.

Chapter 28

FAMILY MATTERS

Lydia Mayer was a small, energetic woman in her late sixties. Under one arm she clutched a bulging leather portfolio that strained at its seams. She looked at me with lively blue eyes, "I'm sixty-nine years old, you know, and I've got a lot of responsibilities for my age. It's so confusing since my husband died. How much can one person do?"

She unzipped the portfolio and began to rummage inside it. Crumpled papers spewed out into her lap and drifted to the floor. Lydia found what she wanted, a folded five by seven metal triptych that opened to reveal three photographs: "This is my husband, Harry. He died six months ago and left me the business, but I never was in business before. Harry did all that, and now it's up to me to keep it going.

"This good-looking fellow here," she continued, pointing to the photograph in the middle, "is my son, Irving. He'll be forty in April. Irving's helping me because he's brilliant in business, but it's hard because he lives in Boston, so it's back and forth, back and forth. This with him is his wife, and these two little darlings are my grandchildren.

"And this over here," Lydia moved a well-polished fingernail across the frame until it rested at the last photograph, a picture of a younger, more casual version of Irving, "this is my youngest, my son Simon. It's Simon who says I need some help, and I don't disagree."

Lydia placed the opened frame on my desk, gathered up all the loose papers, and tried to stuff them back into her portfolio. Check stubs, receipts, and legal forms overflowed the leather case, and the zipper stuck. "Oh, the hell with it," she said, and dumped the whole mess into the seat of the empty chair next to her.

In trying to sort out Lydia's life, it soon became clear that her problems involved not only herself but the whole family. Repeatedly her discussion returned to Irving and Simon and her late husband, Harry. All of Lydia's life was tied up with these three people. To relieve some of her confusion, it was necessary to release her from the intricacies of family life. The two children agreed to join their mother in therapy.

It was an old, silent feud between brothers. Irving, the star of the family, had had a patronizing, condescending attitude toward his little brother from the day he was born. Simon had lived his whole life in his brother's shadow. While Irving excelled at everything, Simon remained quiet, unobtrusive, average.

Since Harry's death, the tension between brothers had exploded into a battle of wills. Simon wanted an independent life of his own. He had no interest in pursuing the family business and would like to see his mother give it up.

Irving insisted that the business must go on, that Lydia must take over as head of the company, and that he and Simon would help her run it. He tried to bully Simon into sharing "family responsibilities."

Irving came by his bullying tactics honestly. His father had been a gruff, successful businessman. "*Overbearing* would be a good word for Harry," Lydia said. "He was hard on the children." Lydia was the mediator between the boys and "their father," and the boys reciprocated by comforting her when Harry browbeat her.

"It wasn't a happy marriage, I'm sorry to say," Lydia admitted. "But it wasn't all his fault. I always put my parents first, and Harry resented that. My mother lived with us for many years, and she never got along with Harry. But she was sick and had no one to take care of her. Harry put up with it. He usually could get people to do things the way he wanted. But I put my foot down where my mother was involved."

It became clear that the family business was not Harry's travel bureau. The family business was to keep the family the same. Instead of looking for a way to release his mother from business responsibilities and help her enjoy a life of her own, Irving was insisting that the business go on. All of his personal responsibilities to his wife and children, and his own job (running his father-in-law's business), fell by the wayside as he tried to handle the details of his mother's life and his father's business. He continued to badger Simon to help out, but Simon was steadfast. He refused to get involved.

At one point Irving yelled at his mother, "Do something about Simon!" Lydia cried. Simon held out. Lydia again found herself in the middle, this time between her volatile older son and her unyielding younger one.

As the battle escalated, Irving's health deteriorated, he began to grow obese, and his marriage started to fall apart. The constant trips back and forth to New York were beginning to tell in his work, and his position at the office became shaky.

Irving believed that if Simon would help with the business, his situation would improve. But the more he tried to get Simon to do it his way, the more obstinate Simon became. The more he pulled away, the more obsessed Irving became with maintaining the status quo. He was the keeper of the family rules, and Simon was breaking with tradition; he was initiating change and exposing the taboo against emotionally leaving the family. By wanting his own life, Simon challenged the terms of loyalty that the family exacted. But he continued to be supportive to his mother, visited her regularly, and paid attention to her needs. He encouraged Lydia to make friends, develop interests, and have a life of her own.

On many levels the Mayers as a family were resisting the departure of family members. Irving, obsessed with continuing his father's business, couldn't stand the idea of Simon leading his own life. He would deny him leave taking, just as he would deny his father's final departure. Death, the most final separation, exaggerated the problem in a family that could not tolerate separation. By assuming Harry's attitudes and keeping the family dynamics the same, Irving ignored the fact that his father had died.

Lydia hadn't begun to mourn the death of her husband, because mourning meant finally letting go. The whole Mayer family needed to let go of each other and find more flexible, less binding ties to one another.

They made progress, thanks largely to Simon's obstinacy and the work of the whole family in therapy. Simon continued to lead his own life, battling Irving tooth and nail. Lydia for the first time visited her younger son's apartment, which he shared with his girl friend. As Lydia said, "I'm thinking modern." It was a positive sign that she was flexible enough to accept her son's way of life.

Lydia had many adjustments to make. The most profound was learning to live alone. But she also had to learn to make smaller changes: write her own checks, pay her own bills, make new friends.

To survive she had to let go of the business, no matter what Irving wanted. Without seeming to choose between her sons, she had to make her own life.

Lydia's future will be entirely different from her past. Some of these changes would have been required even if Harry were still alive. But his death made more extreme the nature of change. Many widows at this stage of family life fail to adjust—the death of a husband, at a time when the last child in the family also leaves, is too great a loss to sustain. But it is necessary to grieve and face the losses.

Some widows languish. Others make the rugged transition and thrive. Lydia was one of these. Several months later she described the adjustment. "I looked around me," she said, "and knew it was going to be whatever I made it. The lady living upstairs from me doesn't play cards, doesn't golf, doesn't like people. Stays in her apartment most of the time and complains. That's not for me. I want to get out and meet people. I'm scared. I don't feel whole since Harry died. I'm not always so happy; I get lonely. But you'd never know it to look at me, would you?"

Chapter 29

BONDS WITHOUT BONDAGE

Everyone faces some of these major life changes as he or she grows older. How well we make the transition is strongly affected by the family system—what we have given and received in our extended families.

A major magazine surveyed the ties between generations.[12] One fascinating discovery was that although patterns of telephoning and visiting among adult children and their parents varied, the guilt a person felt for not visiting enough depended more on a parent's sex and religion than on how often the children actually visited. According to their offspring, Jewish mothers and Catholic fathers are the most demanding and the least satisfied.

Other results of the survey: contact between adult children and their parents was more frequent when grandchildren were involved. "People with children not only see their parents more often than do people without children," the survey reported, "but they telephone them more often and, most dramatically—considering the increase in contact—keep feeling they ought to be having even more contact. . . . The yearning to see more of parents was not a response to parental pressure. . . ."

Surprisingly, the older generation seemed to want slightly *less* contact when there were grandchildren. But the adult children themselves wanted to visit more, perhaps because they wished to give their own children a "feeling of continuity and heritage."

"My daughter," a seventy-year-old grandmother told me recently, "is always pushing family. She's engrossed in the idea of a big, extended, close family. The fact is, her kids are in their teens and, to tell you the truth, they're not that interested. Neither am I. I enjoy my grandchildren, but I'm more interested in my own children." Sometimes the disinterest of adolescents for the family scene brings aging parents and their adult children together naturally. But these studies successfully squelch the idea that only the oldest generation profits by the extended family. All family members not only benefit from the interplay of generations, but actively seek it out.

THE MYTH OF THE THREE-GENERATION HOUSEHOLD

There is another idea afoot that in days gone by—perhaps fifty or a hundred years ago—grandparents lived with their children and the ideal family included several generations living together under one roof. Family moralists berate modern families because this closeness and concern for their oldest generation are absent. But, in fact, the three-generation idyll has never been common in our society.

Contrary to popular belief, there has been no sudden decline in the three- or four-generation household. The evidence suggests that the three-generation household was never a characteristic of American society.

"The structure of the family in America," writes Beth Hess in a *New York Times* editorial

has not changed drastically, and the "extra" adults of previous eras were as likely to be lodgers, apprentices and servants as they were to be kinfolk. The norm has been for young adults to set up their own households. These were often in the same neighborhood as the parents' house, but this is a far cry from extended family living. Among the few exceptions to this pattern were the large households of the upper middle class, whose diaries and well built dwellings have survived to generate the illusion that everyone lived this way. The other exception occurs at certain moments in the immigrant experience where among the very poor, for economic and perhaps emotional support, several generations lived together. But as soon as it was financially possible, the younger generation moved out and on its own.[13]

My maternal grandmother lived with us until the last months of her life. Yet my own mother has always vowed that she would never be a burden to us. This is as much a statement about her feelings toward my grandmother as it is a prediction of mother's future plans. I take it as fact that ours will never be a three-generation household.

In my parent's generation, whether a parent lived in or out depended on economics and also on his or her position in the community. My grandmother, for instance, was an immigrant and always somewhat estranged in the New World. She had no way of supporting herself and was totally dependent on my parents for food and shelter.

One of my strongest memories of my grandmother is her promises to take me to the movies, to the theater, out for a soda. Over and over again we put our heads together and made plans. But we never went. One day my mother explained that Grandma wanted to take me out, but she had no money and was unfamiliar with the neighborhood.

My grandmother was a proud woman. Even though my father put money in the bank for her, she wouldn't take it. She wanted to feel independent. I think it was demeaning for her to depend on her daughter and son-in-law. For that reason she worked around the house, baby-sitting with us, cooking, helping in tangible ways. And as we grew older and she was needed less, she began to withdraw. Over the years Grandma became more and more of a recluse until she was almost invisible in our household.

That both my husband and I lived in three-generation households places us in a specific cultural framework (we both came from immigrant families), and also in the minority. While it's true that one-fourth of all old people share a household with an adult child, only a very small number live in a three-generation household. The majority of aging parents are interdependent with their children, not dependent *on* them.

The main feature of the healthy family is independence and autonomy for all of its members. From the youngest to the oldest, independence is the strength of the contemporary family. The physical decline of the oldest generation eventually may make grandparents and great-grandparents weak and sometimes completely dependent, but for many people this contingency never arises. Better health care, financial protection, and longer life expectancy make possible a long and potentially active period of life in Stage 7.

HEALING FAMILY WOUNDS

The issues of separation and death in Stage 7 cannot be avoided. The two oldest generations realize that time is running out, and the family responds to the impact of aging whether elderly parents are infirm or well. Family relationships flowing from the past create a natural continuity. Even though there are no sudden idiosyncratic changes between parents and children, the normal crisis of aging usually increases the intensity of relationships between generations.

The extended family may have to mobilize itself to cope with a prolonged or serious illness. Or adult children may provide active caretaking for aging parents, a situation that can spark old conflicts that reverberate throughout the family. Sometimes this added stress provides the opportunity to resolve family tensions by forcing concealed resentments into the open. These confrontations, if they occur, tend to take place between brothers and sisters rather than parents and adult children.

Sibling relationships take on a new light in Stage 7, as the middle generation moves into the leadership position in the large extended family.

Old hidden rivalries swell and ignite sibling tensions at this stage. As adult children anticipate their parents' death, brothers and sisters get another chance to resolve original family problems.

INHERITORS

Family patterns repeat themselves as the family goes on and on. We leave to our children and their children our own unsolved problems with our parents. Family problems are seldom solved by breaking away. Staying connected to—and at the same time separate from—our families parallels the lifelong struggle to create intimate/independent relationships throughout our lives. Balancing intimacy and individuality is a major theme of surviving family life.

Family relationships can swallow us up or nurture our continued growth. Each stage of family life presents a turning point which offers an opportunity for growth and renewal.

Stage 7 offers the original nuclear family the momentum to review the family's history, rehash and settle old wounds, and come to terms with hidden tensions. The healing power of a surviving family ripples through the generations, and family ghosts are released.

The extended family—grandparents, great-grandparents, aunts, uncles, cousins, brothers and sisters, and new babies—gathers together in celebration. Sometimes in the commotion, old wounds are reopened, sensibilities are ruffled, bonds are twisted. But just as often, wounds are healed, feelings soothed, desires nurtured.

Ultimately the family comes together to renew itself, to give all its children and adults a sense of belonging, and to mark for them a place in the world. In making the most of the cycle of family crises, we not only improve on the past but also contribute to the family history for future generations.

POSTSCRIPT

When I called Josleen Wilson to help me write this book, I wanted a professional writer to help express my ideas about families. I needed someone with a facility with language, an inquiring mind, and a humanistic writing style. Collaboration seemed a simple matter of two people specializing in separate parts of a joint project.

Over the next year and a half, we developed a partnership that transcends our separate strengths. Our individual contributions to this book are impossible to separate. *Surviving Family Life* is a mixture of *our* concepts, *our* language, and experiences separately as daughters and wives and together as professionals. Like all true partnerships, Josleen's perceptiveness shaped my ideas, new concepts emerged from her language, and case material was transformed by our creativity.

We casually joke that in our next lives, I will be a writer and Josleen a family therapist. I have learned to express myself more clearly. Josleen has become an astute observer of family relationships.

But it didn't come easy. We brought everything we had to this project, and our professional skills were only a small part of our effort. We struggled painfully, sometimes alone, sometimes together. We paid a price. In time we became closer, more intimate, sharing our secrets about the families we grew up in, our marriages, our worries, shames, fears, and hopes.

In this sense we were a family. We learned to know and trust each other. We learned to count on each other. We also had to face our work alone with no one to call on, including each other.

We feel our collaboration duplicates the emotional process that is the heart of this book. It's about connecting and separating; about depending on someone and being exquisitely alone. In our work together some of our uniqueness is lost. We can't tell where my contributions end and where Josleen's begin, we've blended so completely. Yet in the last analysis our work together has helped us grow and become more complete as individuals. This is what intimacy is.

NOTES AND SOURCES

INTRODUCTION

1. Although the life cycle of the family has been widely accepted as a framework for the study of the family, the approach originated as a way of analyzing the changes which take place in the composition and economic characteristics of families from marriage onward. Writings by P. C. Glick on this subject are too numerous to list. Some of his earlier reports are: "The Family Cycle," *American Sociological Review* (April 1947), and "The Life Cycle of the Family," *Marriage and Family Living* (February 1955). Later articles by other authors which continue the same demographic emphasis are: E. M. Duvall, *Family Development* (1962) 2nd ed.; R. H. Rogers and R. Hill "The Developmental Approach" in *Handbook of Marriage and the Family* (1964).

In May 1977 I published an article called "A Developmental Approach to the Life Cycle of the Family" in *Social Casework*. This professional piece includes the original ideas on which *Surviving Family Life* is based. Since then I have come across two other conceptualizations of the life cycle of the family which are similar in approach. J. Haley, *Uncommon Therapy: The Psychiatric Techniques of Milton H. Erikson, M.D.* (1973), and M. A. Solomon, "A Developmental, Conceptual Premise for Family Therapy," *Family Process* (June 1973).

2. Each stage in the life cycle of the family is characterized by an average expectable family crisis, brought about by the convergence of biological, sociological, and psychological processes. This approach is modeled after the ego psychologist Erik H. Erikson, whose original developmental model of the life cycle of the individual inspired recent theories of stages in adult development. E. H. Erikson, "Identity and the Life Cycle," *Psychological Issues* (1959).

3. P. C. Glick, "Updating the Life Cycle of the Family," *Journal of Family and Marriage* (February 1977), p. 12.

STAGE 1: EARLY MARRIAGE: INTIMACY OR GAMES

1. As mentioned by J. M. Lewis, *How's Your Family* (1979), p. 15.

2. This idea is expressed most clearly by H. V. Dicks in *Marital Tensions* (1967): "The partner attracts because he or she represents or promises a rediscovery of an important lost aspect of the subject's own personality, which, owing to earlier conditioning, had been recast as an object for attack or denial" (p. 30).

3. The following are listed to acquaint the reader with the literature on complementarity: N. W. Ackerman, *Treating the Troubled Family* (1966); B. Bittleman, "Complementary Neurotic Reactions in Intimate Relationships," *Psychoanalytic Quarterly* (January 1944); Dicks (1967); L. Eidelberg, "Neurotic Choice of Mate" in *Neurotic Interaction in Marriage* (1956); P. Giovacchini, *Psychoanalysis of Character Disorders* (1975) pp. 177–260.

4. J. Warkentin and C. Whitaker, "The Secret Agenda of the Therapist Doing Couples Therapy," in *Family Therapy and Disturbed Families* (1967). In this article Warkentin and Whitaker discuss how marital relationships reflect reciprocal and interacting problems of each of the spouses.

5. Giovacchini (1975), pp. 191–202.

6. The interplay between unconscious individual conflicts and interpersonal (or relationship) problems in marriage is most thoroughly appreciated by the following authors: C. J. Sager, *Marriage Contracts and Couple Therapy* (1976); F. M. Sander, *Individual and Family Therapy* (1979); A. C. R. Skynner, *Systems of Family and Marital Psychotherapy* (1976).

7. Reporting on research done in Britain, V. Adams states in an article in the *New York Times*, titled "Study Confirms Aiding a Neurotic Can Harm a Marital Relationship": "There is evidence . . . that marriage to a neurotic can help preserve self-esteem in the ostensible non neurotic partner" (August 25, 1979).

8. The technical term which explains this blaming system is *projective identification*. The most lucid explanation of projective identification as a marital problem appears in Dicks (1967), p. 69.

9. M. Bowen, one of the major figures in the development of family theory, calls this pattern the overfunctioning-underfunctioning spouse system. "The Use of Family Theory in Clinical Practice," *Comprehensive Psychiatry* (1966); "A Family Concept of Schizophrenia," in *The Etiology of Schizophrenia* (1960).

10. This analysis is based on a body of psychoanalytic theory called object-relations theory. Readings include: Dicks (1967); W. D. Fairbairn, *An Object Relations Theory of the Personality* (1952); E. Jacobson, *The Self and Object World* (1964).

11. In his early papers M. Bowen developed a scale indicating various levels of human functioning, which he called Differentiation of Self Scale. In an article written in 1976, he contrasts *fusion* (an emotional stuck togeth-

erness) with *differentiation* (closeness without fusion). "A poorly differentiated person is trapped within a feeling world. His effort to gain the comfort of emotional closeness can increase the fusion. . . . A more differentiated person can participate fully in the emotional sphere without the fear of becoming too fused with others. . . ." "Theory in the Practice of Psychotherapy" in *Family Therapy: Theory and Practice*, p. 67.

12. W. J. Lederer and D. D. Jackson, *The Mirages of Marriage* (1968) outline eight techniques which can be employed to drive your spouse crazy. This book uses humor to deliver a serious message and is highly recommended for those who want to understand the complexities of their relationship patterns. J. W. Charney, a family therapist, takes the position that irrationality is the essence of marriage. His article "Marital Love and Hate" in *Family Process* (March 1969) is a classic tribute to the inevitable craziness that surfaces in marriage.

13. Skynner (1976) states that marriage can ". . . either be a process of facilitating growth (when the partners cherish and respect each other as individuals and have no desire to possess or restrict one another), a substitute for personal growth (when the partner is used to contain the lost aspects of the self, without attempt at reintegration), or a defense against growth (where they rely on each other's defenses to maintain the status quo and seek comfort and security only)" (pp. 128–129).

14. Sager (1976).

15–16. S. Minuchin, a leader in the field of family therapy, distinguishes between *enmeshed* and *disengaged* family styles, *Families and Family Therapy* (1974). Our family portraits describe the dangers of enmeshed and disengaged family styles at each stage of the life cycle.

17. Jane Austen, *Mansfield Park*.

18. The notion that every relationship is made up of unspoken rules was first set down in a classic paper by D. D. Jackson, "The Study of the Family," in *Family Process* (March 1965). A synonym for family rules is the Latin phrase *quid pro quo*. In *Mirages of Marriage* (1968), Lederer and Jackson expand on marital quid pro quo for the general reader. *"Quid pro quo* literally means 'something for something.' In the marriage process, it means that if you do so-and-so, then I automatically will respond with such-and-such. It might be called 'tit for tat' or 'point and counterpoint' or 'reciprocal behavior,' but some of these names imply nasty or opprobrious responses, whereas by *quid pro quo* we imply shared, or exchanged, behavior—much of it unconscious" (p. 178).

19. It is my impression that many people expect to change the rules of the relationship "after we get married." Change in the marital contract is an inevitable but difficult process. You overburden the process by consciously holding back what you feel strongly about before marriage.

20. A great deal of family-therapy literature focuses on dysfunctional family patterns, which operate to disguise, detour, and/or hide conflict

between marital partners. In Stages 2 to 7 we will describe (through the use of case material) the various concepts which have evolved to explain how "mutual retreat" affects the functioning of all family members.

21. L. Wynne, "The Study of Intrafamilial Alignments and Splits in Exploratory Family Therapy," in *Exploring the Base for Family Therapy* (1961).

22. This idea is powerfully presented in an article by J. Warkentin and C. Whitaker, "Serial Impasses in Marriage," *Psychiatric Research Report 20* (February 1966).

23. Although most family therapists would agree with this formulation, there are several family therapists who have made notable contributions to the literature. Among these are: Bowen (1960, 1966, 1976); J. Framo, "Family of Origin as a Therapeutic Resource for Adults in Marital and Family Therapy: You Can and Should Go Home Again," *Family Process* (June 1976); A. Y. Napier with C. A. Whitaker, *The Family Crucible* (1978).

24. Napier and Whitaker (1978), p. 119.

25. A large body of psychoanalytic literature is devoted to the subject of psychological separation. M. Mahler, F. Pine, and A. Bergman are the authorities on the complementary processes of separation-individuation for the first three years of life. (*The Psychological Birth of the Human Infant Symbiosis and Individuation,* 1975). P. Blos links the main task of adolescence with this earlier separation in his seminal paper, "The Second Individuation Process of Adolescence," *Psychoanalytic Study of the Child* (1967). E. H. Erikson (1959) has made identity crisis a household term.

26. I am referring to separation as a necessary part of becoming an adult. Blos (1967); Erikson (1959).

27. The phrase "pulling up roots" is used by G. Sheehy, *Passages: Predictable Crises of Adult Life* (1977).

28. Minuchin (1967), p. 30.

29. J. Boszormenyi-Nagy and G. M. Spark, *Invisible Loyalties: Reciprocity in Intergenerational Family Therapy* (1973).

30. Minuchin (1974), p. 22.

31. A. Y. Napier, "The Marriage of Families," *Family Process (1971).*

32. Personal communication with Harold Wise. Dr. Wise is an internist who has created and developed the family reunion as a therapeutic approach with cancer patients. His book, *The Family Reunion,* is in manuscript.

33. A. L. Leader, "The Place of In-Laws in Marital Relationships," *Social Casework* (October 1975), p. 486.

34. Leader (October 1975).

35. Napier (1971): "Two of the clearest trends in the attempt at growth seem to be the desire to integrate disparate elements in the family of origin and to make overt what was covert in the original family" (p. 390).

36. Napier (1971; 1978).

37. Extracted from A. Norton and P. C. Glick, "Marital Instability: Past, Present and Future," *Journal of Social Issues* (May 1976).

38. Extracted from Norton and Glick (May 1976).

39. For an excellent discussion of remarriage, analyzed from the perspective of family boundaries and roles, see K. N. Walker and L. Messinger, "Remarriage After Divorce: Dissolution and Reconstruction of Family Boundaries," *Family Process* (June 1979).

40. Walker and Messinger (June 1979) comment on the time and patience required to integrate two separate households (pp. 189–190).

41. M. McGoldrick, Family Life Cycle Conference, New York City, May 12, 1979.

42. Walker and Messinger (June 1979).

STAGE 2: COPING WITH PARENTHOOD

1. E. E. LeMasters, "Parenthood As Crisis," *Marriage and Family Living* (1957).

2. "The duration specific rates (of marriages ending in divorce) increased slightly in the very early years of marriage, reached a maximum between the second and fourth marriage anniversary. . . ." *Divorce and Divorce Rates United States 1978*, DHEW Publication No. (PHS) 78–1907, p. 9. The interval between marriage and birth of the first child is about two years (Glick, 1977). Putting these two statistics together, we can view early parenthood as a high-risk period of the life cycle of the family.

3. In 1972 Ellen Peck, the founder of National Organization for Non-Parents (NON), brought attention to the fact that the precise term for couples without children is "childfree," not "childless." *The Parent Test: How to Measure and Develop Your Talent for Parenthood*, by E. Peck and W. Granzig (1978), offers a means of self-analysis of possible motives in considering parenthood.

4. J. Prochaska and J. R. Coyle describe a community service which helps couples discuss "their ambivalence, fears and expectations about having children" (p. 289). "Choosing Parenthood: A Needed Family Life Education Group," *Social Casework* (May 1979).

5. The average number of children born to a woman who married in the 1940s was 3.3; for a woman who married in the 1970s, the average number of children she will bear is projected to be 2.5. (Glick, 1977).

6. J. E. Veevers (1974), "The Parenthood Prescription," *Alternatives: Perspectives on Society and Environment* (Spring 1974).

7. Extracted from Glick (1977), p. 9.

8. Extracted from Glick (1977), p. 9.

9. G. Collins, "A New Look at Life With Father," *New York Times Magazine* (June 17, 1979). "Researchers have lately probed the father-infant relationship and found few significant differences in the way children relate to fathers and to mothers. Their studies may sharply alter our concepts of what parenting is all about" (p. 31).

10. B. Friedan discusses the impact of the women's movement on families

and the need for institutional and economic reform to support contemporary American families. "Feminism Takes a New Turn," *New York Times Magazine* (November 18, 1979).

11. R. W. Schram, "Marital Satisfaction Over the Family Life Cycle: A Critique and Proposal," *Journal of Marriage and the Family* (February 1979). This study surveys and critiques the major research studies of the 1960s and 1970s that examined the relationship between marital satisfaction and the family life cycle.

12. C. S. Chilman, "Parent Satisfactions-Dissatisfactions and Their Correlates," *Social Service Review* (June 1979).

13. My figures are extracted from Glick (1977) and reflect the following modification: On the basis of his demographic studies, Glick reports that women who marry in the 1970s average an eighteen-month interval between marriage and the birth of the first child. However, he points out that "the currently short interval between marriage and the birth of the first child results in part from the increase, during recent years, in the proportion of children who are born before their mothers marry" (p. 10). Therefore, for the average married woman the interval between marriage and the birth of her first child will be longer than the projected eighteen-month interval.

14. Figures for current divorce rates vary from 38 percent to 50 percent. The larger figure includes first and subsequent marriages, while the smaller figure refers to first marriages only. The most recent census reports on marital status and living arrangements of Americans as of March 1979 disclosed that the divorce rate continued to rise during the period from 1970 to 1979. *New York Times*, April 2, 1980.

15. Extracted from *Monthly Vital Statistics Report, Final Divorce Statistics 1976* (August 16, 1978). DHEW Publications No. (PHS) 78–1120, p. 2.

16. *Monthly Vital Statistics Report 1976*, p. 3.

17. Trend data from DHEW through 1976 reflect that the likelihood of divorce increases slightly in the very early years of marriage, reaches a peak in between the second and fourth marriage anniversary, and then declines over the duration of the marriage. However, this same report emphasizes that more and more older people are divorcing. The March 1979 Census Report narrows this group down, disclosing that people between the ages of thirty and forty-four had higher divorce rates than any other age group (*New York Times*, April 2, 1980). These figures suggest an increasingly vulnerable period for divorce for the couple married longer and approaching mid-life. ". . . Dissolution of long term marriages (15 years plus) occurs in every 2 out of 5 marriages as opposed to one in 25 before World War II." *Marriage and Divorce Today Newsletter* (March 17, 1980), p. 2.

18. G. Sheehy (1977); R. Gould (November 1972), "The Phases of Adult Life: A Study in Developmental Psychology," *American Journal of Psychiatry*; R. Gould, *Transformations* (1978); D. Levinson, *The Seasons of a Man's Life* (1978).

19. The *average* length of marriages that end in divorce was 6.5 years in

1974 and 1975 (DHEW Publication No. 78–1120). This figure is arrived at by adding the length of marriage at divorce of all the sample population, then dividing by the number of the sample. Therefore the figure 6.5 is an average (rather than a mode), and is not the same thing as saying that most couples divorce 6.5 years after they marry. Thus, G. Sheehy's (1977) analysis of the "Catch-30" couple crisis is, in my opinion, in error (p. 202).

20. Sheehy (1977), pp. 213–216.

21. For a review of trends in age composition and its relation to marital breakup, see Norton and Glick (May 1976).

22. J. V. Sawhill and her researchers estimate that for each year of a person's life in which getting married is delayed, the annual separation rate is reduced by 0.1 percent. *Income Transfer and Family Structure* (1975).

23. See C. Bird, *The Two-Paycheck Marriage* (1979), for an analysis of factors contributing to "The Baby Panic."

24. National Center for Health Statistics, *Advance Report Final Natality Statistics, 1978.*

25. *New York Times* (January 2, 1979).

26. J. E. Dizard, "The Price of Success," in *The Future of the Family* (1972), p. 195.

27. R. O. Blood and D. M. Wolfe, *Husbands and Wives: The Dynamics of Married Living* (1960).

28. *New York Times* (January 2, 1979).

29. My reading of P. C. Glick's (1977) statistical tables and commentary.

30. Department of Health, Education and Welfare, No. 79–1120 (1979).

31. See E. Greenspan, "Work Begins at 35," *New York Times Magazine* (July 6, 1980).

32. See P. Bart (1977), "The Loneliness of the Long-Distance Mother," in *The Family.*

33. B. Friedan, *The Feminine Mystique* (1963).

34. *National Statistical Analysis of Child Neglect and Abuse Reporting* (1977).

35. *National Statistical Analysis of Child Neglect and Abuse Reporting* (1977).

36. See S. L. Rhodes, "Trends in Child Development Research Important to Day-Care Policy," *Social Service Review* (June 1979).

37. See J. Kagan, *Infancy: Its Place in Human Development* (1978).

38. J. M. Lewis (1979).

39. A Jolles, *In Praise of Mothers* (1980), manuscript.

40. T. B. Tully, "A New Breed of Mamas?" *Wheaton College Alumnae Magazine* (Fall 1979).

41. Norton and Glick (1976).

42. US Bureau of the Census, "Households and Families by Type: March 1978," *Current Population Reports*, Series P-20, No. 327 (1978).

43. US Bureau of the Census, "Money Income in 1976 of Families and

Persons in the United States," *Current Population Reports*, Series P-60, No. 114 (1978).

44. B. Blum, quoted in the *New York Times* (May 2, 1980).

45. The terms *disengaged* and *enmeshed* families used throughout this book were first used and conceptualized by S. Minuchin (1974).

46. Wynne (1961).

47. The triangle is a basic concept used in family therapy. According to M. Bowen's family-systems theory, a triangle is the basic structure in dysfunctional relationships. The triangled family member takes the heat off a dyadic relationship that is getting too intense. M. Bowen, "The Use of Family Theory in Clinical Practice," in *Changing Families* (1971).

48. Although scapegoating is a commonly used family therapy term, the process and purpose of scapegoating was first described by E. Vogel and N. Bell in 1960 in an article called "The Emotionally Disturbed Child as a Family Scapegoat," in *Psychoanalysis and Psychoanalytic Review* 47.

49. For a discussion of the relationship between triangles, coalitions, stable coalitions, and cross-generational coalitions, see Minuchin (1974), pp. 101–102.

50. J. M. Lewis, W. R. Beavers, T. Gossett, V. A. Phillips, *No Single Thread* (1976), pp. 209–211.

51. Minuchin (1974).

52. *Fusion* is M. Bowen's term (1971).

53. L. Wynne, I. Ryckoff, J. Day, and S. Hirsch, "Pseudo-mutuality in the Family Relations of Schizophrenics," *Psychiatry* (May 1958).

54. H. Gavron states that new parents have to erect "a marital defense against the institution of parenthood." *The Captive Wife* (1966).

55. Minuchin (1974), pp. 97–98.

56. Minuchin (1974), pp. 97–98.

STAGE 3: WHEN CHILDREN GO TO SCHOOL

1. The term *latency* is Freudian. The years of a child's life between six and puberty are designated by the psychoanalysts as *latent* because of an assumed diminution of sexual energy.

2. E. H. Erikson, an ego psychologist, goes beyond instinct theory by placing the latency-aged child in a social environment of peer and school activities. In "Identity and the Life Cycle" he describes a dialectic between industry and inferiority in the self-image of the latency-aged child (1959).

3. Gould (1972), p. 39.

4. Sheehy (1977), p. 198.

5. Sheehy (1977), pp. 198–217.

6. Gould (1972) comments that his subjects often told anecdotes about their children that were hard to separate from memories of their own past (p. 36).

7. Although the term *boundary* is commonly used by family therapists, my approach to the concept closely follows Minuchin's structural analysis of families presented in his book *Families and Family Therapy* (1974), pp. 51–56.

8. Gavron (1966).

9. The *New York Times,* September 12, 1976, p. 49.

10. Bird (1979), pp. 80–83.

11. Sawhill, et al. (1975).

12. N. O'Neill and G. O'Neill, *Open Marriage: A New Style for Couples* (1972).

13. The classic family-therapy paper, on which my discussion is based, is M. Barrigan, "The Child Centered Family," in *Family Therapy Theory and Practice* (1976), pp. 234–248.

14. Minuchin (1974).

15. Following discussion based on Barrigan (1976).

16. A. A. Milne, *When We Were Very Young* (1924).

17. M. Bowen (1976) summarizes his contribution to the "multigenerational transmission process," which is a basic concept in his family-systems therapy, p. 86.

STAGE 4: FAMILIES WITH ADOLESCENTS

1. P. Blos, *The Adolescent Passage: Developmental Issues* (1979), pp. 264–265.

2. Blos (1979), pp. 264–265.

3. "People between the ages of 30 and 44 had a higher divorce rate than any other age group." *The New York Times,* April 2, 1980. Also, " . . . Dissolution of long term marriages (15 years plus) occurs in every 2 out of 5 marriages as opposed to one in 25 before World War II." *Marriage and Divorce Today Newsletter* (March 17, 1980), p. 2.

4. Sheehy (1977), pp. 120–194.

5. J. Bernard, *The Future of Marriage* (1973).

6. L. Walker et al., "An Annotated Bibliography of the Remarried, The Living Together, and Their Children," *Family Process* (June 1979), p. 208. Walker et al. are reporting on the research of J. S. Wallerstein and Joan B. Kelly, *The Effects of Parental Divorce: The Adolescent Experience. The Child in His Family.* A. Koupernik (Ed.), New York: John Wiley and Sons, 1974.

7. J. S. Wallerstein and J. B. Kelly, "Children and Divorce: A Review," *Social Work* (November 1979), p. 470.

8. Bateson, et al. (1956).

9. For compendiums of the major articles written and presented by the communications theorists, I refer the reader to the following two volumes edited by the late Don D. Jackson: *Communication, Family and Marriage,* Vol. I (1968); *Therapy, Communication and Change,* Vol. 2 (1968).

10. Ackerman (1966).

11. S. Minuchin et al., *Families of the Slums: An Exploration of Their Structure and Treatment* (1967).

12. S. Minuchin et al., *Psychosomatic Families: Anorexia in Context* (1978).

13. Bowen (1960, 1966, 1971, 1976).

14. T. Lidz, "Family Organization and Personality Structure," in *A Modern Introduction to the Family* (1968).

15. Haley (1973).

16. This term was developed by the following authors to conceptualize a family pattern with schizophrenics. The text is self-explanatory in developing the term. L. C. Wynne, J. M. Ryckoff, J. Day, and S. I. Hirsch, "Pseudo-Mutuality in the Family Relations of Schizophrenics," *Psychiatry* (May 1958).

17. Wynne (1961).

18. The double-bind theory is an explanation of schizophrenic behavior in the context of communication in the family. G. Bateson, D. D. Jackson, J. Haley, and J.H. Weakland, "Towards a Theory of Schizophrenia," *Behavioral Science* (October 1956). This is a family-therapy "classic."

19. The idea of breakaway guilt as binding children to parents is convincingly presented by H. Stierlin, *Psychoanalysis and Family Therapy* (1977). Stierlin's analysis, beautifully written and full of clinical data, helped me understand and work with many families.

20. G. Zuk, *Family Therapy: A Triadic-Based Approach* (1972).

21. *The Family Crucible* (1978), p. 10. This book is highly recommended to the reader interested in family therapy.

STAGE 5: THE SHRINKING FAMILY

1. Bart (1977).

2. S. Bank and M. D. Kahn, "Sisterhood-Brotherhood is Powerful: Sibling Sub-Systems and Family Therapy," *Family Process* (September 1975). The section of "Sibling Support" relies on the conceptual contribution of Bank and Kahn. Their discussion of "Sibling Functions" is, in my opinion, a major breakthrough in our understanding of sibling relationships.

3. Bank and Kahn (1975), p. 324.

4. Minuchin (1974).

5. B. Carter, speaker, Family Life Cycle Conference, New York City, May 12, 1979, used this phrase to title the process by which older parents recognize their adult children.

6. Stierlin (1977).

7. Wynne, et al. (1958).

8. The concept of the family myth has been developed by the following authors: D. Block and K. La Perriere, "Techniques of Family Therapy: A Conceptual Frame," in *Techniques of Family Psychotherapy* (1973).

STAGE 6: THE EMPTY NEST

1. " . . . dissolution of long term marriages (15 years plus) occurs in 2 out of 5 as opposed to one in 25 before World War II." *Marriage and Divorce Today Newsletter* (March 17, 1980), p. 2.

2. H. Grunebaum identifies some of the marital conflicts of middle-aged couples that derive from the fact that in mid-life women become more assertive and men more affiliative. "Middle Age and Marriage: Affiliative Men and Assertive Women," in *The American Journal of Family Therapy* (Fall 1979).

3. Glick (1977).

4.,5. "The average at which men and women become grandparents is 57 and 54 respectively . . . ; they become great grandparents at 75 and 72." E. M. Brody, "Aging and Family Personality: A Developmental View," *Family Process* (March 1974). Brody is quoting statistics cited in P. Townsend, "Emergence of the Four-Generation Family in Industrial Society," in B. L. Neugarten, *Middle-Age and Aging* (1968).

6. Reported in *Marriage and Divorce Today Newsletter* (July 14, 1980), p. 3.

7. M. Blenkner (1965), "Social Work and Family Relationships in Later Life with Some Thoughts on Filial Maturity."

8. The concept of *filial maturity* was created by Margaret Blenkner (1965). It is discussed at length in Brody (March 1974) and G. M. Spark and E. M. Brody, "The Aged Are Family Members," *Family Process* (1970). My discussion is drawn from their analysis.

9. Spark and Brody (1970), p. 200.

10. Spark and Brody (1970).

11. E. M. Brody and G. M. Spark, "Institutionalization of the Aged: A Family Crisis," *Family Process* (1966). In this article Brody and Spark develop the role of "burden bearer" for middle-aged adults vis-à-vis their parents.

12., 13. Brody (1974) cites statistics from M. W. Riley and A. Foner, *Aging and Society, Vol. One: An Inventory of Research Findings* (1968).

15. Haley (1973).

STAGE 7: THREE GENERATIONS TOGETHER

1. Spark and Brody (1970).

2. Erikson (1959) describes the crisis of aging as a struggle to achieve integrity over despair.

3. S. Cath has written eloquently on the interdependence between physical and emotional deteriorations in older people and the opportunity provided in the social environment to enhance or destroy self-esteem. "Some Dynamics of the Middle and Later Years," in *Crisis Intervention: Selected Readings* (1965), p. 182.

4. Cath (1965) compares the marital crises of the young person with that of the older person, and offers the analysis given in the text.

5. Cath (1965), p. 182.

6. Cath (1965), p. 183.

7. Haley (1973), p. 64.

8. US Department of Health, Education and Welfare, Vital Statistics Report No. 79–1120 (December 1978).

9. The 1977 death rate for the female population was 1.3 times the corresponding rate for the male population. DHEW No. 79–1120.

10. Spark and Brody (1970) give a thorough analysis of the difference between pathological dependency and healthy interdependence among family members in this stage of the life cycle. My discussion is based on their concept differentiating intergenerational relations along the dimensions of dependence-independence.

11. The concept is taken from Spark and Brody (1970).

12. L. Wolfe (1979), reports the findings of the *New York* magazine survey, "When Was the Last Time You Called Your Mother?"

13. B. Hess, "Family Myths," the *New York Times* (January 9, 1979), p. A19.

BIBLIOGRAPHY

Ackerman, N. *Treating the Troubled Family*. New York: Basic Books, 1966.

Adams, V. "Study Confirms Aiding a Neurotic Can Harm a Marital Relationship." *New York Times*, August 25, 1979.

Austen, Jane. *Mansfield Park*. New York: New American Library, 1964.

Bank, S., and Kahn, M. D. "Sisterhood-Brotherhood is Powerful: Sibling Sub-Systems and Family Therapy." *Family Process*, September 1975.

Barrigan, M. "The Child Centered Family." In *Family Therapy Theory & Practice*. Guerin, P. J., ed. New York: Gardner Press, 1976.

Bart, P. "The Loneliness of the Long-Distance Mother." In *The Family*, Stein, P. J., Richman, J., and Hannon, N., eds. Reading, Mass.: Addison-Wesley, 1977.

Bateson, G., Jackson, D. D., Haley, J., and Weakland, J. H. "Toward a Theory of Schizophrenia." *Behavioral Science*, October 1956.

Bernard, J. *The Future of Marriage*. New York: Bantam Books, 1973.

Bird, C. *The Two-Paycheck Marriage*. New York: Rawson, Wade Publishers, 1979.

Bittleman, B. "Complementary Neurotic Reactions in Intimate Relationships." *Psychoanalytic Quarterly*, January 1944.

Blenkner, M. "Social Work and Family Relationships in Later Life with Some Thoughts on Filial Maturity." Chap. 3 in Shanis, E. and Streib, G. (eds.), *Social Structure and the Family: Generational Relations*. Englewood Cliffs, N.J.: Prentice-Hall, 1965.

Bloch, D., and La Perriere, K. "Techniques of Family Therapy: A Conceptual Frame." In Bloch, D., ed., *Techniques of Family Psychotherapy*. New York: Gruen and Stratton, 1973.

Blood, R. O., and Wolfe, D. M. *Husbands and Wives: The Dynamics of Married Living*. Glencoe, Ill.: Free Press, 1960.

Blos, P. "The Second Individuation Process of Adolescence." In *The Psycho-*

analytic Study of the Child. New York: International Universities Press, 1967.

———. *The Adolescent Passage: Developmental Issues.* New York: International Universities Press, 1979.

Blum, B. Quoted in *New York Times,* May 2, 1980, p. B3.

Boszormenyi-Nagy, I., and Spark, G. M. *Invisible Loyalties: Reciprocity in Intergenerational Family Therapy.* New York: Harper & Row, 1973.

Bowen, M. "A Family Concept of Schizophrenia." In *The Etiology of Schizophrenia.* Jackson, D., ed., New York: Basic Books, 1960.

———. "The Use of Family Theory in Clinical Practice." *Comprehensive Psychiatry,* 1966.

———. "The Use of Family Theory in Clinical Practice." In *Changing Families,* Haley, J., ed. New York: Gruen & Stratton, 1971.

———. "Theory in the Practice of Psychotherapy." In *Family Therapy: Theory and Practice.* P. J. Guerin, ed. New York: Gardner Press, 1976.

Brody, E. M. and Spark, G. M. "Institutionalization of the Aged: A Family Crisis." *Family Process,* 1966.

Cath, S. "Some Dynamics of the Middle and Later Years." In *Crisis Intervention: Selected Readings.* Parad, H. J., ed. New York: Family Service Association of America, 1965.

Charney, J. W. "Marital Love and Hate." *Family Process,* March 1969.

Chilman, C. S. "Parent Satisfactions-Dissatisfactions and Their Correlates." *Social Service Review,* June 1979.

Collins, G. "A New Look at Life with Father." *New York Times Magazine,* June 17, 1979.

Dicks, H. V. *Marital Tensions.* Boston: Routledge & Kegan Paul, 1967.

Dizard, J. E. "The Price of Success." In *The Future of the Family.* Louise Kapp Howe, ed. New York: Simon and Schuster, 1972.

Duvall, E. M. *Family Development.* 2nd ed. New York: J. B. Lippincott Co., 1962.

Eidelberg, L. "Neurotic Choice of Mate." In *Neurotic Interaction in Marriage.* Eisenstein, V., ed. New York: Basic Books, 1956.

Erikson, E. H. "Identity and the Life Cycle." In *Psychological Issues.* New York: International Universities Press, 1959.

Fairbairn, W. D. *An Object-Relations Theory of the Personality.* New York: Basic Books, 1952.

Framo, J. "Family of Origin as a Therapeutic Resource for Adults in Marital & Family Therapy: You Can & Should Go Home Again." *Family Process,* June 1976.

Friedan, B. *The Feminine Mystique.* New York: Dell, 1963.

———. "Feminism Takes a New Turn." *New York Times Magazine,* November 18, 1979.

Gavron, H. *The Captive Wife.* London: Routledge & Kegan Paul, 1966.

Giovacchini, P. *Psychoanalysis of Character Disorders*. New York: Jason Aronson, 1975.

Glick, P. C. "The Family Cycle." *American Sociological Review*, April 1947.

———. "The Life Cycle of the Family." *Marriage and Family Living*, February 1955.

———. "Updating the Life Cycle of the Family." In *Journal of Family and Marriage*, February 1977.

Gould, R. "The Phases of Adult Life: A Study in Developmental Psychology." *American Journal of Psychiatry*, November 1972.

———. *Transformations*. New York: Simon and Schuster, 1978.

Grunebaum, H. "Middle Age and Marriage: Affiliative Men and Assertive Women." *The American Journal of Family Therapy*, Fall, 1979.

Greenspan, E. "Work Begins at 35." *New York Times Magazine*, July 6, 1980.

Haley, J. *Uncommon Therapy: The Psychiatric Techniques of Milton H. Erikson, M.D.* New York: W. W. Norton, 1973.

Hess, B. "Family Myths." *New York Times*, January 9, 1979.

Jackson, D. D. "The Study of the Family." *Family Process*, March 1965.

———. (Ed.) *Communication, Family and Marriage* I. Palo Alto, Calif.: Science and Behavior Books, 1968.

———. (Ed.) *Therapy, Communication and Change* 2. Science and Behavior Books, 1968.

Jacobson, E. *The Self and the Object World*. New York: International Universities Press, 1964.

Jolles, A. *In Praise of Mothers* (Manuscript), 1980.

Kagan, J. *Infancy: Its Place in Human Development*. Cambridge, Mass.: Harvard University Press, 1978.

Leader, A. L. "The Place of In-Laws in Marital Relationships." *Social Casework*, October 1975.

Lederer, W. J. and Jackson, D. D. *Mirages of Marriage*. New York: W. W. Norton, 1968.

LeMasters, E. E. "Parenthood as Crisis." *Marriage and Family Living*, 1957.

Levinson, D. *The Seasons of a Man's Life*. New York: Knopf, 1978.

Lewis, J. M., Beavers, W. R., Gossett, J. T., and Phillips, V. A. *No Single Thread*. New York: Brunner/Mazel, 1976.

Lewis, J. M. *How's Your Family?* New York: Brunner/Mazel, 1979.

Lidz, T. "Family Organization and Personality Structure." In Bell, N. and Vogel, E., eds. *A Modern Introduction to the Family*. New York: Free Press, 1968.

Mahler, M., Pine, F., and Bergman, Anni. *The Psychological Birth of the Human Infant: Symbiosis and Individuation*. New York: Basic Books, 1975.

Marriage and Divorce Today Newsletter. New York: Atcom, July 14, 1980.

Marriage and Divorce Today Newsletter. New York: Atcom, March 17, 1980.

Milne, A. A. *When We Were Very Young.* New York: E. P. Dutton, 1924.

Minuchin, S. *Families and Family Therapy.* Cambridge, Mass.: Harvard University Press, 1974.

————, et. al. *Families of the Slums: An Exploration of Their Structure and Treatment.* New York: Basic Books, 1967.

————, Rosman, B. L., and Baher, L. *Psychosomatic Families: Anorexia in Context.* Cambridge: Harvard University Press, 1978.

Napier, A. Y. "The Marriage of Families." *Family Process,* December 1971.

———— with Whitaker, C. *The Family Crucible.* New York: Harper & Row, 1978.

National Statistical Analysis of Child Neglect and Abuse Reporting 1977. Denver: American Humane Association, 1977.

Norton, A., and Glick, P. C. "Marital Instability: Past, Present and Future." *Journal of Social Issues,* May 1976.

O'Neill, N., and O'Neill, G. *Open Marriage: A New Style for Couples.* New York: Evans, 1972.

Peck E., and Granzig, W. *The Parent Test: How to Measure and Develop Your Talent for Parenthood.* New York: G. P. Putnam's Sons, 1978.

Prochaska, J., and Coyle, J. P. "Choosing Parenthood: A Needed Family Life Education Group." *Social Casework,* May 1979.

Rhodes, S. L. "A Developmental Approach to the Life Cycle of the Family." *Social Casework,* May 1977.

————. "Trends in Child Development Research Important to Day Care Policy." *Social Service Review,* June 1979.

Rogers, R. H., and Hill, R. "The Developmental Approach." In Christensen, H., ed. *Handbook of Marriage and the Family.* Chicago: Rand McNally, 1964.

Sager, C. J. *Marriage Contracts and Couple Therapy.* New York: Brunner/Mazel, 1976.

Sander, F. M. *Individual and Family Therapy.* New York; Jason Aronson, 1979.

Sawhill, J. V., et.al. *Income Transfers and Family Structure.* Urban Institute Working Paper 179–03 Washington, D.C.: Urban Institute, September 1975.

Schram, R. W. "Marital Satisfaction Over the Family Life Cycle: A Critique and Proposal." *Journal of Marriage and the Family,* February 1979.

Sheehy, G. *Passages: Predictable Crises of Adult Life.* New York: Bantam, 1977.

Skynner, A. C. R. *Systems of Family and Marital Psychotherapy.* New York. Jason Aronson, 1976.

Solomon, M. A. "A Developmental Conceptual Premise for Family Therapy." *Family Process,* June 1973.

Spark, G. M., and Brody, E. M. "The Aged Are Family Members." *Family Process*, 1970.

Stierlin, H. *Psychoanalysis and Family Therapy*. New York: Jason Aronson, 1977.

Tully, T. B. "A New Breed of Mamas?" *Wheaton College Alumnae Magazine*, Norton, Mass., Fall 1979.

U.S. Bureau of the Census. "Households and Families by Type: March 1978." *Current Population Reports*, Series P-20, No. 327. Washington, D.C.: U.S. Government Printing Office, 1978.

U.S. Bureau of the Census. "Money Income in 1976 of Families and Persons in the United States." *Current Population Reports*, Series P-60, No. 114. Washington, D.C.: U.S. Government Printing Office, 1978.

U.S. Department of Health, Education and Welfare. *Monthly Vital Statistics Report, Final Divorce Statistics 1976*, No. (PHS) 78–1120, 1978.

U.S. Department of Health, Education and Welfare. *Divorce and Divorce Rates U.S.* No. (PHS) 78-1907, 1978.

U.S. Department of Health, Education and Welfare. *Monthly Vital Statistics Report Annual Summary for the United States*, No. (PHS) 79–1120, 1979.

Veevers, J. E. "The Parenthood Prescription." *Alternatives: Perspectives in Society and Environment*. Spring 1974.

Vogel, E., and Bell, N. "The Emotionally Disturbed Child as a Family Scapegoat." *Psychoanalysis and Psychoanalytic Review*, 47, 1960.

Walker, L., et. al. "An Annotated Bibliography of the Remarried, the Living Together, and Their Children." *Family Process*, June 1979.

Walker, K. N., and Messinger, L. "Remarriage after Divorce: Dissolution and Reconstruction of Family Boundaries." *Family Process*, June 1979.

Wallerstein, J. S., and Kelly, J. B. "Children and Divorce: A Review." *Social Work*, November 1979.

Warkentin, J., and Whitaker, C. "Serial Impasses in Marriage." *Psychiatric Research Report 20*, February 1966.

———. "The Secret Agenda of the Therapist Giving Couples Therapy." In *Family Therapy and Disturbed Families*. Zuk, G. H., and Boszormenyi-Nagy, I. (Eds.) Palo Alto, Calif.: Science and Behavior Books, 1967.

Wise, H. (in manuscript) *The Family Reunion*.

Wolfe, L. "When Was the Last Time You Called Your Mother? A *New York* Magazine Survey of Readers and Their Parents." *New York Magazine*, May 7, 1979.

Wynne, L. "The Study of Intrafamilial Alignments and Splits in Exploratory Family Therapy." In *Exploring the Base for Family Therapy*. Ackerman, N., Beatman, F., and Sherman, S. (Eds.) New York: Family Service Association, 1961.

Wynne, L. C., Ryckoff, I. M., Day, J., and Hirsch, S. I. "Pseudo-Mutuality in the Family Relations of Schizophrenics." *Psychiatry*, May 1958.

Zuk, G. *Family Therapy: A Triadic-Based Approach*. New York: Behavioral Publications, 1972.

Index